SIXTY YEARS OF HURT

The

Report

Love great sportswriting? So do we.

Every month, Pitch Publishing brings together the best of our world through our monthly newsletter — a space for readers, writers and fans to connect over the books, people and moments that make sport so captivating.

You'll find previews of new releases, extracts from our latest titles, behind-the-scenes interviews with authors and the occasional giveaway or competition thrown in for good measure.

We also dip into our back catalogue to unearth forgotten gems and celebrate timeless tales that shaped sporting culture.

Scan the **QR code** and join the growing Pitch Publishing reader community today.

JONNY BRICK

SIXTY YEARS OF HURT

England, and the England Football Team

First published by Pitch Publishing, 2026

1

Pitch Publishing
9 Donnington Park, 85 Birdham Road
Chichester, West Sussex, PO20 7AJ
www.pitchpublishing.co.uk
info@pitchpublishing.co.uk

© 2026, Jonny Brick

The moral right of the author and illustrator has been asserted in accordance with the Copyright, Designs and Patents Act 1988

Every effort has been made to trace the copyright.
Any oversight will be rectified in future editions at the earliest opportunity by the publisher.

No part of this book may be used or reproduced in any manner for the purpose of training artificial intelligence technologies or systems. In accordance with Article 4(3) of the DSM Directive 2019/790, Pitch Publishing expressly reserves this work from the text and data mining exception.

Set in Adobe Caslon 10.8/13.6

Typeset by Pitch Publishing

Cover design by Olner Design

Printed and bound in India by Replika Press Pvt. Ltd.

The authorised representative in the EEA is
Easy Access System Europe OÜ, Mustamäe tee 50, 10621 Tallinn, Estonia gpsr.requests@easproject.com

A CIP catalogue record for this book is available from the British Library

ISBN 978 1 83680 255 6

Papers used by Pitch Publishing are from
well-managed forests and other responsible sources

Contents

Introduction 7

1970. 11

1974. 30

1978. 46

1982. 58

1986. 70

1990. 86

1994. 104

1998. 119

2002 141

2006 157

2010. 174

2014. 193

2018. 219

2022. 245

2026. 270

Acknowledgements. 296

Bibliography 299

Introduction

ENGLAND WON the FIFA World Cup in 1966. They haven't won it since.

In the 60 years that have followed this victory, England as a nation has harked back to that one glorious summer day. The last survivor of the 11 players who started the match, at the time of writing, was Geoff Hurst, the man whose hat-trick won the final. He and those other ten footballers lived with the status that came with winning the competition, which overshadowed everything else that happened in their playing and post-playing careers. They were living legends who were all mourned on their passing, as if they were Battle of Britain pilots or soldiers who won the Victoria Cross.

I was born in England and, aside from five years studying in Scotland, have lived here all my life. The first World Cup I remember was in 1998, where David Beckham became the totemic figure whose sending-off against Argentina remains the largest blip in an otherwise stellar career. In 2006, England expected from the 'Golden Generation', which included Rio Ferdinand, Ashley Cole, Steven Gerrard, Frank Lampard and Wayne Rooney. In 2022 the modern England team of Bukayo Saka, Marcus Rashford and Harry Kane lost to the eventual beaten finalists; Kylian Mbappé, the French wizard, became the first player to score a hat-trick in a men's World Cup Final since Hurst.

This book is as much about those players and those who managed them as about the nation whose hopes they shoulder on a quadrennial basis. As the anniversary of the World Cup win reaches a year ending in zero, I want to run back over the 60 years since that triumph to turn the focus away from the team and on to the country. Notable journalists have written books about the England team, from which I will quote selectively and which I recommend wholeheartedly for a fuller picture, particularly for the European competitions that come in between World Cup years.

Across the following pages, I will quote from prime ministers, chancellors and ministers whose job has been to safeguard the nation's economy and prosperity. I will consider committee reports and government debates into footballing matters, including the reconstruction of Wembley Stadium and how laws have been made to combat hooliganism and gambling addiction. I will ask if the way in which the country was being governed has matched the way the team was being managed. Was the team of 1990, for instance, in any way representative of the society and politics of 1990?

Above all, how did the nation look every time the tournament came around? What were the cultural issues and the worries within society? Whenever England failed to qualify for a World Cup, who was to blame?

I will also examine how the Football Association, who play a custodial role in looking after the national game, have tried to push the England team towards success even as the Premier League has become a behemoth and European competitions have grown in importance.

Before this, I will run through how the failure to qualify for the 1974 and 1978 World Cups ran alongside the political difficulties that successive governments had

INTRODUCTION

with energy prices and disputes with miners. In 1982 and 1986, England did make it to the finals, at a time when the government went to war with Argentina and when football fans were creating their own conflict at home and abroad.

I will then proceed to the run to the semi-final at the 1990 tournament, the year that saw a new Conservative prime minister who would eventually be assailed by a problematic economy and a resurgent Labour movement. John Major and England manager Graham Taylor, who were well prepared for their respective leadership roles, are not remembered with great fondness today.

In 1998, keen to change formation and his team's fortunes, Glenn Hoddle took the team to a tournament where young superstar David Beckham was hero one minute, villain the next and tabloid fodder throughout. New prime minister and football fan Tony Blair – at 43 the youngest person to move into Number 10 since 1812 – was keen for his country to host the 2006 World Cup, whose bidding process is recounted within these pages.

Blair once asked Sven-Göran Eriksson who would outlast the other in their jobs, which might have been the highest profile of all in England. The first non-English manager of the England football team was in the dugout at the 2002 and 2006 World Cups, both of which saw them lose to nations whose people spoke Portuguese. Blair and his government, including chancellor Gordon Brown, were eager to bring in legislation to help the country enjoy an important place in global affairs, and to feel confident and healthy within themselves.

Brown was occupied by a global financial crisis when he took over as prime minister, a position he lost just before the 2010 World Cup, where England were managed by a strict Italian. At least they did better than in 2014, where disaster befell Roy Hodgson's team in Brazil, while back at home the Conservative Party were promoting a long-term plan for the economy.

Out in Russia in 2018, an accidental manager led a team which was more cohesive and united than ever, and England finally won a World Cup penalty shoot-out to give a country some happiness amid the fallout of the EU referendum. By 2022, at a World Cup held in a desert, England had gone through a pandemic and the football team had reached a European Championship Final which was as memorable for fan trouble as for the climax of the game.

As we head towards the 2026 tournament in North America, can we predict how England will look, with a manager recruited from abroad whose contract will expire at the end of the competition? In 1966, the coach was from Dagenham and every player was white, which was typical of the make-up of a contemporary domestic side. As the years progress, and the triumph of 1966 recedes into the past, the faces of both the country and the England football team have a greater variety among them.

This book is a catalogue of events that celebrates how football can distract a country or bring it together, how it can concentrate English minds on societal issues, and how it can create durable memories which add to the folk history of the nation.

1970

IN THE spring of 1970, Paul McCartney announced the dissolution of his band The Beatles via a press release for his new solo album. A few weeks after the final Beatles single, 'Let It Be', reached number two in the UK charts, two dozen men went one place better.

'Back Home' was the official England World Cup song. It began with a military fanfare and ended with a promise to 'fight until the whistle blows'. The faces of the 1970 squad, who would defend the World Cup won by the 1966 side, were also minted on silver coins sold at Esso garages.

One such voice, and face, was central midfielder Alan Mullery. 'I felt extremely proud that a snotty-nosed kid from Notting Hill had achieved what every kid I played football with in the streets and parks dreamed of: to become an England footballer,' he told Henry Winter. When Mullery was sent off for England in 1968, manager Sir Alf Ramsey paid his fine, commending his player for defending his honour. He also recalls how the players obeyed Ramsey's dictum to go to bed at 10pm, in a deferential era where memories of the officer class were still keenly felt.

England qualified automatically for the 1970 World Cup, which took place in Mexico. In what would become common in the England camp at tournaments, there were strict ground rules: no ice in drinks that players consumed; no room service; no walking outdoors in the early afternoons; and a 20-minute limit for sunbathing. The food that England had taken with them to Mexico had unfortunately been destroyed upon entry to the country, denying the team their comforts, although the Football Association ensured that local caterers could whip up English cuisine.

The England team benefitted from a group of players who were part of domestic teams that had won European competitions, something which had not been the case in 1966. Manchester United, Chelsea, Manchester City and Newcastle United all won various continental trophies between 1967 and 1970, so the squad included three European Cup winners in Bobby Charlton, Nobby Stiles and Alex Stepney, as well as Peter Bonetti of Chelsea and Colin Bell of Manchester City.

Charlton and Stiles could thus boast World Cup and European Cup triumphs, and their experience was carried over into the 1970 side. Since 1966, striker Roger Hunt had retired and gone into the family haulage business, while left-back Ray Wilson, who at 31 had been the oldest of the XI, worked as an undertaker at a funeral home. His place in the team was taken by Terry Cooper, with Keith Newton or Tommy Wright replacing George Cohen on the right.

In his book *Answered Prayers*, a comprehensive examination of Ramsey and his team, Duncan Hamilton reckoned that the successful tournament was both 'the ultimate pyrrhic victory' and 'a punishment'. For many years after it, members of the victorious team would attend functions, trot out their recollections and sign memorabilia. They were 'benign prisoners of that final' whose entire careers were reduced to those 120 minutes. Other than those 11 men, no Englishman has become similarly trapped.

The demands of club football affected the players of the era. They would tread in heavy boots on muddy pitches which were unassisted by undersoil heating; this led to postponements and logjams in fixtures, and squads were not large enough to spread the burden between players to protect the ones who were most talented and pivotal to the side's success. Centre-back Jack Charlton recalled in his autobiography that he missed a lot of international games between the two World Cups because of the pressure of playing for his club, Leeds United. Their manager Don Revie was eager to win every trophy the club competed in but suffered from the inability to rotate his squad in the manner he would be able to today.

Charlton still made the England squad for the 1970 tournament at the age of 35, as an experienced understudy to Brian Labone, who in turn had been Charlton's deputy in 1966. The future Republic of Ireland manager, whose team would play England at two international tournaments and who, unlike England, would qualify for the 1994 World Cup, was concerned that Francis Lee was in the team despite having trouble with the heat of Mexico.

Lee, who played with Bell for Manchester City, wore the number seven shirt which Alan Ball had worn in the home tournament; Ball took number eight for Mexico, with Bobby Charlton again wearing the number nine even though he was not a centre-forward. Lee went into business during his playing career, setting up a company which recycled wastepaper to make toilet tissue, and he eventually became City chairman for a tumultuous four years in the 1990s. He is to the blue side of Manchester what Charlton was to the red, although Charlton was merely a director of the club for whom he had played. The pair died within three weeks of each other in October 2023.

Speaking to *The Telegraph* in 2018, Lee remembered that England 'wore special Aertex shirts that were supposed to keep us cooler. The doctor tested our blood all the time. We had to take these sodium tablets which were meant to replace salt while we were playing. There was no stone unturned.' Sports science not yet being what it is today, this was commendable planning. On the topic of the heat, which exceeded 38ºC, Lee said that no player could take on fluids, with the dehydration so severe that after a match 'all you could do was lie on your hotel bed'.

Helped by a skilful squad, England came through the group stage with 1-0 wins against Romania and Czechoslovakia, with goals from Geoff Hurst and Allan Clarke respectively. The 1-0 defeat to eventual champions Brazil echoes through the decades, not least because of a Gordon Banks save from Pelé and the post-match shirt-swapping of the Brazilian and Bobby Moore.

The fact that the game was broadcast in colour, which accentuated the glamour of Brazil's golden apparel, also helped make memories which linger across the ages. Such a noble defeat would be followed by a pair against Argentina in 1986 and 1998, and it supports the theory that losing in a gallant manner to South American sides – excepting the hapless loss to Uruguay in 2014 – could also provide important signposts in the story of the England football team.

Mullery was the player deputed to track Pelé throughout the game, while Lee missed a good opportunity with a header. Jeff Astle, after he was introduced as a sub, passed up an even better chance. Pelé revealed that he and his team were more afraid of England than other European teams because they didn't mark man-to-man or adopt the sweeper system. Formations and playing styles would be a common cavil among critics and players as England reached successive tournaments, although this suggests that in 1970 it worked to their advantage.

One tactical tweak came with the reintroduction of wingers for Mexico. In 1966, Ramsey had famously employed an XI without them, choosing to leave out Ian Callaghan, Terry Paine and John Connelly for the knockout rounds. Instead, he used Stiles behind Charlton, Ball and Martin Peters. Peters wore the number 11 shirt usually given to a left-winger, which he retained for the 1970 tournament. 'We were the symbol of English austerity and coldness,' Peters told Andrew Downie for his book *The Greatest Show on Earth*, remembering how Mexico's fans kept them all awake before the game with constant chanting and beeping outside their hotel windows.

Plans for the quarter-final against West Germany were thrown into disarray when Banks was ruled out with illness. His replacement was Bonetti, who had been England's number two at the home tournament and was thrown in at short notice ahead of the third choice, Alex Stepney. 'The London press picked the goalkeeper' is something Francis Lee often maintained of the Chelsea player with little justification, in a manner which shows the geographical divisions of the media at the time. *The Guardian* had been called *The Manchester Guardian* until 1959, while London had several daily newspapers including the *Evening News*, the *West London Observer* and the *Evening Standard*.

Lee and Charlton both subsequently said that Banks would not have let Franz Beckenbauer's shot go past him for Germany's first goal, as Bonetti had done. In mitigation, Paul Hayward noted in his biography of the England team that there was the 'invisible element' of tiredness through dehydration, which likely caused lapses in concentration. These would have been particularly acute for goalkeepers who were away from the main action for great stretches of a typical game, let alone for Bonetti who had sat on the subs' bench throughout the group games.

As with Rob Green 40 years later in a World Cup match against the USA, for all his domestic successes – which included helping Chelsea win the FA Cup weeks before he headed to Mexico – Bonetti would be defined by an error in a high-profile game. Although David James, who started the 2010 finals, did not fall ill in the same manner Banks did, Green was still forced to come into the team in the middle of the tournament.

In future World Cups, there was a definitive number one who played every match: Peter Shilton in 1982, 1986 and 1990; David Seaman in 1998 and 2002; Paul Robinson in 2006; and Jordan Pickford in 2018 and 2022. Aside from a freak goal conceded by Seaman against Brazil in 2002, no goalkeeper was blamed in any respect for England failing to win a World Cup.

On Bonetti's death in April 2020, Brian Glanville's obituary of him in *The Guardian* noted that the German equaliser, headed backwards by Uwe Seeler, was 'something of a freak' and the England defence were equally culpable for that goal and Gerd Müller's winner; football, after all, is a team game, even though it is easy at the final whistle to look for a sacrificial lamb. Bonetti conceded more goals in that World Cup game than in his other six international caps combined; his 729 appearances for Chelsea places him second in the club's rankings, and he was an early inspiration to Shilton.

Jack Charlton failed to make the substitutes' bench for the game and, although England were 2-1 up, he wrote in his memoir that he 'couldn't stand it any more' and walked out of the stadium to sit in a cafe, returning to watch England lose in extra time. 'I've never seen a team come off the field so down,' he recalled. Brother Bobby had been substituted, as was common practice during the tournament because Ramsey was trying to protect him before the semi-final after three hard matches in the heat. Like Bonetti, neither Charlton brother ever played for England again.

After Germany equalised, Geoff Hurst headed a shot inches wide, and then the tie went into extra time, which saw Müller grab the winner. Had he not done so, because penalties had not yet been introduced to break a deadlock, lots would have had to be drawn to decide a victor. 'If you ever hear that footballers are mercenary types whose minds are stuffed with thoughts of how much they can squeeze out of the game and nothing else,' recalled Peters, 'tell them about the scene in our dressing room ... The place was like a disaster area.'

'I always loved watching England,' wrote Glenn Hoddle in his book *Playmaker*; the future midfielder and manager was 'desperate for us to win'. He had been very upset when Germany equalised to take the 1966 final into extra time, and he was equally frustrated when England lost to the Germans in Mexico, admitting, 'I was just a 12-year-old boy who didn't like losing.'

At the time, a typical 12-year-old was not able to watch a great deal of live football on TV, barring the FA Cup Final and World Cup games. *Match of the Day* had become a pivotal part of a football fan's diet by 1970, providing extended highlights of First Division matches. This was complemented by the print magazine *Charles Buchan's Football Monthly*, which would cease publication in 1974 having been joined by other titles like *Goal* and *Shoot!*

Arthur Hopcraft's taxonomical study into *The Football Man* was published in 1968, in which he wrote that the job of the England manager was to put together 'a team whose individual talents and personalities would cohere'. The focus on the latter was what led Ramsey to include all those central midfielders over wingers.

In all the conversation surrounding Ramsey's side, nobody has ever salivated over them in the manner people have purred over the era-defining teams of Brazil or the Netherlands; winning was all that mattered and 'attractiveness was incidental'. Ramsey himself, though 'not a popular man', had what Hopcraft called 'a cold dignity' whose players 'reflected his character truthfully ... He aimed at removing risk.' Far from the matinee idols who would take the job in the future, such as Kevin Keegan and Glenn Hoddle – who, like Ramsey, had both played for the national team – Ramsey was 'a poor talker' and 'tongue-tied' with the media, although Hopcraft did compliment how he was 'impeccably groomed'.

With more and more English people renting TVs, perhaps watching them while browsing a glossy magazine that came with the Sunday newspapers, 1970 saw a focus on the visual. To complement this, the World Cup brought the pub debate to the TV studio, with Malcolm Allison, Pat Crerand, Derek Dougan and Bob McNab arguing the toss and Jimmy Hill in the role of ebullient referee.

Alan Mullery was given a right to reply after Allison blamed him for the defeat against Germany, asking how many England caps the manager had won (zero). It made for a great moment of TV which drove the public conversation. Today, more would have been written about the bulldog called Winston who actually accompanied the England team to Mexico; indeed, the dog who travelled to the Women's European Championship in 2025 made several cameo appearances in the coverage of the tournament.

There has always been a focus on the men in FA blazers who act as custodians of the game even though they might come from outside football; once again, the officer class makes its presence felt among the infantry. Sir

Harold Thompson, a chemist, was the deputy chairman of the Football Association, the organisation which latterly referred to the long drought after the World Cup win as 'the 66 Overhang'.

In what would become a quadrennial FA event, Thompson wrote a postmortem after the 1970 World Cup which blamed members of the association itself for not being 'worldly' enough and manager Ramsey for his 'silent arrogance'. With a great deal of hyperbole, he wrote that the image of the English game was 'blurred, almost tarnished', although Thompson could not precisely pin the responsibility on high player wages, ill-disciplined fans or Ramsey's 'idiosyncrasies'. Such things, of course, would never have been questioned four years previously.

Unsurprisingly, as Duncan Hamilton wrote in *Answered Prayers*, the animosity between Thompson and Ramsey was a matter of 'class and upbringing'. How dare a former footballer have more authority than he. This recalls the TV sketch, also from 1966, where John Cleese portrayed an upper-class man, Ronnie Barker a middle-class one and Ronnie Corbett a member of the working class who intones, 'I know my place.'

As mentioned, there was more deference within society at the time, with little by way of social mobility which could help people rise through the levels of the class system. Ramsey's attempt to change how he spoke, adopting a clipped diction that belied his east London roots, was his attempt to be of the managerial class. Given that he had been born in 1920, his generation had served in wartime when the concept of a teenager was yet to be invented. Bobby Charlton, born in 1937, came along at the very end of the era, but he and Jack were children of wartime who grew up in the coal mining village of Ashington in Northumberland.

The youngest member of the 1970 squad was 22-year-old Emlyn Hughes, one of several born after the end of the Second World War. He would enjoy a career as captain of Liverpool, which saw him play dozens of games in European competition and, testament to the new TV era, would become a team captain on *A Question of Sport*. Famously, he gave Princess Anne a hug when she appeared on the programme, something nobody of Ramsey's generation, or even the Charltons', would have dared do.

When Ramsey was fired in 1974, he garnered sympathy from Celtic manager Jock Stein, who wrote that 'amateur legislators' had acted to remove him. Many years later, Ramsey himself revealed that he never enjoyed working for the FA, although he was proud that he had given the nation 'some glory, an identity to be proud of'. For Trevor Brooking, the manager had 'a passion about passing', telling players to 'treat the ball like a precious jewel' and to be positive in going forward rather than negatively 'stopping opponents'.

Ramsey took charge of the national team in the early 1960s, having won the First Division with Ipswich Town. At the time, the nation was still only two decades removed from the end of Empire, a time when Britain had granted independence to India and Pakistan. With the Queen at the head of the Commonwealth of former imperial countries, Britain was now attempting to forge closer links with Europe as part of the European Economic Community, the forerunner of the European Union.

Foreign secretary Sir Alec Douglas-Home asked in the House of Commons in July 1970, 'Is Britain to be in or out of this movement, which not only covers economic integration but looks beyond into the political and defence fields, this movement which in Europe has unquestionably been born of political will?'

1970

This question would reverberate across the decades during which England took part in many World Cups. The Second World War, the end of which was only 25 years in the past, was still a dominating theme of popular entertainment, all the better to remind people of the sacrifices and glories of the conflict. *Where Eagles Dare* and *The Battle of Britain* were still showing in cinemas months after their initial release, while on TV there was the fourth series of *Dad's Army*, which put a comedic spin on the war as it chronicled the goings-on of the Home Guard in Walmington-on-Sea.

The big new films of 1970 came in the form of *Ryan's Daughter*, directed by David Lean and set during the Easter Rising of 1916, and *The Go-Between*, which boasted a script by playwright Harold Pinter and starred Julie Christie and Alan Bates. *The Railway Children*, a novel published in 1905, was turned into a popular family film which was still being shown in schools in the 1990s, while rock 'n' roll pinup Mick Jagger (born in 1943) starred in *Performance*, where he played a rock 'n' roll pinup opposite the Eton-educated James Fox. The film touched on East End gangsterism as well as the new era of free-loving hippies.

For something less risqué, screen versions of stage musicals abounded, including *Hello, Dolly!* and *Funny Girl*, making it a very good time for fans of Barbra Streisand, who played the title role in both of the latter two productions. *Oliver!* was also still popular, updating Charles Dickens a century after he wrote about orphans and street urchins. A new version of the show played in London during 2025, with greater sensitivity shown towards the Jewish character of Fagin.

Entertainers peppered football pitches too. Midfielder Rodney Marsh was given his England debut by Ramsey, but he despaired that the manager had tried to change how he played and 'never allowed me to express myself'.

He wrote in his memoir *I Was Born a Loose Cannon*, 'I had complete respect for Ramsey the football man. I didn't have so much respect for Ramsey the person.' Ramsey once swore at a Scottish journalist before the teams met at Hampden Park and it was also 'pathetic' to Marsh that he had taken those elocution lessons to refine his accent.

'In the dressing room he was completely expressionless,' Marsh continued, 'like a mouse, standing there with a clipboard.' He was nonetheless 'meticulous with detail' and 'demanded loyalty, and if you didn't respect that you were out'. Alan Mullery was loyal to Ramsey, saying that he gained 'tremendous respect' from the players, who acknowledged that the boss knew their strong and weak points when it came to how they played the game. He also, helpfully, 'didn't complicate' the game of football.

For Bobby Charlton, Ramsey simply 'elected to play his best team' and gave them 'pride and an unprecedented belief that we could compete in the wider football world'. This served to inspire younger coaches 'in a new climate of confidence', although one such coach, Bobby Robson, called Ramsey 'a bizarre fellow' who never replied to Robson's invitations to attend England games in the 1980s.

When Ramsey was manager, a player like Charlton had to play within the team, in contrast to how Sven-Göran Eriksson would later shoehorn central midfielders into playing in wide positions. Charlton himself famously annulled the influence of Franz Beckenbauer in the 1966 World Cup Final, which lessened his own importance on the game and sublimated himself into the team's overall effort. Naturally, had England lost, history would have declared this tactic a mistake, just as taking off Charlton in the 1970 tournament was said to be one contributing factor to the defeat.

The captain of Ramsey's two England tournament sides was Bobby Moore. Rodney Marsh wrote that he was 'someone who meant everything to everybody' and 'a people's champion ... When he looked you in the eye and shook your hand, he made you feel special.' Moore led the team by example, as per England's future captains Terry Butcher, David Beckham, Steven Gerrard and Harry Kane. As a player, Marsh wrote that Moore was 'always a step ahead ... He played the game in slow motion.'

Yet by 1983, far from enjoying the high-profile punditry careers of defenders like Jamie Carragher and Rio Ferdinand, Moore was coaching an American side of which Marsh was chief executive, the old defender 'scratching around for a living'. His own media presence was limited to a column in tabloid newspaper the *Sunday Sport* and summarising matches on radio station Capital Gold.

In a sign of the more parochial nature of football fandom at the time, when Moore died in 1993 and West Ham fans left flowers at Upton Park, the only acknowledgement of his passing came during their game. It was different in 2023 when Bobby Charlton's death was greeted with tributes across the country. Whereas Charlton was immortalised in bronze outside Old Trafford during his lifetime, a statue of Moore was put up posthumously at Wembley Stadium in 2007: the writing under it reads 'immaculate footballer, imperial defender ... captain extraordinary, gentleman of all time'. The bridge by Wembley Park station also bears his name.

Over the years, clubs have come to honour their esteemed former talent, as a way for future generations of supporters to keep their name alive. At Stoke City, there are statues of Gordon Banks and Stanley Matthews, while at Newcastle United there is a statue of and a stand named after Jackie Milburn. Jack Leslie, a black man who would have played for England in the 1920s had the selection committee not withdrawn his name on discovering his ethnicity, is memorialised at Plymouth Argyle and in Matt Tiller's book *The Lion Who Never Roared*.

Jeff Astle has a set of gates named after him at The Hawthorns, home ground of West Bromwich Albion. He died in 2002 of Alzheimer's, a cause of which was confirmed in 2014 to be chronic traumatic encephalopathy, a brain disease that resulted from repeatedly heading a football. Although there was a great deal of pushback from the FA and other organisations, who called for more evidence linking the two, these days younger footballers are discouraged from heading the ball. Several reports have outlined that there are dozens of players whose time in the game contributed to the onset of dementia and brain injury. They were over three times more likely than an average person to suffer such issues.

Outside Huddersfield rail station stands Harold Wilson, who was the Labour prime minister on the day England won the 1966 World Cup. Denis Howell, who was his sports minister in charge of delivering the tournament, had been a league referee, and Wilson had asked him why Ramsey had withdrawn Charlton against Germany. Niall Edworthy wrote in his book on England's managers, *The Second Most Important Job in the Country*, that during the 1970 World Cup 'politicians giving local lectures in the run-up to the general election addressed near-empty town halls'.

It may well be true that England's loss at the 1970 World Cup cost Wilson the election. Howell remembered a meeting the morning after the match where football, not politics, was discussed, 'And whether Ramsey or Bonetti was the major culprit. I tried to be good-humoured about my answers, but for the first time I had real doubts and knew the mood was changing fast.'

A key objective of this book is to tie together the national team and political life in England. It helps the opening chapter that Wilson was a football fan himself; when he was a young child, his local team won three First Division titles in a row, and he carried a postcard with the 1924 team on it in his wallet. He maintained his West Yorkshire accent when he was prime minister, and he was known to smoke a pipe in public in an image-conscious manner. Only Steve McClaren has been associated with a prop of his own, an umbrella, while managing England, although Gareth Southgate briefly started a trend for wearing waistcoats at the 2018 tournament.

When he was elected Labour Party leader in 1963, *The Guardian* called Wilson a performer 'unequalled in the present House of Commons'. He was certainly more of a rhetorician than Ramsey, 'like a battering ram with a mind behind it'. Unlike the England manager, however, according to a biography by Nick Thomas-Symonds, Wilson was keen on 'preventive action', particularly when avoiding sending troops to fight foreign wars. The Wilson government was in the right place to abolish the death penalty, commuting it to life imprisonment.

Wilson was a keen social reformer. In the 1960s, the quota of pupils educated in comprehensive schools rose from one in ten to one in three, then up to two in three by the mid-1970s. He also spearheaded the introduction of the Open University in 1969, a so-called 'university of the air' that prioritised distance learning; students would be sent course materials by post. Radio and television were seen as conduits of education as well as entertainment.

When it came to abortion, an act for which he brought before parliament in 1967, Wilson saw that opinion polls showed majority support for his reforms, especially among those who voted Labour. Social mores were changing, with the Theatres Act of 1968 abolishing the need for censorship, which soon saw risqué contemporary musicals like *Hair* and *The Rocky Horror Picture Show* reach the London stage.

Wilson's chancellor and home secretary had swapped roles halfway through his six years in government between 1964 and 1970: Roy Jenkins became chancellor in 1967, taking the role from James Callaghan. When the latter became prime minister, he would be the last to have fought in a war, having served in the navy.

In the 1970 Budget, Jenkins argued that it had been necessary to devalue the pound in order to repay British debts, which at the end of 1968 came to £3.36bn. 'This meant higher taxes, a strict pruning of public sector expenditure programmes, and a firm monetary policy,' he said. Jenkins also noted the 24 per cent increase in exported goods and services in the previous two years, a period which also saw a wage rise of ten per cent.

The 1970 general election cast Wilson's Labour Party out of power on 19 June, five days after the Germany defeat. A 1997 BBC news report noted that the election 'was the first in the postwar era to focus on the leaders and not the parties', with Wilson busy outlining to TV viewers, unsuccessfully, why they should continue with more of the same. He was accompanied by his wife Mary, all the better to portray him as a family man.

For his part, Conservative leader Ted Heath pursued a campaign to label the contest the 'Shopping Basket Election', attacking Labour's handling of the economy in the time-honoured fashion to which the Conservatives have often defaulted. There was a complete reversal in the number of seats: the Conservatives won 77, Labour lost 76 and the majority was 42, with over a million more votes cast for the new party of government than for the party who had implemented all these social reforms.

1970

No matter the trophies you accrue, and the joy you bring to supporters, you are only as good as the most recent tournament performance. This is as true in politics as it is in football. Just as how a manager's best-laid pre-season plans are ruined by injury to a key player, Heath's chancellor Iain Macleod died of a heart attack a month into his premiership.

In 1968, the government had expanded the Race Relations Act of 1965, which had helped second-generation immigrants to secure housing and employment. In 1970 the focus was on equality between the sexes, and Labour introduced the Equal Pay Act, spearheaded by employment minister Barbara Castle: sewing machinists at the Dagenham-based Ford factory had, two years previously, gone on strike in protest at being paid 15 per cent less than the men who did the same job.

The act, however, took until 1975 to come into force and, all these years on, plenty of women are still not paid an equivalent wage to their male counterparts. It should be noted that women were still not allowed to play football in 1970, with the game's status as 'unsuitable for females' still in force decades after the official FA ban, something not even a World Cup triumph could reverse, although the ban was lifted in 1971. We shall see later how a combination of investment and FA guidance contributed, half a century on, to the England women's side reaching three major tournament finals in a row.

But what precisely was the England that the football team was representing at every World Cup? Throughout this investigation, it is instructive to look at the sort of laws the government was bringing to the statute books. They were supplied to Her Majesty the Queen each year for a speech to open each annual session of parliament, and we can thus look at transcripts of Queen's Speeches across the decades.

At the very start of the 1970 schedule was the earlier mentioned start of negotiations for Britain to become a member of what was then the European Community. The country also sought stronger ties with NATO at a time when the USA was waging a disastrous war in Vietnam. Wilson opted not to send British troops to the Far East, which in hindsight was a shrewd decision. In 1960, national service had been phased out, allowing people either to enter the job market without first serving in the armed forces, to go straight on to university or, indeed, to represent their football club as a young man.

The Queen also announced reviews of company law and the running of primary schools, and that the government would encourage home ownership. Almost three decades before it actually came to pass, plans were made to give more powers to Wales and Scotland. It would only take three years for commercial radio to launch as a competition to the BBC. Capital Radio was the major London pop music station, providing a home for the irreverent genius Kenny Everett, while Piccadilly Radio in Manchester and City Radio in Liverpool were essential listening for local football fanatics.

In May 1970, the prime minister fielded a question about the potential of there being too much football on TV during the World Cup, 'over-saturation ... on both channels' as the Labour MP Charles Pannell put it; that is, on BBC1 and BBC2, rather than the regionally broadcast ITV. This was especially true in the year of a general election. In a reply that reflected the patrician times, Wilson reckoned, 'The ladies are less keen on seeing it, football, on both channels.'

When Wilson died in 1995, prime minister John Major noted that he had been 'the only man to preside over England's winning the World Cup'. Unlike Ramsey, he was able to stand down on his own terms, in 1976, having won four general elections across a decade. To Tony Blair, then the Labour leader in opposition, his predecessor 'was to politics what The Beatles were to popular culture. He simply dominated the nation's political landscape, and he personified the new era, not stuffy or hidebound but classless, forward-looking, modern.'

Ramsey and the FA who paid his wages were nothing of the sort. Blair's remarks when Ramsey died in 1999, which coincided with a drive to host the 2006 World Cup, were to say that he 'gave England the greatest moment in its sporting history', words which were echoed by Bobby Charlton. 'He was professional to his fingertips,' said the midfielder who had himself acted in a highly professional manner in his attempt to deliver the World Cup tournament to England's pitches three decades after he won it at Wembley.

Alan Mullery, whose words opened this chapter, was keen to remind England fans that when Ramsey said something 'he said it quietly but you listened, otherwise you didn't play in the next game'. The age of player power was still a long way off.

1974

ENGLAND AS a nation was troubled in the middle of the 1970s, and not just because the football team failed to qualify for the 1974 World Cup in West Germany.

Post Office workers were routinely on strike, inflation reached nine per cent and, for the first time since the 1930s, over a million people were registered unemployed. In 1971 Rolls-Royce, which had been founded in Manchester in the early part of the century, had gone bankrupt and had been brought into state control by the government.

The new Conservative government had introduced the Industrial Relations Act of 1971, which attempted to limit strikes to official trade unions only. In 1972, prime minister Ted Heath had announced a 90-day freeze on prices and wages, and at the end of the year he ordered a close-down of TV channels at 10.30pm. *Match of the Day* was thus broadcast earlier in the evening.

The country's reliance on oil cost it dearly in 1973, when the OPEC group reduced production and suspended the supply of oil to the USA. They could weather the storm because they had their own resources but, given that the UK imported it for half its energy needs, prices quadrupled. A TV campaign was launched in January 1974 to 'Switch Off Something' and save energy, with the country working a three-day week and with a ban in place on overtime. This helped football experiment with matches on a Sunday, a practice which quickly petered out once energy supplies were more plentiful.

Chancellor Denis Healey delivered the 1974 Budget in March after Labour had won back power in a minority government. Although they had four seats more than the Conservatives, they were 17 seats short of an overall majority. 'These are in no sense normal circumstances,' Healey said, having been in his post for all of three weeks. 'It is as if I have been sent into the arena to fight the monstrous problems now confronting me with one hand tied behind my back.' Had he used a football metaphor, he would have been 2-0 down with ten men deep into the second half of a cup final.

The deficit had increased to £4bn, which would be eased by a ten-year loan of $2.5bn. Healey also brought up the potential dividends from North Sea oil, although he was careful to confirm it would not be 'the answer to all our problems'. Britain, he went on pessimistically, 'is moving fast in the wrong direction. Serious dangers lie very close ahead. Somehow we must steer ourselves on to a safer course' and into 'a just and fair society'. Even though he denied saying it, Healey's catchphrase was to 'squeeze the rich and make the pips squeak'. The average footballer would not find himself among these rich Englishmen just yet, even if they played for their country.

Key to Healey's plans was to reduce waste and put a lid on any rise in inflation, and to 'recreate that sense of social unity on which Britain has always had to rely at a time of national crisis. This means convincing the whole nation that the burden of our sacrifices and the rewards of our successes are fairly shared.' Electricity, coal and rail travel prices would increase, the first of these at an average of 30 per cent, although, without negotiation, it would have gone up as high as 50 per cent. Given that these were all state-owned industries, the consumer would be hit hard and somewhat unfairly. Additionally, steel prices would go up by 25 per cent to match how much it now cost to produce it.

Healey chose not to lower VAT on crisps, ice cream and soft drinks, which raised £125m inside a year; he did realise that his decision would be 'unpopular with the children'. He was equally keen to add 20p to a bottle of whiskey or gin, ten pence to a bottle of wine and a penny to a pint of beer, levies which would raise a quite incredible £165m in one year. The highest rate of investment income tax, meanwhile, rose to 98 per cent.

Now speaking in opposition, Ted Heath said Healey had left out of his statement the £2bn rise in oil prices and the risk of still rising unemployment. He also pointed out that Healey had sought advice from a Cambridge-based academic rather than one from Oxford University, which suggests that in some places even a selection such as this becomes a matter of interest.

Heath also declared, in solidarity with the sort of person who votes for Labour, that Healey 'has found that he cannot raise the money from the rich ... The great burden is being carried by the great mass of the people.' He concluded that the chancellor was adopting 'the usual socialist policies of increasing taxation, of squeezing the profits, of giving no additional opportunities or incentives to those who work in industry or to those who produce the goods or to those responsible for our exports'.

Healey's speech lasted two hours and 20 minutes, or the length of a football match that goes to penalties. He immediately promised a second Budget later in the year, thanks to Britain's 'unique economic difficulties'; he gave it in July, with a third following in November. This was because, in October, Labour had won an overall majority of three seats in the year's second general election, having crossed the threshold with 319 MPs.

Heath had, without success, promised a government of national unity, akin to the one which governed Britain during the Second World War. He was, however, aware that he would find difficulty in winning the election because the Conservatives were unpopular after the disagreements with the miners. As the political journalist Steve Richards wrote in his book *Turning Points*, 'A union made a pay demand. Heath resisted. There were strikes as a result. An independent body came down more or less on the side of the union's demands.'

This was in spite of his efforts arguing for Britain's place in the European Community. He also enabled package holiday businesses, which had previously been yet another industry that fell under government control, to operate as private companies, something which helped football fans follow their teams abroad. The first few years of the 1970s saw more success for British clubs, especially in the newly established UEFA Cup.

Tottenham beat Wolves in an all-English final in 1972, with Liverpool winning the 1973 trophy; they would win it again in 1976 with a side that included Ian Callaghan, who played in the 1966 World Cup, and Kevin Keegan, who would be the talisman of the 1982 England team. The Cup Winners' Cup went to Chelsea in 1971, when they beat Real Madrid after a replay two days after the first attempt at settling the final.

Talk of unity in the March Budget and the October election was solidified by what Healey called 'the social contract'. He sought to replace 'the politics of confrontation', mainly between the government and trade unionists, to stall any further increase in unemployment levels which would have resulted from layoffs and redundancies. His plan to keep their wages lower and to curb inflation backfired because workers wanted fairer wages and, as Heath had discovered, they were willing to go on strike to get them. Dominic Sandbrook, in his BBC TV series *The 70s*, called this 'a victory for aspiration' rather than for socialism, where 'ordinary people's ambitions were outrunning the nation's ability to pay for them'.

Healey and the second Wilson government found the same problems as Heath had done, proving that merely changing the parties in power did not magically make major issues disappear. For the England football team, managers still have to cope with shallow talent pools, disruptive talents and older or off-form players whom nobody dares drop. Yet the narratives still spin around these leaders or managers as an easy shorthand for readers, driving their attention away from the issues and towards the personalities.

For his part, in 1974 Healey was worried about the global oil crisis, where prices had gone up fivefold in the past 12 months, and of the cost of sugar, which had gone up sixfold. In late 1973, basic foodstuffs including meat and eggs had also risen by double-digit percentages. Ironically, given the theme of Heath's 1970 election campaign, it was once again the shopping basket that convinced voters to eject the Conservatives. Politicians are at the mercy of global events, just as Alf Ramsey was powerless when his goalkeeper was ill before the 1970 World Cup quarter-final, but there was no Peter Bonetti for Ted Heath to fall back on. Nor would there be for Denis Healey.

'There is grave risk that we shall once again be plunged into a depression on a scale as great as we encountered over 40 years ago,' the chancellor said in his Budget, with the unmentioned peril of what that depression of the 1930s led to. Back in July, in spite of the country's financial hardship,

Labour had found the room to raise pensions by 30 per cent in order to keep a portion of the electorate on their side. They had also raised miners' wages by 35 per cent, in the same manner that the Labour government elected in 2024 gave pay rises to doctors and nurses, who can be seen as the modern equivalent to the coal miner struggling to do their job in very difficult conditions.

Of the new estate duty he had levied, Healey said he was 'somewhat shocked by the volume and intensity of protest generated in some quarters' to make it a compulsory tax. 'I should have expected the moderation of my proposals, particularly the exemption for transfers between husband and wife, to have brought me gratitude rather than abuse from those concerned,' he said, sounding like a football manager who still elicits grumbles from people despite acceding to their demands to pick a popular player. These people will always find another fault elsewhere, usually in playing style or not converting as many chances as they ought. In politics and football, satisfaction is as elusive as the Golden Snitch.

Back on the other side of the House of Commons, Heath's Budget reply for the Conservatives picked up on a figure of £6.3bn, the new deficit, and complained of Labour's 'statistical deceit' over the unemployment figures and the 'fraudulent prospectus' in its election campaign concerning local government financing. 'We have to accept a socialist state,' Heath said, returning to his theme from March. He would hand the party leadership over in 1975; Heath would, just as Geoff Hurst would later do, become an author of books, in his case on music and sailing, which he would sign for readers at public appearances.

Alf Ramsey would also, as mentioned, relinquish his job in 1974. Like Ramsey, and unlike Wilson, Heath adopted an upper-class accent which was entirely different from the one he was born in Kent with. Ramsey, however, would tell people he would not discuss the events of 1966 because he was at work on a book and did not want to breach a contract; needless to say, the book did not exist. Brian Glanville wrote in his book on England managers, which as per its subtitle he called 'the toughest job in football', that Ramsey 'had no real hinterland: football had been the warp and weft on his life, given an almost religious importance'.

Peter Shilton replaced Gordon Banks in goal after the 1966 medal winner injured his eye in a car accident; he wrote that Ramsey was like 'a mother hen' to his players. In *Answered Prayers*, Duncan Hamilton mentioned a celebratory 'testimonial dinner' at London's Café Royal which attracted over 60 England players whom Ramsey had managed, as well as prime minister Harold Wilson, who presented him with a replica World Cup trophy.

Losing the job was 'like a bereavement', although he was approached by Ajax, who were one of the continent's dominant clubs. He became a pundit on the TV coverage of the tournament for which his team had failed to qualify. Following this, Ramsey was first a director then short-term manager at Birmingham City. The only two other managers who did not guide England to a World Cup went to the Middle East and Watford, although happily England have reached the final tournament every fourth year since 1994.

Even after England missed out on the 1974 World Cup, however, Ramsey asked for a doubling of his salary, perhaps hoping the FA would focus on 12 good years rather than one poor one. This would have brought him much closer to, but still would not have matched, the salaries of Don Revie or Brian Clough, whose Leeds United and Derby County teams were near the summit of the First Division.

Such a disparity in domestic and international team salaries continued into the 1990s, with Gerry Francis noting that he would have had a wage that was 50 per cent lower than his Tottenham one if he accepted the England job, even though the latter was 'the ultimate in English football'. Prestige used to make up for financial shortfalls, but at some point, a few years into the Premier League era, money would start to matter as managers sought compensation at the market rate.

According to Martin Peters, by the end of his time as manager Ramsey 'had very few friends left in the press box and he found himself isolated and without support, except from the players'. A more hostile media environment may well have seen a new manager appointed after the 1970 tournament, as the FA bowed to pressure from the outside; it would take until the circulation wars of the 1980s for the England manager's job to be subject to extreme criticism from the printed press.

Ultimately, however, Ramsey didn't adjust to a time when substitutions could change the game; they had previously only been permitted in non-competitive games, which meant that a manager was dependent on the 11 starters at the 1966 World Cup. As to his style of management, Alan Mullery said it was simply a matter of Ramsey picking the team and formation, then letting the players 'get on with it'.

In training sessions Ramsey would 'stand on the touchline watching, saying virtually nothing'. Duncan Hamilton called his team one of 'functionality rather than flair ... not the kind of side that made you gasp'. It was enough for him that he could choose his own squad, something a group of FA selectors formerly did.

England played Poland in a must-win qualifier for the 1974 World Cup, as part of a three-team group where only one could advance to the finals. The starting XI contained only one member of the 1966 team, in Peters, with Alan Ball suspended and Bobby Moore dropped to the bench after a bad game out in Warsaw. England enjoyed 35 attempts on goal, with one goal disallowed, four shots cleared off the line and only a penalty from Allan Clarke putting them on the scoresheet.

Amazingly, Wembley had no clock to alert the manager to the remaining time, so he instead blamed a broken watch on his decision to make a change with only a minute of the match left. Given that defender Norman Hunter made the error for the Poland goal, one would expect him to have been made the scapegoat, even by the media, but Ramsey refused to criticise him. History recalls the Polish goalkeeper Jan Tomaszewski having the game of his life, which seems an act of transference and an easy solution to explain away England's poor conversion rate.

Remembering the game in 2013 for the BBC Sport website, commentator Barry Davies mentioned English exceptionalism, given that they had qualified for every World Cup since 1950, having sat out the first few tournaments, 'I don't think anybody seriously thought England would fail. This was still in the age when everybody felt we had an entitlement to be in the World Cup finals.' At the final whistle, 'There was a stunned silence … It was more disbelief than anything else.'

In 2021, Jonathan Wilson recalled the game for *The Observer* and noted how England 'late on lumped ball after ball into the box without much variety or imagination'. With Ramsey's style passé, 'the template of decline was already in place', but the match can be read either as an unfortunate draw or a deserving defeat. To Wilson, it 'reflects back almost whatever the viewer wants to see'. At the 1990 World Cup, when England lost to West Germany in the semi-final, the endlessly replayed pictures inform how agonising a first penalty shoot-out loss was, rather than how fortunate England had been just to be playing the game following two extra-time knockout victories.

Often, just as how governments are blamed for things outside their general control, people pointed fingers at the FA when it was the players who had failed to convert more of their three dozen opportunities. In 1973, the association was keen to let fans across the country watch the team. Writing in his memoir *The First Voice You Will Hear Is...*, FA secretary Ted Croker realised sales for the game at Wembley against Austria had been rather low. He advertised the match in newspapers and, for the first time, on TV. The sellout fixture against Poland was screened on ITV, opening up the audience to millions, who would enjoy it in full rather than be served highlights.

Nonetheless, in a short but withering chapter of his biography of the England football team, Paul Hayward called the group of the time 'subservient to the Blazers'; players and coaches flew economy while the executives sat in the front part of the plane. Officer class still ruled, but they were not the most effective leaders of their men.

The coach of Ajax, Ștefan Kovács, said that Ramsey's late-period England team were like '11 faceless gladiators chasing around as if the clubhouse were on fire'. In Amsterdam, spearheaded by Johan Cruyff, Ajax were reinventing positional play with their total football, whereas England still played as they did in, yes, 1966. The German playmaker Günter Netzer had complained the previous year that his English opponents 'had autographed my leg', although he had a clue of the challenge he faced because the team included Norman Hunter, whose infamous nickname was 'Bites Yer Legs'. Defenders like him and Jack Charlton had been taught to tackle and were not shy to do so.

For Henry Winter, writing of the failure to qualify for the World Cup in his book *Fifty Years of Hurt*, 'The hysterical reaction merely accentuates the anxiety. A more cerebral nation would analyse the stats, inspect the performance against Poland and coldly put it down to experience, not trigger panic stations. This is a serial fault of the English, this tendency of players, managers, administrators and reporters to respond with emotion rather than thought.'

Perhaps this makes for better newspaper copy than rationalising defeat with cold detachment. Across this investigation, there will be very little quotation of tabloid newspaper commentary on the England side, given that they are prone to hyperbole and viciousness. To give a single illustrative example, in 1973 one reporter for *The Sun*, Peter Batt, called for 'euthanasia' of the English game, to 'blow soccer up and build on the ashes', all because England had failed to beat Poland in two matches at the rough end of Alf Ramsey's time as manager. Forgotten amid all this is that Poland went on to reach the semi-finals of the 1974 World Cup.

At this point, it is customary to bring into the discussion the flair players who never found a regular place in an England side managed by Ramsey. Peter Shilton has written that it was coaches, not players, who dictated the game, and that these coaches saw it much safer to pick a stopper or a clogger than a dribbler or an entertainer. These players would attract audiences to their clubs over a 42-game season but they were less trusted for the few international fixtures against a home nation like Scotland or when England needed to advance to a tournament finals.

Frank Worthington was quoted by Rob Steen in his book *The Mavericks* as saying that football 'became part of the pop industry' in the 1970s, where haircuts and clothes were as important as stepovers and half-volleys. The striker himself was an enormous Elvis Presley fanatic, so he was in a way responsible for this. Steen wrote that 'football's reluctance to market itself left the job to the tabloids', who were delighted to feature the game's attacking playmakers in their pages. George Best led the charge, and there were plenty of English equivalents, including Rodney Marsh and his QPR team-mate Stan Bowles.

Bowles wrote in his autobiography of a clique among Derby County's England internationals of the 1973 team: Colin Todd, Roy McFarland and Kevin Hector would keep apart from the rest of the squad, Bowles joked, 'for fear of being contaminated' by them. Marsh had also mentioned a clique, 'with some players always sniping at others behind their backs'. This meant the England squad 'always felt fragmented'. Perhaps they were in need of the kind of social contract that Denis Healey wanted the English nation to have.

The environment was perfect to help bring in football's commercial era, from which today's multimillion-pound business would emerge. Players would be offered a £50 bonus if they were pictured in the newspapers wearing a branded T-shirt or boots; Bowles famously wore a shoe of one brand on one foot, and another on the other. He wrote that his mum's dog had turned one of his five caps into a chew toy, while he lost another while playing cards. All the same, Bowles remained proud of representing his country, 'I had shown I was good enough to play for England. I had done something that they said I couldn't do.'

As we shall discover, the modern focus on elite player development means that England's 2026 World Cup squad will contain very few surprises because the FA has known about players since they were in the younger age groups, welcoming them to the national centre at St George's

Park across the years of their development. In the past, however, players like Bowles have blossomed and made their England debuts in spite of a modest path to the top of the game: Jamie Vardy and Rickie Lambert both went to a finals tournament in the 2010s having never been considered for the England teams below senior level. Ian Wright only missed out on travelling to France in 1998 because of an injury.

Bowles was picked by Joe Mercer, whose biography was called *Football with a Smile*. Appropriately, across his short spell as caretaker manager he was 'determined to put the fun back into international football', with Worthington also picked for the team. Mercer, whom Peter Shilton memorably described as having 'a banana grin, bandy legs and a heart bigger than his head', did not take the job permanently due to bad sciatica.

In spite of the rising energy prices and industrial disputes, which were mentioned at the beginning of this chapter, the 1970s was an extraordinary time for home ownership. The historian Dominic Sandbrook called the early part of the decade 'the Wimpey years', with homes built by that constructor springing up in towns like Peterborough to resettle slum residents from 'damp and dilapidated' London. The government encouraged people to take out a mortgage and own their own home, at a time when the Bank of England was less strict about who could borrow money.

This, naturally, created the same kind of market that always springs up when a state-owned enterprise, be it energy or telecommunications, falls into private ownership. Mortgage companies began to compete for the attention of homebuyers as house prices rose by ten times between 1970 and 1980. All modern conveniences filled these homes, which gave people more leisure time and moved

Britain into the new, technological era. It also pulled them away from the pub, even if it was one owned by a retired footballer.

David Goldblatt wrote in his book *The Game of Our Lives* that English football of the 1970s was 'conservative, paternalist, racist and sexist, but then so was everything else in the country'. Benny Hill chased women in sped-up film in a TV show that was not brought to an end until 1989, while actors blacked up as minstrels. Attitudes to race were examined, complete with words that have now become eradicated from society, on primetime shows like *Love Thy Neighbour* and *Till Death Us Do Part*.

One of the most popular shows on TV was *The Good Old Days*, which from 1953 to 1983 comprised prewar singalongs in a studio in Leeds which replicated an old music hall. People who attended tapings of the show would dress up in appropriate period costumes, which were anachronistic and smacked of nostalgia, but it would be no different to an England fan of 2026 watching a game dressed in an old Admiral kit from the 1980s.

The Good Old Days was as old-fashioned as an Alf Ramsey England side, especially at a time when David Bowie and Marc Bolan were bringing androgyny and glitter to *Top of the Pops*; to Dominic Sandbrook, by the end of the decade this was perhaps the only programme that could offer a viewer 'more than an occasional black face'. The England team who lost to Poland was entirely white, although Ramsey and his successor Don Revie could have picked West Ham striker Clyde Best, one of his side's black players whom Bobby Moore protected from racist abuse.

Brendon Batson, Laurie Cunningham and Cyrille Regis played for West Bromwich Albion, and the trio gave fans an appreciation for otherwise marginalised players.

Bananas were thrown towards black players like these four, who were also compared to golliwog toys. Goldblatt called such players 'the most visible black men in British public life', especially because there was no black member of parliament until 1987.

Oddly, as Goldblatt also noted, the hooligan firms were 'among the most mixed parts' of the crowd, with the Cool Cats of Manchester City and Birmingham Zulus fighting the National Front, on whom more in the next chapter. Sports minister Denis Howell set up a group to deal with the problem, realising that English football hooliganism didn't help sell the image of the game. Nor did old stadiums and 'rusting terrace barriers', he said, but there was also far more competition for leisure time than in previous years, including from 'DIY, gardening and shopping'.

In an eclectic period for British cinema, 1974 was the year of the sex comedy *Confessions of a Window Cleaner*, the latest Bond movie *The Man with the Golden Gun* and the adaptation of *Murder on the Orient Express* starring Lauren Bacall, Sean Connery and Albert Finney. After the success of *The Railway Children*, the 1930 novel *Swallows and Amazons* was plucked off the shelves of children's literature and turned into a motion picture which depicted adventures in the Lake District. This was a world away from the footballing heartland of the nation, although Stan Bowles did play a season for Carlisle United.

The Queen's Speech of 1974 alluded to a referendum on membership of the European Economic Community; Britain voted 'in' in 1975. Another clause posited that goods carried their price on labels, while the government also mooted the removal of entrance charges to museums. As with Scottish and Welsh devolution, it would take over 20 years for this to become law, in this case in 2001; the National Football Museum in Manchester does carry a charge, in the form of an annual season ticket, unless you are a resident of the city.

The government also wrote that it would 'oppose all forms of racial discrimination', which would have proven impossible to enforce in football stadiums, as well as a restatement of the purpose of the Race Relations Act referred to earlier; this was paired with a mention of the country still called Rhodesia, the modern-day Zimbabwe.

In the four months that led up to the Queen's Speech, there had been a state of emergency surrounding the dispute over coal mining as well as the election, which had been such a close call that there had to be another one later in the year. Compared with not qualifying for a World Cup, political events were far more important to the life of the country, but there would be no England team to support during the summer of 1974 – as there had been every fourth year since 1950.

The Queen's Christmas message, in a year which also saw bombings by the Irish Republican Army, sought to remind viewers that 'we have much more in common than there is dividing us … Goodwill is better than resentment, tolerance is better than revenge, compassion is better than anger.' She added that it was the 'comradeship of adversity' that served to bring out the best in people, although the England football team who represented the Queen still believed themselves to be superior to most opponents they faced.

1978

ONCE AGAIN, England failed to qualify for the 1978 World Cup, which took place in Argentina and was won by the hosts. Weeks after they contributed to the team's victory, Osvaldo Ardiles and Ricardo Villa, who were room-mates during the tournament, landed in England to sign for Tottenham. The FA had finally removed the rule that forbade clubs from buying talent from outside Europe, having been pushed to do so by a European court ruling. Previously, players born in countries outside the British Commonwealth had to have lived in England for two years.

It had taken the England football team 20 years to participate in the World Cup, having refused to do so until 1950. Three years later, two heavy losses against Hungary, who became the first non-British or Irish team to triumph at Wembley Stadium, demolished any sense of superiority among other European nations. As we learned in the previous chapter, some critics were shocked when England did not qualify for the 1974 World Cup, even though the tactical approach was out of date and Poland had achieved the right result in their home match which set them up for qualification.

How much better might it have been for English players to mix with international talent in their dressing room in the 1970s, or even for more Englishmen to have gone abroad? Preventing clubs from signing global talent was another sign of insularity and protectionism, and a few decades later the balance would tip the other way. By that stage, the FA were powerless to stop clubs from stacking their rosters with South American or European journeymen, although the game was enriched by the presence of Eric Cantona, Dennis Bergkamp and Thierry Henry. Ardiles and Villa, when they signed for Tottenham, were a welcome addition to football in England.

Between 1974 and 1977, the national team manager was Don Revie, another man who is immortalised in a statue; his stands outside Elland Road thanks to the success he led Leeds United to. Revie died in 1989 of motor neurone disease, but nobody from the FA turned up to his funeral; conversely, Bobby Robson's memorial was attended by several former England managers and players.

Amazingly, Revie lacked the necessary full coaching qualifications to manage England, which seems in keeping with the amateur ethos of the governing body who appointed him; two members of the 1966 World Cup squad, Gordon Banks and George Eastham, coached the under-23s side. In the senior game against Czechoslovakia at Wembley, fans were handed a piece of paper with a thank you note from the new manager on one side and the lyrics to 'Land of Hope and Glory' on the other. Just as Revie's Leeds sang of marching on together, so it was thought that Revie's England could enjoy vocal and stirring support from spectators.

This was also the game in which England first wore a shirt with a sponsor's logo on it, that of the Leicester-based sportswear maker Admiral. The shirt was sold in stores so the FA could raise some money to plough back into the national game. Revie initiated the idea to be more commercial, something over which Alf Ramsey had demurred; at the time, the FA were still stumping up for balls and kits. Trevor Brooking, who would later work for the association as director of football development, argued that private finance had supported the development of English coaching centres, which allowed for more full-time professionals, so such commercialism was a good thing for the game.

Not everybody agreed with the new developments. In February 1977, the MP Roy Hughes brought up Admiral in a parliamentary debate on sports equipment. 'Children are being exploited,' he fulminated; what was more, Admiral was also using the same lions that were meant for cars and jewellery, as laid down by the Copyright Act of 1968. 'In return for this privilege, money is put into the coffers of the English Football Association,' Hughes continued. 'The company is able to exploit the market in trendy children's football gear. The price of its products is excessive … Starstruck youngsters who wish to wear the colours of their favourite teams are having to pay through the nose for the pleasure.'

Responding for the government, Robert Maclennan in part blamed the power of colour TV for encouraging kids to pester their parents for a shirt. He hoped the craze for replica shirts 'becomes unfashionable as quickly as did the fashion for hula hoops'; he had no such luck.

Some of the men who wore those England shirts were appalled at being made to read dossiers on the opposition, although Kevin Keegan was in favour of them, writing, 'In six years at Liverpool, I was never given a file on the opposition.' According to Peter Shilton, Keegan 'was not a flair player but he made the most of what he had'. He was accordingly chosen by Revie to be his captain, and he was a very visible presence outside of the game, promoting road safety awareness via the Green Cross Code TV advert and appearing on the game show *Superstars* and vinyl records.

Keegan also negotiated his own sponsorship deals and transfers, which took him to Hamburg in 1977 as one of very few Englishmen who played abroad during the decade the national team spent in the doldrums. Wages of £2,000 a week were an enormous improvement on his Liverpool salary. At the time, Stan Bowles applauded Revie for fighting for better pay for those who represented England, seeking £200 for each of them, although Emlyn Hughes told Revie he'd play for free. 'In that case, I'll have yours!' Bowles quipped.

Revie also criticised pundits like Jimmy Hill for throwing stones in his direction, even though he admitted, 'It's part of a manager's job to be criticised.' As Alf Ramsey had suffered before him, Revie also had to endure the meddling of FA deputy chairman Sir Harold Thompson, who often suggested which players should be picked or dropped. Christopher Evans wrote in his biography of Revie that the manager handled some players badly: in 1975 Alan Ball was made captain for a game against West Germany, with Arsenal's game postponed to allow him to play for England. A few months later Revie sent an unsigned letter relieving the World Cup-winning midfielder of the duty.

Even with a new manager, the style of play still refused to come up to date. Brian Glanville wrote that the style in which Revie made England play in a game against the Netherlands 'seemed as archaic' as the hymn the fans sang, with full-backs who 'simply trundled down the flanks and booted in high crosses'. This sat in sharp contrast to the modern Dutch style, pioneered by Rinus Michels, which took them to the 1974 World Cup Final. Having emerged from the First Division with its 'football played at 100 miles per hour', Revie wanted to change England's style to one that was slower and more technical.

He also played Kevin Beattie out of position: a centre-back for his club, Revie put him on the left, so that he was the one walloping in those crosses. Beattie, whose playing style was compared to Bobby Moore, only made nine appearances for England because of injury, retiring from the game at the age of 28.

'Lazy coaching' was how Glenn Hoddle explained the lull in England's achievements in the 1970s, with a litany of complaints in his memoir *Playmaker*: 'creative football was frowned upon'; 'we were so stagnant'; 'the style of play was so sad'; 'the blood and thunder wasn't for me'. He added, 'We didn't think creatively. The British bulldog spirit helped win the war but it kept us repressed and isolated in other walks of life.'

Speaking to *FourFourTwo* magazine in 2019, Ossie Ardiles complimented Hoddle for playing like an Argentinean in a football environment where 'there was one way to play and it was not particularly our style'. As Matthew Syed put it in *The Times* in 2018, Hoddle did not fit 'the conceptual matrix of the English game'. The same can be said of those mavericks mentioned in the previous chapter, including Stan Bowles and Frank Worthington. Like Ramsey, Revie had enjoyed success with Leeds with a certain playing style and he transferred that to the national team, even though the side which won the 1973/74 First Division boasted as many Scots as Englishmen.

'He was the teacher and you were the pupil,' Leeds and England defender Norman Hunter told the fanzine *The Square Ball*. 'Whatever he told us to do was basically law ... You always had to be on time.' Hunter told *The Independent* that Revie was 'a father figure' to him, especially because his own father had died before he was born. He added that it was Revie who pioneered the time-killing method of taking the ball to the corner flag to preserve a lead, so at least he had updated one aspect of England's play.

At the time, football boots were supposed to be tough, all the better to lump it long. Writing in *The Guardian* in 2009, Hunter Davies recalled that modern, lightweight boots which were 'more like slippers or ballet shoes' used to be called 'continental'. This made it seem as though the English 'were still trying to distance ourselves from this poncey, pansy notion'. Davies reckoned that winning the World Cup, and the associated 'feeling of superiority' was to blame for England's stasis: foreign nations could teach the victorious team nothing, which led to 'laziness, stupidity and then downright sloth, encouraging us to lumber on in our old, traditional lumpen ways'.

There was little chance of England repeating their 1966 success any time soon. To Paul Hayward, it was the 'wilful blindness' they showed to other nations improving how they played that led to a 'spiral of hysterical pessimism'. In his newspaper column Revie once wrote that only Leeds residents would be annoyed at their team losing, but 'with England it is tantamount to a national disaster'.

When they watched the team play Cyprus in 1975, England fans booed the opposing players and their national anthem. The following year, fans jeered a qualifying game against Finland even though England won, with Revie saying, 'We lost our passing and our positional sense.' Then came a friendly defeat, again against the Netherlands, inspired as ever by Johan Cruyff, in spite of the England starting XI including Keegan, Bowles, Brooking and Trevor Francis.

The Dutch coach Jan Zwartkruis thought England had 'no brain behind all the bustle', while Revie told a newspaper it would be a while until his team could challenge the best in the world. Such realism was incompatible with the demand for victory at all costs, against any opponent. For his part, Brooking complained how he was forced to fit his way of playing into a more rigid set of tactics, rather than finding space in the manner of a Dutch player. He placed the blame of Revie's failure on the turnover of players, 52 in 29 games. 'He judged everything on the results,' he wrote. 'If we failed to win, he would try more players.'

Revie also complained to the Football League about the overload suffered by the players in playing so many games. It was a schedule he called 'amateurish' and which contributed to England failing to qualify for the 1976 European Championship. It was fixed the following year, which only irritated the secretary of the Football League, Alan Hardaker, who had once asked why people made such a fuss about the World Cup. Brian Glanville thought that another of Revie's complaints, about not having players for long enough, would have had merit if he had succeeded 'in getting and keeping together a better conceived and more impressive squad'.

Francis, who came off the bench to appear against Italy, noted how Revie 'tried to create a club atmosphere', with bingo and carpet bowls laid on as entertainment. Kevin Keegan went from considering Revie 'the enemy', given the domestic rivalry between Liverpool and Leeds, to judging him well by his focus on the opposition, thanks to those dossiers. He placed such importance on those strengths and weaknesses, however, that he 'overlooked what our own players could do'.

England had little hope in qualifying for the World Cup before a match at home to Italy, by which time Revie had taken a coaching position in the Middle East, the England job 'no longer worth the aggravation'. He told the *Daily Mail*, with an awareness of how the public treated the manager of the national team, 'Nearly everyone in the country seems to want me out, so I am giving them what they want.' His behaviour was greatly different to that of Alf Ramsey, who seemed impervious to public criticism of him. Ron Greenwood was in the dugout for that Italy game, and even though England won it, they failed to qualify via goal difference.

The starting XI, captained by Emlyn Hughes, included young stars Ray Wilkins, Peter Barnes and Steve Coppell, as well as Trevor Cherry from the 1970 World Cup squad. Future England manager Fabio Capello was an unused substitute for Italy, who started with six Juventus players. A few months later Viv Anderson would become the first of several black players to regularly play for England in the 1980s.

Rather quaintly, Ted Croker took issue with the big screen which had been installed at Wembley to show replays of match incidents. 'It was a frightening thought that the match officials could find their decisions questioned,' he wrote. 'There cannot be outside interference in the running of a game of football.' One wonders what he would make of video assistant referees half a century later, when the exploits of his grandson Eric Dier would be beamed on to that screen as he played for Tottenham and England.

In 1975, the government had brought in the Safety of Sports Grounds Act, supporting the redevelopment of stadiums with the Spot the Ball competition run by the football pools. The act also imposed a safety certificate on many club grounds, including those of the top two divisions but not the leagues below. This did not stem the dangers that would eventually lead to the tragic fire at Valley Parade in Bradford in 1985.

Denis Healey had delivered a Labour Budget in April 1978, which began on a sombre note about 'the deepest and most prolonged recession since the 1930s combined with an unprecedented inflation' across the world. Prime minister James Callaghan had limited public sector pay rises in his attempt to curb inflation, which he later called 'socialism in action', but in 1976 the International Monetary Fund had to bail out Britain, which owed billions of pounds to other countries and had run out of credit. At the end of 1975, even the health service had been affected by strikes: hospitals closed their emergency departments and maternity services after disagreements over new contracts for doctors.

Across Britain in the late 1970s, Healey said that unemployment was still 'intolerably high' but it was important to oppose any thought of protectionism, so that the country would not be cut off from the rest of the world. England could have taken its lead from football clubs, who, as mentioned, were able to look abroad to secure top talent. Healey commended his party for raising the value of a pension 20 per cent in their time in office. The popularity of UK tourism encouraged him to grant allowances to people building hotels. His concluding remarks included the mollifying line, 'I do not in this Budget make any call for sacrifice.'

A 1979 feature on BBC show *Nationwide* laid bare the struggles facing the UK manufacturing industry. Corby was a new town where one in every two residents worked at the British Steel factory, but the images showed housing developments boarded up and trade unionists deliberating on the next steps to take. One man in a hard hat bemoaned how Corby was 'a victim of change'; after the Second World War there was a demand for steel, but it had trickled away by the end of the 1970s.

The man wanted the government to support British Steel in the creation of new jobs in the town, while another contributor noted the vandalism and antisocial behaviour which he felt might serve to disincline new enterprise to invest in the town 'because of the security risk'. The reporter Tony Wilkinson's voiceover stoically mentioned the lack of hospital or railway station in Corby, with the technical college now closed.

The 1970s, to David Goldblatt in his book *The Ball Is Round*, was the decade which saw 'the last act in the long death of social democratic Britain. The intellectual assumptions, institutional mechanisms and class alliances of the postwar consensus fragmented.' Dominic Sandbrook summarised the change as going from 'a collective culture to a domesticated individualistic one'. During this period, football crowds were down at the very moment English clubs were doing very well in European competitions, with Liverpool, Nottingham Forest and Aston Villa winning the European Cup each year from the Merseysiders' victory in 1977 to Villa's success in 1982.

It is customary to note the rise of the punk ethos on British life in the late 1970s, a youth movement which told of 'no future' and whose bands tackled social and political issues; 'everybody's sitting round watching television,' sang The Clash on *London's Burning*, while The Jam sang about 'Eton Rifles', bringing class divisions back into the top ten. The Specials, whose members were black and white and who recorded on the Two Tone label, advised 'wearing a cap' to avoid falling pregnant on 'Too Much Too Young'.

Also in 1977, a band whom the punks were set against, Genesis, put out a song called 'Match of the Day', which was 'the only way to spend your Saturday'. The players, however, were 'inciting riots, causing chaos ... from the terraces you can see your men do battle'. Punk started in London and spread throughout the country, with different areas boasting their own bands, but the movement flared out quickly, as youth movements tend to do. It nonetheless sowed the seeds for the football fanzine movement of the mid-1980s.

The National Front, which had been set up in 1967, preyed on the disaffection of young men by making them identify with a nationalist cause. The England football team offered people a healthy way of expressing pride in their country, but the National Front was far nastier in their intentions, pitting white Britons against those of other ethnicities and backgrounds. In August 1977, in an echo of the Cable Street gathering of 1936, the organisation was met by over 4,000 anti-racist demonstrators in the multicultural area of Lewisham, south London. Police used horses and, for the first time in England, riot shields to contain the fighting.

Members of the far-right group found football terraces a prime recruitment ground, where they handed out copies of their magazine *The Flag*. Brendon Batson remembered being spat on when he and the other black West Bromwich Albion players walked into an away ground. This was an environment where, as mentioned in the previous chapter, *The Black and White Minstrel Show* was still running on the BBC.

Entire books have now been written on why those times are different from these, but the main reason the show ended its long run in 1978 was because the executives who green-lit each series finally listened to a part of its audience. There seemed no reason at the time why a black man should not play for the England football team, either, although we shall see that not every fan was entirely accepting of it.

This was also the year of *Grease* and *Saturday Night Fever*, both starring John Travolta, as well as Christopher Reeve playing Superman. *Death on the Nile* was the latest Agatha Christie adaptation and animators turned the novel

Watership Down into a motion picture; that movie's theme song, 'Bright Eyes', was one of the year's biggest hits.

The Conservative Party were in opposition, with their leader Margaret Thatcher following Alf Ramsey in taking elocution lessons, in her case to better connect with the electorate. In 1978, Thatcher had spoken in an ITV interview of potentially four million people from India and Pakistan coming to Britain, intimating that Britons would feel 'rather swamped' by the new arrivals, who bring with them 'a different culture'. This would serve to worsen relations between immigrants and natives. 'The big political parties have not been talking about this,' she added, with an inference to more nativist parties on the 'extremes' like the National Front who made reducing immigration numbers the pillar of their offering to the electorate.

'We are a British nation with British characteristics,' Thatcher continued. 'Every country can take some small minorities and in many ways they add to the richness and variety of this country. The moment the minority threatens to become a big one, people get frightened.' Four million South Asian immigrants should not equate to the millions more who lived in England, but if this sophistry helped the Conservatives win votes in the next general election, so much the better.

A vote for the Conservatives, therefore, would help ease this fear by introducing policies to cut immigration, something the party would still be pushing to voters over 40 years later. Even though football supporters could admire international talent, for whose signatures clubs could compete in a Europe-wide marketplace to bring to their ground, in politics nativism was still alive and well.

1982

FOR THE first time since 1970, England would travel to a World Cup. Famously it was the first time they had qualified for one, without being hosts or holders, in 20 years. It took place in Spain, and the team's symbol was Bobby, the English bulldog.

In the opening group game against France it took England 27 seconds to score, the goal coming from a totally unmarked Bryan Robson. The final score was 3-1, with Robson rising high to direct a glancing header into the French net for the second goal. The win was followed by two more, 2-0 against Czechoslovakia and 1-0 against Kuwait. For that last game, Trevor Brooking wrote, 'None of the players wanted to be injured.'

The manager was Ron Greenwood, the former West Ham United boss who had coached three members of the 1966 side: Geoff Hurst, Bobby Moore and Martin Peters. In fact, he had found new positions for the first two of them. Greenwood grew up poor in Burnley and moved to London, where he worked on the Wembley Stadium scoreboard. When in charge of the national team he knew he was 'a public servant, like a politician ... answerable to the country'.

Brooking enjoyed the best years of his England career under Greenwood, which made sense given that he too had been a West Ham player. In his 1982 autobiography, he wrote that being called up for England 'signifies the peak of a footballer's career and that he is in the top 16 out of 2,000 or more professional footballers who are eligible in the country'. He kept every cap he was given after every appearance.

To Brooking, Greenwood was as passionate about football as Alf Ramsey was: 'He will talk about it for hours and no other subject will intrude ... Football is his hobby.' Peter Shilton, who for several years was rotated with Ray Clemence in goal because his manager could not decide on a permanent number one, referred to him as 'Reverend Ron', such was 'his tendency to almost preach when talking tactics'. In an old-fashioned manner Greenwood also allowed players to nip into a pub for a pint while on international service. After the victory against the Czechs, Greenwood ordered the players to go out drinking to celebrate.

As for Terry Butcher, to whom Greenwood gave his England debut, he commended him for initiating a players' committee to increase the harmony and mutual respect between the squad and coaches. He was, however, less amenable to the media than Don Revie had been. Niall Edworthy wrote that Greenwood 'believed that speed of foot was no replacement for speed of mind. Football was a battle of wits, a rapidly moving game of physical chess.'

Greenwood felt the English game was 'too defensive, too physical and was not producing enough skilful players'. It would take a generation or two for him to get his wish, thanks in part to the introduction of foreign talent into the English domestic game which was mentioned in the last chapter, as well as greater investment into coaching from the FA and player development from the clubs.

To Brian Glanville, writing in his *Story of the World Cup*, the manager was 'hapless' and 'thin-skinned', while Eamon Dunphy saw him as 'scorned as often as he was appreciated'. Ted Croker of the FA agreed, calling him 'oversensitive in the face of criticism' in a job where 'it needs a strong personality' to accept being told that you are wrong. In any case, a manager like Greenwood did not have to cope 'with a variety of trade unions whose paid officials are constantly making demands', as in an ordinary industry, or have round-the-clock security like a government minister.

Shilton has said that Greenwood 'liked to play the game the right way', but Glenn Hoddle, one of those few skilful players and a future national team manager, thought his England side lacked 'enough of a strategy. The message was that we were good enough to sort it out ourselves on the pitch.' The same had been said of Alf Ramsey. Steve Coppell remembered how Greenwood would boast of having '11 captains' in his team. Yet those players were deficient in technique compared to continental players, and they once told the manager that the Wembley crowd was 'tribal and impatient'.

'We had our head in the sand ... we didn't evolve,' Hoddle noted, calling England 'painfully small-minded' in how they coached young players. It would have helped them greatly to work on ball control by playing on smaller pitches, something he would teach in his own soccer school later in his career. When it came to flair, 'Our eyes were not yet open ... Most of the players were physical. Foreign players scoffed at our long-ball tactics.'

Bryan Robson, meanwhile, lamented how England players would for ever give the ball away. 'You're rushing everything, when you've got more time on the ball than you think,' he said, adding that it was hard to play the English game, where the team went 'flat out', in the punishing heat of Spain or Mexico. Tactically, other nations would have a sweeper, or *libero*, behind the back four, something

England had not yet adopted in 1982. Failing to adapt to the modern game was becoming a pattern.

César Luis Menotti, the celebrated coach of Argentina, wrote that Kevin Keegan, who had been so dynamic at Liverpool, was wasted in the national side. 'It was a sad team,' he thought, 'with no joy in playing.' Keegan, who had returned to English football and was playing at Southampton, wore the number seven shirt at the 1982 tournament; he admitted in his autobiography *My Life in Football* that he 'was not what you would call a good watcher', especially at the 1978 World Cup in which he and England did not participate.

He was thrilled to captain his country. 'The national anthem would start and I would sing the words,' he wrote, and he put his caps on display too, as proud as Trevor Brooking was in representing his country. In 1980, just before that year's European Championship, Keegan and his fellow Liverpool midfielder Emlyn Hughes were photographed with the now prime minister Margaret Thatcher on the doorstep of 10 Downing Street. Thatcher held a football while the players made to kiss her on each cheek and Hughes, who was a team captain on TV panel show *A Question of Sport*, joked that she might want to hold the unmentionables of her nemesis Arthur Scargill. Only one member of the 1982 World Cup squad, Paul Mariner, confessed to being a Labour voter.

Scargill was a voluble member of the National Union of Mineworkers, who became its president in 1982. 'He told the miners what they wanted to hear,' said Dominic Sandbrook in his BBC documentary *The 70s*, 'his promise to get them more money.' Football agents would have doubtless approved of his intentions. Scargill was so ubiquitous across the media that he became a figure to rival the England football manager. At the end of the 1970s,

Britain had sold off some of its coal mining equipment to China, allowing it to double its profits at a time when energy came more from oil than coal, but it also precipitated a Chinese manufacturing boom.

As for Keegan, he wrote about the injury he was carrying at the 1982 tournament and how he snuck out of camp to meet a doctor who had treated him in Hamburg, 'wearing sunglasses and a hat to conceal my curls'. It was Keegan who, when he was brought off the bench in a match against Spain, missed a header from close range, which is 'probably the only moment of my England career that people remember now'. Such are the perils of a game watched live by millions of viewers. Brooking, who also appeared as a sub in that fixture, pinned the blame on the side being 'too cautious'. England had played hosts Spain as part of a second group stage, the other team being West Germany. England drew both games 0-0.

Trevor Francis, who started against the Germans, didn't feel like he was comfortably an England regular until 1982, five years after his debut, so fierce was the competition for a place in the team. He saw every game 'as a big occasion' and was sad when injury so often denied him the chance to be called up. Terry Butcher found out he had made the 1982 squad on the car radio; three months earlier he had undergone a blood transfusion after he took a boot to the face.

Qualification for the tournament had been difficult. In September 1981, Norway overcame England in a game made memorable for the commentator Bjørge Lillelien telling the prime minister, 'Your boys took a hell of a beating!' The clip circulated across British media and even moved politicians to comment on the defeat in parliament. Even after England beat Hungary in Budapest, Greenwood was set on resigning from the job, only to be talked out of it on the plane home by his players. Would they have done the same with Revie or Ramsey, or would they have accepted their offer to quit, if indeed they had been informed at all?

By this time, Ted Croker wrote, each player was awarded £1,000 per match, with clubs being paid £400 for each player. One MP, Marcus Lipton, saw this as a kind of bribery that would 'kill the sport'. Croker was also pleased that transfer fees had settled down after they had gone 'haywire' in the late 1970s; seven-figure sums paid for players like Francis had helped raise the total league wage bill by 44 per cent. The FA executive once told Margaret Thatcher, who was not a football enthusiast, that players were paid far less handsomely than jockeys, and that some horses cost far more than a player's transfer fee.

A series of fortunate results put England in a position to qualify for the World Cup, and they sealed it with a closing victory against Hungary. At the tournament itself, there was complete lockdown at the England hotel, with over a dozen armed policemen on guard who escorted the squad in and out of the camp. There was a near miss when a stunt was set up involving so-called ballet players who wanted to visit the squad, a press ruse which would have provided some lovely photos for the folks back home.

At the cinema, there was Ben Kingsley playing Gandhi and Monty Python playing the Hollywood Bowl. *The Wall* by Pink Floyd was adapted into a movie starring Bob Geldof, and *Who Dares Wins* put on film the SAS's actions in the siege of the Iranian Embassy. In parliament, the Queen's Speech of 1982 included a note about 'continued restraint in public spending', including private investment in British Telecom via a bond scheme and a new Youth Training Scheme. With the popularity of computers, there was a mention of laws to protect personal information.

The 1982 Budget was delivered by Geoffrey Howe, who adopted a pessimistic tone as he addressed the rate of unemployment, which stood at three million. 'Until quite recently, we took it for granted that we had one of the highest living standards in Europe, if not in the world,' he said. 'Fewer than half the new cars bought in Britain were being made here ... Our share of world trade had been halved.' Above all, Howe sought in his Budget to restore Britain as 'a trading nation'.

In spite of the oil in the North Sea which Britain could tap into and 'the skill and enterprise displayed, and risks accepted, by the private sector', a price of $34 a barrel was 26 times what it had been in 1970, a boon for industry but wretched for consumers forced to pay far more to fill up their car or van. There was a great focus in the opening few sections of the Budget on comparing the economy with other nations, including the USA, to disprove the notion that Britain's own was 'foredoomed'.

In 1979, prime minister James Callaghan had tried to keep pay rises at five per cent but Ford workers and lorry drivers led the revolt. Rubbish piled up on the streets, gravediggers did not bury the dead and NHS workers were out on the picket line to block entrances to hospitals, hence the Winter of Discontent, a phrase borrowed from Shakespeare that conjured up the mood of the country. The British people put the Conservative Party back in power, but, as ever, the same issues remained in spite of the new faces elected to sort out the mess.

A year into the Conservative government in 1980, in the middle of a recession, inflation stood at 22 per cent, with Howe seeking to raise taxes to ease the burden on the public purse. He increased pensions by 11 per cent and raised child benefit 23 per cent over the course of two years. He also put a 30p duty on spirits and added 2p to a pint of beer. It is striking to see mention of *Space Invaders* in the section on taxing and licensing arcade machines, and for 1982 to be labelled Information Technology Year.

Given the increased interest in 'the property-owning democracy', Howe announced that the exemption on stamp duty would increase 25 per cent to £25,000. 'By the end of this parliament,' the chancellor said, referring to 1983, 'nearly three out of every five families will own their own homes.' They would be helped in this cause by being permitted to purchase their council houses via the Right to Buy scheme, which helped people buy for themselves 175,000 homes in 1982 alone.

There was also mention of the government's initiative to allow employees to buy shares in the companies for whom they worked 'to develop a greater sense of commitment to the success of the business'. By the time Howe delivered the Budget, there were now over 400 companies, a rise from 30 at the start of the scheme, who offered this option to their employees.

Independent regulation was the order of the day, as Thatcher's government replaced state monopolies with private ones which the state then regulated; this accounts for the setup of arm's-length bodies such as Ofcom and Ofwat. Employees of private companies who worked for state bodies like the NHS were at a remove from their employers, who themselves were unaccountable to people who used the services. As political journalist Steve Richards put it, when a train company underperformed, the shareholders still earned their dividends; if the government were in charge, they would receive all of the blame. Four decades later, such a status would recur in the water industry.

In football, criticism of the FA is easy because they are a constant presence. New players and managers can be found for the national team, just as new chancellors and home secretaries can be appointed, but the blazer-wearing committee members preside over the team and are sought for comment about the man they have appointed who has, once again, failed to bring England a World Cup victory. Sir Harold Thompson, Graham Kelly, Mark Palios and Brian Barwick would all become bogeymen across the decades, simply for being the public face of the FA.

There were also developments on the political party front. Spearheaded by a quartet of Labour MPs nicknamed the 'Gang of Four' – Roy Jenkins, David Owen, Shirley Williams and Bill Rodgers – the Social Democratic Party (SDP) was founded in 1981 to carve a new movement out of a Labour Party that was moving leftwards after losing power in 1979. Labour leader Michael Foot resigned in 1983 after a general election where votes for his party had gone to the SDP/Liberal alliance, which as per their manifesto sought to relieve Britain of the main two parties.

Together, they had served to create 'an industrial wasteland out of a country which was once the workshop of the world', where the Conservative Party put their faith in 'the blind forces of the marketplace' and Labour sought to enforce 'rigid controls over enterprise'. It was a choice between 'neglect and interference', between two parties who were 'prisoners of ideology'. There was now an enticing third way, where there was 'no need for hopelessness'.

The SDP/Liberal manifesto also claimed that society was 'at war with itself', and that the new party would 'call a halt to confrontation politics', which recalls Denis Healey's desire for a social contract a decade previously. Proving that the spectre of the Second World War still had not diminished, it called on 'the vision and sense of enlightened self-interest which produced the Marshall Plan and pulled post-war Europe together … We cannot live in a bunker.'

1982

Steve Richards doubted that the new party could have impacted Tory rule, given that Labour was still dominant in the north of England and the whole of Scotland, but it added an extra note of interest in the political environment. Richards also wrote that, after 1979, the UK 'became paradoxically more closed-minded and far more open to global players to arrive and flourish on its insular stage'. You could say this equally for enterprise and for football.

The Ipswich Town side of 1982, which gave the England squad Terry Butcher, Paul Mariner and Mick Mills, also included the Dutch wingers Arnold Mühren and Frans Thijssen. Viv Anderson and Peter Shilton's Nottingham Forest team-mates included Jürgen Röber from Germany and Einar Jan Aas from Norway. César Luis Menotti noticed that Ossie Ardiles had begun to be more defensive in his play, including in his passing, directly due to playing in England.

A few talented England internationals went abroad to escape the straitjacket of First Division football, given that there was less tackling and more risk in how teams played; Kevin Keegan went to Hamburg, Glenn Hoddle to Monaco, and Tony Woodcock to FC Köln. The last of these was the only English player in the 1982 World Cup squad to be playing abroad, and it is interesting to note that only one Frenchman, Didier Six of Stuttgart, also plied his trade outside of his home country.

Trevor Brooking, who stayed in England, wrote in his 1982 autobiography that the English game would suffer if players left, with the crowds preferring 'whole-hearted commitment and enthusiasm' in the football they watched. To counter this, there should be 'more emphasis on ball work and fewer competitive matches'.

In a chapter titled 'Are we too insular?', he discussed the general state of the sport, lamenting that the league was often given preference over the England team, which meant the country could not take part in a 1981 international tournament. The British Home Championship was also about to draw to a close, which was ideal given that it 'raises no enthusiasm among the players'. Its cessation also forced England to play more matches outside Scotland, Wales and Northern Ireland, which allowed them to test themselves more regularly against different European nations and their tactical styles.

Manager Ron Greenwood, Brooking wrote, could pick from 'a lot of very good players' but 'few great ones'. On top of this, a spate of injuries including pelvic strains affected Ray Wilkins, with the English game 'more physically demanding' on muddy and icy pitches. As we have learned, the standard of football had been overtaken by those of other countries, with an overly negative attitude in England's play resulting from a 'fear of losing'. As well as defenders who were unable to attack, there were few attacking players 'with the technical ability to control the ball and who are prepared to take on opponents in areas of the field where there is a risk that a mistake could be punished by a goal'.

The Thatcher government was anything but negative when it came to foreign policy. As England prepared to return to a World Cup, the Falklands conflict dominated news reports in the spring and summer of 1982. The army, navy and RAF were all deployed to retake the islands. 'They do not want to be Argentine,' Thatcher said in a rare Saturday session of parliament, referring to people on an island which had been under British rule for 150 years. 'Their way of life is British; their allegiance is to the Crown.'

This defence of the realm, which allowed England to enforce their sovereignty, was useful when Thatcher sought re-election in 1983 and held off the revolutionary zeal of the SDP/Liberal alliance. The Falklands conflict was her own World Cup Final, and, as they might be in their football coverage, the war enabled newspapers to be jingoistic and patriotic.

The Sun, whose news editor wore a tin hat in the office, splashed one issue with pictures of Winston Churchill and the headline 'We'll Smash 'Em'. The sinking of the *Belgrano* battleship led to the famous 'Gotcha' cover, which quickly became seen as grossly insensitive. There was a chance that the government would order the England team to withdraw from the World Cup, but the FA was eventually given the final say on the matter. This pleased Ted Croker, who wrote that 'sport will break down barriers between countries faster than politicians can build them'.

The FA also ignored a directive not to attend the opening game, lest an Englishman cross paths with one from Argentina. Croker even had to turn down a request for an injured soldier to meet the team, so as not to appear as if the national team were publicly taking a side in the conflict. Once again, England's World Cup involvement saw them embroiled in issues off the field, supporting the view that football is part of a country's diplomatic efforts.

1986

EVERY DISCUSSION of English football in the middle of the 1980s must begin with the line from the *Sunday Times* which called it 'a slum sport played in slum stadiums'. One codicil to this was that Highbury got a jumbo screen in 1984, but otherwise it was a time of security fences, crammed terraces and omnipresent fighting outside and often inside the grounds.

In 1981 the FA had relaxed the rules on directors' pay, encouraging less amateurism and anticipating the current business-focused manner in which football clubs were run. Two years later, the Chester Report concluded that football should undergo 'a form of rationally managed decline', with more such professionals in charge of running the game including 'a more commercially minded outlook'. Lord Chester also suggested reducing the First Division in size and regionalising the lower leagues, but both proposals were ignored at the time, although the report did lead to the removal of the rule which enabled an away side to share a home team's gate receipts.

Given that some grounds were far bigger than others, the rich became richer, with football reflecting contemporary society. Tottenham Hotspur became a PLC, with the FA never replying to the club when it alerted the governing body to its wish; chairman and property tycoon Irving Scholar was also ahead of the curve when he introduced advertising around the pitch. Scholar had initially become involved with Spurs after they had poured £5m into redeveloping White Hart Lane, and he astutely saw merchandise as a way to plug the hole in their accounts.

As Alex Fynn and Lynton Guest wrote in *The Secret Life of Football*, in the 1980s boardroom figures like Scholar and David Dein of Arsenal became fixtures of news reports. All but nine of the 92 Football League clubs were in debt, with crowds still down from their previous highs and transfer fees returning to relative normality after the seven-figure sums exchanged for players at the end of the previous decade. The struggles of the England team, meanwhile, 'sapped confidence' in the national game, although it did precipitate the rise in football literature and fan involvement. In 1985 the Football Supporters' Association was founded, and punk fanzine culture came to football with the launch of *When Saturday Comes*, a magazine with the fans' interests at heart.

Highlander was one of the movies of the summer of 1986. It was directed by Russell Mulcahy, the man who gave Duran Duran their image through their music videos. David Bowie was in two movies: *Absolute Beginners*, set in 1950s London; and *Labyrinth*, the Jim Henson fantasy film. Meanwhile, *The Mission* headed to 18th-century South America, which was coincidentally where the World Cup was due to be held. War in Colombia forced FIFA to move it to Mexico.

Bobby Robson had replaced Ron Greenwood as England manager after the 1982 World Cup but it should not surprise you that there was no modern reboot to the tactical approach he took. Brian Glanville, who had covered swashbuckling Austrian and Hungarian sides in the 1950s, had no time for Robson's tactics, writing in his book *England Managers* of the 'sterility, technical inadequacy, bleak lack of imagination, [and] addiction to the shortest and crudest route to goal by the long ball'.

Gary Lineker wrote that Robson 'understood footballers and was very loyal to them', although he did allude to his 'fairly basic' coaching. Peter Shilton, who resumed his place as first-choice keeper for his country, called him 'a coach-manager' who was usually kind enough to explain his justifications for leaving a player out of the team. Conversely, however, Trevor Francis recalled in his memoir *One in a Million* that Robson did not tell him he had missed out on the 1986 World Cup squad.

Robson's coaching, however simple, had brought success to the provincial club Ipswich Town two decades after Alf Ramsey had done the same. His captain Terry Butcher wrote in his own memoir *Both Sides of the Border* that Robson would be so keen on meetings that players would joke about him 'calling a meeting to decide when to have the next meeting'. He was fully committed to the job, sitting mute in the dressing room and 'shaking his head in disbelief' when England lost, aware that it would take months rather than days before he could help the side win their next match.

The manager was one of the forces behind the National Football School at Lilleshall, which gathered schoolboys to develop their skills that, with luck, they would one day use as an England player. John Cartwright, however, was not convinced by its outcomes in his two years as technical director there. 'They were still short on the basic skills. Kicking techniques were very poor. Most of them were one-footed,' he told the BBC TV documentary *Kicking & Screaming*. 'It was basically about knocking the ball forward, scrapping for things in midfield. There was no grace, no art and no imaginative football.'

In conversation with *FourFourTwo* magazine, one anonymous player said that Lilleshall was a training camp for 'workhorse athletes, players who could run all day and tackle hard'. Effort triumphed over skill. The boys had school every morning and trained in the afternoons; if they did badly in lessons or homework, they would be punished with a missed game.

Robson's widow Lady Elsie told Henry Winter that he would travel from Surrey to Ipswich to prove his worth to the club's chairman, who did not give him a contract until six months into the job. He then took a pay cut even though he was also the FA coaching director. He was 'deeply interested in the science of football coaching' as per the establishment of Lilleshall. As Gareth Southgate would do with Wayne Rooney, Robson decided to move on without Kevin Keegan, blooding young players including John Barnes and Mark Hateley, who would both go to the 1986 World Cup.

'I had entered a jungle,' Robson wrote of his 1982 appointment in his book *Farewell but not Goodbye*, on account of 'the hysterical expectations of some England fans'; after a game against Russia, he was sprayed with beer and spittle. At the time, due to circulation wars, the tabloid papers were engaged in a war for readers which Robson called 'medieval', and former England players were given space in their sports sections to vent about the current team. One *Mirror* journalist boasted of his desire to 'fry' Robson. 'I was lampooned and vilified,' he complained with some justification and no way of stopping it, given the nature of a free press in a competitive news marketplace.

The FA's then press officer David Bloomfield told Niall Edworthy that the news guys 'felt no obligation to build up any relationship with the England camp' because they were not the ones assigned to the team full-time. Brian Glanville pinned the blame on those reporters who sought to uncover any scandals for the front part of the paper. 'There is a paranoia floating around football,' Glanville explained to Edworthy. 'There has been an entire conspiracy of silence among football reporters to hush up these stories.' This was still a time when the press hunted in a pack, agreeing on the information they should either hold back or which was fine to publish.

The famous headline 'In the name of Allah, go!' emerged after Robson had not noticed, in a question about Saudi Arabia's manager, that he had been asked about the previous one. This tabloid agenda towards England managers was, to David Goldblatt, 'highly personalised and vindictive', with the men in charge receiving the opprobrium which is usually aimed at politicians. Robson was 'pursued with a new relentlessness, his private life becoming fair game'. For his part, Robson disliked the media, telling them, 'If you people didn't exist, my job would be twice as easy and twice as pleasurable.'

Peter Shilton noted the change in the 'relaxed relationship' shared between players and the press; the latter were 'not beyond manipulating the truth' to spice up stories. One tabloid reporter offered money to the manager of the hotel England were staying at so he could pass on any confidential titbits. Robson himself overheard one football writer telling his editor that he refused to make up quotes or twist his words into new shapes, so at least there was some humanity and decency amid those who worked in an often nasty trade.

Terry Butcher listed the home comforts England took to Mexico – '1,000 sachets of shampoo, 600 bars of soap ... 4,000 teabags, 500 bars of chocolate, 108 bottles of HP sauce, our own mustard, 144 tins of baked beans' and board games including Scrabble and Monopoly. Quirkily, England also took two defenders called Gary Stevens to the 1986 World Cup, as well as midfielder Trevor Steven.

1986

Wearing the number ten shirt, Gary Lineker finished top scorer at the tournament. Robson called him 'a one-touch finisher', saying that 'simplicity was at the core of his art'. Lineker himself remembered how players could only phone home or pick up a call from home once a week; it was like 'being in the army or boarding school'. The squad would even skip sunbathing sessions to avoid the attention of camera crews, so they were like celebrities as well as soldiers or boarders.

Graeme Souness made the point in his book that teams would be 'locked up in a hotel or in training camps', without even interacting with the locals. He suggested that the ideal location for a base camp would be near a golf course, 'keeping them entertained without going mad'. In the early 2000s, David Beckham would also complain about having to socialise 'with the doors shut and the curtains drawn'. This did not seem a healthy way to cool down in preparation for doing your job in far-flung places with millions cheering you on at home.

Bobby Robson spent press conferences updating journalists on the condition of his captain Bryan Robson's shoulder; the Manchester United man required an operation to stop it popping out, and in the first game of the 1986 tournament he was 'not the real Bryan Robson [who] went into everything like a locomotive'. Bobby had wanted United to rest Bryan so he could make the World Cup squad, which was rather fatuous given that United, not England, paid his salary.

The manager went on to call Robson's replacement midfielder Peter Reid 'a competitive little bugger. His game was about nudges, tackles, putting his foot in, winning it, giving it five yards.' This made Reid sound like an old-fashioned English midfielder, in the mould of Nobby Stiles or a player moulded at Lilleshall. In 2020, Reid admitted that he was injured himself during the tournament, courtesy of a problem with his ankle.

Robson admitted that Glenn Hoddle was 'not a recoverer of the ball' but had 'a good brain and extraordinary vision, two lovely feet'. In games preceding the World Cup, Hoddle was stuck out on the right wing, where he felt 'suffocated', with his fellow England players shuffling around on the pitch so that the playmaker could move into the centre of it. One wonders if Alf Ramsey would have allowed such insubordination.

Playing for England, Hoddle 'often fought against the side … There was never a coach who truly trusted me.' Besides, given that they were playing in the Mexican heat, he realised 'we weren't going to be able to play the English way' and would instead try to conserve energy and not press the opposition so much. Ron Greenwood once noted that Hoddle would 'duck out' of some periods of matches, 'His shoulders would slump and he seemed short of breath.' For his part, Hoddle would be 'more knackered' playing for England than for Tottenham because the ball was being passed around him and his fellow midfielders.

'We had nowhere to go when we had the ball: our defenders looked to the forwards and bypassed the midfield. It got on my nerves,' Hoddle wrote of Bobby Robson's tactics. 'We wasted so much energy chasing good players who were playing in clever systems.' He lamented that he was 'born in the wrong country', given that other nations 'built their teams around players like me'. Brian Glanville put Hoddle in the same category as the old England winger Stanley Matthews, calling him a 'brilliant, unorthodox footballer … who worries the mediocrities'.

In 1986 Barney Ronay, who would grow up to cover England at international tournaments, had been made to sob, by Hoddle's miss against Morocco. 'I can still see it now,' he recalled in 2018, 'the casual shrug as he jogged back, mane flapping, the sense of infuriating insouciance.' The match was a goalless draw, coming between a 1-0 defeat to Portugal and a 3-0 win against Poland in which Lineker scored all three England goals. Ray Wilkins and Mark Hateley had moved to AC Milan to circumvent the ban on English clubs in Europe but both, according to Brian Glanville, were out of form.

The Times's obituary of Wilkins, who died in 2018, noted that he was a player who divided opinion: some thought him 'cerebral' with an 'elegant touch', while others saw him as a man who passed the ball sideways and slowed the game down. Glanville was in the latter camp, describing how Wilkins 'sat in front of his defence, playing square balls and seldom getting forward', then received a red card in the Morocco match for being adjudged too vehement in his complaints after an offside decision.

The last-16 match against Paraguay was a 3-0 win, with Shilton making several useful saves and Butcher and Lineker both taking punches to the throat from their zealous opponents; perhaps they really were like soldiers after all. The victory set up a quarter-final against Argentina, whose lynchpin was Diego Maradona. The day before the game, Butcher recalled, England needed help from a policeman to enter the ground they were to train on, after being forbidden from entering their initial choice. 'We had to climb over fences and down the terraces to get on to the pitch,' he wrote, once again imitating army combatants.

When it came to the match itself, Hoddle argued that players 'couldn't fool ourselves' into the match being 'bigger than football', although Robson had told the media that he would walk out of the pre-game press conference if the Falkland Islands came up. Security was extraordinary, with armoured cars and helicopter gunships deployed in case of supporter violence and a decoy coach made available to the England team for any emergencies after the match.

In conversation with Henry Winter, Peter Reid said that it wasn't 'the England way' to deploy a man to mark Maradona, given that 'it would have been negative', even though he forgot that Bobby Charlton did a man-marking job in the 1966 World Cup Final. Hoddle also fell back on national traits of fair play to excuse any England player for even thinking about punching the ball into the goal and claiming he had headed it, as Maradona infamously did. 'We had no idea how to do it, so we looked stupid when we tried to con the referee,' he wrote.

Butcher sighed that England were not 'cynical' enough to bring Maradona down as he danced through to score his second goal, which Shilton wrote should never have counted because of the tackle on Hoddle that turned the ball over to Argentina. The playmaker also had a propensity to dive, even after a fair tackle. 'Such playacting doesn't happen very often in British football and I don't think the fans here would stand for it,' Butcher correctly wrote.

Views had changed within a generation, though. Jamie Carragher wrote of his desire for players to go down more when they received contact; come 2002, England fans were congratulating Michael Owen on winning a penalty in this way against Argentina. They have the 'irrational belief the country has a divine right to be the best in the world by playing "the English way",' Carragher wrote, 'whatever that is'.

But, of course, other countries do not play by the same rules. This merely brings into focus how England operates under a certain, unwritten code which clashes with those of other countries. In the same manner, the English constitution is not codified and operates on a series of unwritten rules including the royal prerogative, which states that the government makes the monarch's decisions for them, so as not to cause constitutional chaos should they intervene and overrule the legislators. Parliament has been called 'monarchy, deferred' for this reason.

Carragher, incidentally, was more of a fan of fellow Evertonian Peter Reid than the England team. After the loss to Argentina, he was 'playing with my mates copying the handball goal'; had it been an Everton loss, 'I wouldn't have wanted to speak to anyone for the rest of the day.' Even when it came to 1966, Everton's FA Cup win trumped England's World Cup victory in his own household.

Writing on his Substack account, Jonathan Wilson criticised Peter Shilton for not doing enough to stop Diego Maradona getting to the ball for his first goal. 'Yes, Maradona cheated,' Wilson wrote, 'but Shilton played his part in that goal as well. Look at the still shot from side-on: Shilton's feet have barely left the ground. The top of his head is at roughly the level of Maradona's collar. Shilton was a touch over six feet tall; Maradona was about five feet five. Even with a seven-inch advantage, even with the goalkeeper's benefit of being able – legitimately – to use his hands and, in those days, to clatter through an opponent, Shilton was outjumped.'

Shilton, who was 36 years old at the time, wrote about his surprise that nobody asked him for his side of events. He has suffered with gambling issues in recent years, and he has not been shy to air his strident political views. It is to politics to which we now turn, in an attempt to discover what England's lawmakers were busy with while the football team were once more coming up short at the World Cup.

Nigel Lawson's Budget of March 1986 opened with a mention of 'the dramatic and unprecedented fall in the world oil price', which had returned to its 1973 levels.

Incredibly, these had helped Britain's net overseas assets reach £90bn, a sevenfold increase since the Conservatives took office in 1979. This would boost exports and direct investment to its native industries, which was greatly needed after the year-long strike that saw Britain switch its non-renewable energy, in a reverse of 1973/74, from coal to oil. It is interesting to see Lawson mention 'lead-free petrol', since it had by then become the more affordable way to fill up a car, but it is also no surprise to note an 11p rise on the price of a 20-pack of cigarettes.

Lawson complained about global markets, mentioning the high exchange rate with the dollar and the USA's 'protectionist pressures'. He also noted the £6bn that the City of London contributed to the UK economy, which accounted for Lawson's desire to help it dominate the global securities market. As well as being a property-owning democracy, Britain was now a share-owning one too, with an introduction of a 'personal equity plan' to help people invest £200 per month in shares of UK businesses. It was in 1986 that British Gas launched a campaign to encourage people to buy shares in the newly privatised company via its Tell Sid-themed advertisement.

Britain had enjoyed five years of growth, with inflation kept low, but Labour MPs were keen to point to 'record unemployment'. Accepting this, wrote Steve Richards, 'severely limited the power of the unions' who had gone on strike for their rights in the prior decade. Replying to the Budget for Labour, the party which represented the unions' interests, leader Neil Kinnock called the expansion of job clubs, which advised people who were seeking work, 'nothing more than an additional opportunity to have a chat and a cup of tea'.

Lawson had himself addressed unemployment by turning to 'the rigidity of the pay system' and the 'inertia' of businesses to adapt to changing economic circumstances. There was also, remembered Richards, 'a curious reverse-imperialism' whereby companies from abroad made their home in the UK, helping to train domestic employees. One business was Nissan, which opened a plant in Sunderland, followed by Toyota and Honda elsewhere in the UK. Come the end of the 2010s, Nissan and its manufacturing plants had become a political football.

To bring under-18s into the workforce, Lawson reiterated what he had said in the 1985 Budget about introducing a Youth Training Scheme and an expansion of the Enterprise Allowance Scheme. The latter gave a £40-a-week payment for people wishing to start their own business. Musicians, artists and promoters, including Jarvis Cocker, Jeremy Deller and Alan McGee, took advantage of it, while Julian Dunkerton used the sum to fund his market stall which, several years down the line, led him to running the clothing business Superdry.

Pertinent to some members of the World Cup squad, Lawson sought a reciprocal tax arrangement which would allow foreign players, and any other entertainer, to withhold tax on their earnings. Gary Lineker, for instance, would enjoy this in Spain, but Ossie Ardiles would not enjoy it in England. There were also moves to reform income tax to make it more favourable to women, because in 1986 a wife's income was absorbed into her husband's.

The 1986 Queen's Speech outlining the government's agenda for the forthcoming parliamentary session naturally mentioned privatisation. This would 'improve economic efficiency and encourage wider share ownership' while also, in a euphemistic phrase, 'provide further financial assistance to support the coal industry's progress to commercial viability'. In the aftermath of the Bradford City FC fire, there would be a bill concerning fire risks at sports grounds, while also setting in motion the Channel Tunnel and the one at Dartford.

When British people travelled to the continent, Steve Richards wrote, they would 'note cleaner streets, better transport provision and, if they fell ill, more efficient healthcare', whereas back home there was a disconnect between 'private affluence for some and the public squalor'. There was also a tremendous problem with hooligans: in March 1985, Millwall and Luton Town fans had clashed during a televised FA Cup quarter-final at Kenilworth Road. Those supporting Millwall threw bottles and coins, then lifted the seats out to attack the home faithful. After Luton won the game 1-0, there was a pitch invasion, with more seats tossed on to the playing surface and fans lobbing missiles while the police were running from them.

Ted Croker witnessed England fans upsetting a banana stall in Switzerland, where he realised 'the apparent hopelessness' of dealing with unruly young men. 'The host country does not want the bother of putting these people in jail and charging them,' he wrote, 'so few are punished.' It also dragged down the FA's attempts to help fans enjoy travelling to watch the side; they paused the travel club which had enabled 8,000 of them to go to Italy in 1978. The government refused to enact a blacklist of names and addresses, pleading restrictions on people's civil liberties.

There was a parliamentary debate on hooliganism in April 1985, led by Labour MP Tony Banks. Crowd trouble of the sort which had happened at Luton was 'partly a reflection of our increasingly violent society. Therefore, it is nonsense to single out football violence.' Banks complained that hooliganism had led to 'too many knee-jerk reactions and far too little real action', and in any case, as had been noted by MPs before, football was dealing with the heightened competition for leisure time. The solution that was offered was to ban away fans, although one member of the House of Lords went further and suggested the stocks.

Rather daringly, Banks posited that matches should be played on Sunday mornings, but more sensibly he thought grounds should be entirely seated and fans could only be admitted with a membership card. Any offenders should be punished with community service because 'having to weed someone's garden when an FA Cup match is being played' is punishment enough.

Banks noted the cohesion between clubs and their communities, spotlighting the two major Manchester clubs and Arsenal and Fulham; the last two clubs respectively ran an indoor and an all-weather pitch. He also suggested that clubs should be run by supporters rather than have directors who would rule them 'like 19th-century mill owners'. In the coming decades, clubs like Northampton Town, Exeter City and AFC Wimbledon would all be run by fans, but this was not yet the case in the mid-1980s.

Minister Neil Macfarlane, replying for the Conservative government, was a Leyton Orient supporter who had 'visited about four-fifths of all First and Second Division football grounds'. Recently he had suggested that clubs segregate home and away supporters, and that they introduce both fences and CCTV. He also referred to an incident in 1977 when England played Luxembourg and fans damaged the stadium and 'went on a rampage through the city', for which the FA compensated their hosts in apology. Such supporters have an effect, Macfarlane said, 'on the good name of this country. Clearly there is more than just national pride at stake.' This would be a keen focus of the efforts to stop any problems at the 1990 World Cup.

For Ted Croker, segregation led to 'them and us. First there are chants, then it becomes coins and missiles and the police are caught in between.' As part of an FA commission, he suggested plain-clothed policemen travel with away fans. He also saw a problem with ID cards, 'If each holder of a card had to be checked by a turnstile operator, the delays would be such that most people would not see the start of a match.' What's more, it would be hard to identify them at evening games.

At the end of May 1985, crowd trouble at the European Cup Final between Liverpool and Juventus at the decrepit Heysel Stadium in Brussels led to 39 deaths. The *Daily Mirror* called the disaster 'the final shame'. English clubs were banned for playing in European competitions for five years, although the national team were spared such a punishment. Agreeing with what Tony Banks had said, Neil Kinnock suggested that crowd violence was generally caused by 'long-term unemployment, especially among the young'.

Linking the miners' strikes with the issues in football, Tony Evans wrote in his book Two Tribes that 'working-class culture was under assault on all fronts. The prevailing Tory viewpoint sneered at the men down the pit shafts, seeing them as brutish, semi-educated and violent. The terraces were populated by similar lower-class oiks, they thought.'

Coal mining as an industry was being wound down, although the miners continued striking throughout 1984. Jeremy Paxman wrote in his book *Black Gold* that the terraces provided inspiration for some of the chants at the pickets, with 'There's only one Arthur Scargill' emanating from them in celebration of the man who was the visible face of the protests. Any ruckus with the police was met with 'Here we go'.

The Sporting Events (Control of Alcohol etc) Act, which became law in 1985, was a misnomer because the only sport it applied to was football. It forbade alcohol on coaches and in terrace bars, although clubs could sell it in their executive lounges. During the following season, in the absence of European matches, instead of being given a much-needed rest players had to compete in various competitions which sprung up to help their employers earn money to pay their wages and, given the expenditure resulting from the new act, improve the safety of their stadiums. They had to install CCTV and hire security staff to prevent and identify crowd trouble.

In the middle of the 1980s, First Division matches had been screened on Friday nights and Saturday afternoons, but the first half of the 1985/86 season suffered from the blackout. England's World Cup qualifying match against Romania was not broadcast for a different reason: the BBC didn't think enough people wanted to watch it. A nadir had been reached.

1990

THE YEAR 1986 saw the financial Big Bang in the City of London. It was yet another example of the deregulation of, and foreign interest in, British industry. It amalgamated the roles of stockbrokers and investment advisers, and it also removed the limitations of fixed commissions. This served to increase competition and improve the revenues of the sector, which boosted the financial industry's contribution towards the UK economy.

In the years that followed, there was no longer a requirement for banks to be within a short walk of the Bank of England. To that end, London's Docklands were being redeveloped to become desirable for bankers, residents and business. A 1987 report for the BBC programme *Newsnight* showed the tensions between investors, who were buying out local businesses and training people at a skills centre, and existing residents, who painted 'homes for locals, not snobs' on to walls.

'House prices are rising giddily. The real industry is estate agency,' reported Martin Young as he was shown around a flat in a location which offered good access to London, subsequently pricing out less affluent Docklanders in favour of 'penthouses for yuppies'. It was a 'David and Goliath encounter' where the giant financial centre of Canary Wharf would transform the Isle of Dogs, a microcosm of the growth of the final years of the century in the London sprawl. The Development Corporation was the sole planning authority, with the ability to override whatever plans the local authority was drawing up, 'with no appeal, no public enquiry' and with board meetings closed to the public.

At the same time as the financial industry was benefitting from increased competition, an internal market under the title 'Working for Patients' was introduced to the NHS whereby service providers could compete for contracts with hospitals, with the hope of improving standards and finding the best value for money. There was also the Don't Die of Ignorance campaign to raise awareness of HIV/AIDS. The Princess of Wales was filmed meeting victims of the disease to remove its stigma; in 2009 footballers including Michael Ballack and Emmanuel Adebayor, would lend their support to the UN's campaign as goodwill ambassadors.

Also in 1990, members of the English public rose up in outrage after the government unveiled plans for a Community Charge, which became known as the Poll Tax and was replaced by the Council Tax. Whereas nowadays it is levied according to the tax band of the property you live in, in the late 1980s the sum was to be identical regardless of income or housing status. When in 2016 The National Archives released information about how the government discussed the charge, Nick Higham of the BBC wrote that it was 'supposed to make local council finance fairer and more accountable' but instead it rebounded on the Conservatives.

The BBC reported on riots in London, following a peaceful march, at the end of March 1990. Cars were set on fire in the West End, police were injured and there was a black cloud over Trafalgar Square. It came at the end of a month of protests across England, including in Bristol and Hackney, and precipitated the demise of the policy.

The 1990 Queen's Speech was still name-checking the Falkland Islands, as well as South Africa, where apartheid was soon to conclude. Privatisation also remained a key pillar of government policy, in terms of roads and 'trust ports'. When chancellor John Major delivered the Budget in March, he used the dawning of the decade to call on Britain 'to take the opportunities of the 1990s', especially in post-communist Germany and in the Soviet Union, given 'the astonishing developments' there that led to the fall of the Iron Curtain of communism. Geopolitical events were moving rapidly, with England watching on, as they had done with football tactics.

Four years after Nigel Lawson's complaints, this Budget brought in separate taxes for married women and delivered a victory for enterprise, with 1,500 new businesses a week opening up. Inflation was down but borrowing was up, sending interest rates above ten per cent. Major was apologetic about the sluggish growth but celebrated the investment from other countries into the UK, which had resulted in 'a trade surplus in colour television sets', all the better to watch the World Cup.

The deficit had grown to £20bn, although £5bn had been raised for local authorities. For the first time in five years the government put a duty on spirits, raising the price by 54p, while Major also mooted a gift aid scheme on large charitable donations. In opposition to the focus on the banking sector and their uncapped commissions, Major also wanted to bring back 'the culture of thrift', encouraging people to deposit money into a savings account, rather than to seek cheap credit.

Major noted the criticism of 'the widespread marketing' of such credit and the push for people to borrow money, as well as the propensity for European countries to use interest rates rather than credit controls to limit inflation. Hence financial markets 'have become more open to competition', which meant London was vying with other European destinations as a place to set up branches of American or Asian banks.

There was also a section in Major's address on football, following the publication of the Taylor Report that recommended the urgent modernisation of stadiums to ensure a better fan experience. Many clubs 'are in a weak financial position, and only a handful are profitable' Major said, keen to prevent grounds closing and for football itself to contribute to repairs.

Tottenham Hotspur chief executive Irving Scholar noted that the recession Britain was suffering at least lowered the cost of making grounds compatible with the recommendations in the report, which followed the Hillsborough disaster of April 1989. With remarkable prescience, the prime minister Margaret Thatcher added, 'Millions of people watch football every year. With better and safer grounds, I hope that many more will join them.'

Those football fans were fixed on the 1990 World Cup. England, having qualified without conceding a single goal, were drawn in a group with Egypt, the Netherlands and the Republic of Ireland. Because English clubs were still banned from European competition, the Italian police were hugely concerned about visiting hooligans, meaning all three group games were played in the Sardinian city of Cagliari. The island was 'a nice prison camp' for the England team, said defender Paul Parker wryly in the three-part documentary *Italia 90: When Football Changed Forever*, broadcast on Channel 4 in 2022.

Incredibly, there was only one win across all six group matches. England's draw against Ireland was, to Stuart Pearce, 'an affront to football, two teams kicking lumps out of each other'. Reporter Ian Wooldridge likened it to 'watching Aldershot play Aldershot reserves'. The game against the Netherlands, where a Pearce goal from a free kick was disallowed, was the main reason for England being marooned on an island, such was the risk of violence between the two sets of fans.

In fact, as The National Archives revealed in 2012, a government committee had briefly suggested withdrawing the team from the tournament. It was still possible, wrote Conservative minister Geoffrey Howe, for 'determined hooligans' to head to Italy 'and find a different cause to champion', so any thoughts of England not participating were thankfully abandoned.

The strict police presence is evident in the documentary footage, as they sought to counteract the beer-bellied England fans in Sardinia. Sports minister Colin Moynihan met with the police and told them to clamp down on any violence; we see him describe hooligans as worse than animals. Thanks to the FA membership scheme to crack down on the risks of such fighting, in lieu of a mooted blacklist, fans had to give their passport number and criminal record, which only served to drive tickets to the black market. The media began to write stories about what broadcaster Adrian Goldberg called 'superhooligans'.

Back home, football mirrored the violence that was present in society, and there is plenty of footage of punch-ups inside and outside grounds, taking us from the early 1980s to the tournament itself, via the aforementioned incidents in Luton and Heysel. Goldberg noted the fine line between 'boisterous, and outright aggressive and hostile, behaviour' from the Italian police, who would 'arrest first, ask questions later'. At the end of the first episode, it is revealed that two contributors are English police officers who posed as hooligans and were working undercover during the tournament, building on the work done in the domestic game to stop particularly violent individuals at source before they could travel to the World Cup.

Garry Rogers was drawn to the ringleaders who 'drank and drank all day', and he phoned intelligence through of a march on the stadium before the game against the Netherlands. Although there were St George's Crosses draped across the stands during matches, the footage shows several Union Flags held aloft and choruses of 'Rule, Britannia'. The fans then become violent towards the police who escorted them to the ground; as with the violence between Luton and Millwall fans in 1985, cameras are present, which emboldens the police in attacking fans and spraying them with tear gas to prove to the world that they are capable of handling the disorder.

Moynihan, however, was more concerned about England's international stature than the wellbeing of the fans. He was in Italy to oversee their deportation home, some of whom maintained their innocence. Was it a publicity stunt, to make it seem that the government was doing something, just as the Italians were proactive in their encounters with English fans?

Brian Glanville called the narrow margin of England's 1-0 victory over Egypt to take top spot in the group 'a travesty', again complimenting Peter Shilton on his goalkeeping performance. The victory set up a second-round match against Belgium in Rimini, where England fans had discovered the Rose & Crown pub and, unfortunately, more policemen, who administered truncheons to their bodies and heads, as well as spraying more tear gas. 'The tabloids and the government saw the headline that they wanted,' Goldberg sighed.

The only goal in the game – which, once again, was set up by a Paul Gascoigne free kick – came from a David Platt volley over the shoulder; as per the line of commentary used in the song 'Three Lions', it came in the last minute of extra time. Glanville wrote that Platt had justified his manager's 'excessive belief'.

Talking to the FA website in 2020, Platt said the goal 'changed my life'. He had often tried such volleys in training and chose to replicate it during the match, acting on an instinct which he had honed in private. 'The next day, I did a press conference. I was used to a handful of journalists turning up, but this was different. This was a packed room with hundreds of reporters from all over the world.' He would not be the only Englishman to have his career boosted, for good and ill, by something he did at a World Cup.

Cameroon were the opponents in the quarter-final, and during the second half the Africans scored two goals in three minutes to lead 2-1. Bobby Robson rejigged his defence, Gary Lineker scored a penalty and the game went into extra time. Lineker scored another spot kick to take England into the last four. Journalist Barney Ronay recalled cycling with a Union Flag on his shoulders, joining in the celebrations after England's victory.

Pete Davies was given thousands of words, while he was covering the 1990 tournament in Italy, to tell readers that English football was, as per the title of his book, *All Played Out*, 'a squalid, hooligan-ridden, embarrassing sump of gormless violence'. Speaking to the *Irish Times* in 2021, Davies called football 'a window into a country's soul'. He recalled that publishers wouldn't commission football titles at the time 'because they assumed that all football fans were sub-human morons who didn't read books'.

To Davies, Robson was 'a genuinely decent bloke ... He lived and breathed football.' It seems a prerequisite of the England coach, as we saw with Alf Ramsey and Ron Greenwood, to be immersed in the game. Brian Glanville, meanwhile, was once again critical of the manager, this time because he gave the chronicler too much leeway in what he could write about, especially in the inclusion of Gascoigne angrily talking on the phone.

Like their managers, footballers were about to become fair game to tabloid reporters, treated like movie stars and with their every move tracked and their every pronouncement repeated in print. During the 1990 World Cup, their relations with the press were so bad that players treated those who engaged with them as if they were scabs who crossed the picket lines. This meant Davies could enjoy the confidence of the England camp.

These days, thanks to the demands of social media, fans prefer to see well-rounded characters, some of whom are pundits, and others, like Kyle Walker and Jermaine Jenas, hosts of chatty podcasts. Daniel Storey, who wrote a book about Paul Gascoigne's time in Italy, called the midfielder 'our first true street footballer'. To Henry Winter he was ahead of his time, with his flaws on display off the pitch, while on it he was cheeky, 'impudence becoming imperious ... Gascoigne plays the game every kid dreams of: dribbling, daring, chasing goals and glory'.

Gascoigne was 'football unplugged, the sport stripped to its elemental joys'. It was no surprise that he became a public figure, beloved in a way that today's superstars never were. It may not be a coincidence that, like Kevin Keegan before him and David Beckham and Jude Bellingham after him, Gascoigne left England to play abroad, in his case in Italy and Scotland.

Paul Hayward wrote of his 'childlike enthusiasm' and 'endearing innocence', while Winter also labelled Gascoigne 'a man of two halves, insecure and inspirational', and considered that 'we seem to have forgotten the spirit of Gascoigne, certainly in academies where character is discouraged'. Bobby Robson called him 'a Labrador pup' and an 'eccentric, loveable Geordie', as well as 'a bonny lad who trained like a demon as though his life depended on it'. These are the types of figures the public cherishes, helped by a media environment driven by stars and characters.

Winter argued that, before David Beckham and Wayne Rooney, Gascoigne was the player who caught 'the zeitgeist of a nation increasingly in thrall to the cult of celebrity'. He was like George Best, but this time he was an Englishman. Much has been made of Gascoigne's tears when, in the semi-final against West Germany, he realised that by picking up a yellow card he would miss the World Cup Final should England have qualified. The fact that millions of English fans were watching it at home and in pubs provided a water-cooler moment akin to a sitcom death, and soon the player was appearing on talk shows where he was introduced as a cuddly character called Gazza.

In the modern era, Gascoigne has complained of how his phone was hacked by tabloid journalists who would abandon ethics in pursuit of a story. 'I didn't become a professional footballer so I could get hounded to bits for the rest of my life,' he said, but this is what happens when footballers become public property. They were paying a fame tax that was at its sharpest before the internet ate into the hegemony of printed media.

In the semi-final itself, England had fallen behind against West Germany due to a deflection on an Andreas Brehme shot, before Lineker equalised after a mix-up in the German defence. Chris Waddle went on to hit the post, which meant it would be penalties to decide the place in the final. Waddle and Stuart Pearce missed their kicks. The semi-final was such a close-run and exciting match that, in his book *Psycho*, Pearce wrote, 'When we came home to a heroes' welcome, the early matches were glossed over.' Against West Germany, 'the pressure was off' because they had already overachieved by getting to the semi-final. Finally, England did not think it a divine right that they should win a World Cup.

Better still, the squad's families had been flown out to watch them, as the manager had promised they would be. Peter Beardsley remembered a 'siege mentality' adopted by the players on behalf of Robson, who was assailed, as usual, by the media. The forward admitted, 'As players, we had to shoulder some of the blame.' Mark Wright, who scored the decisive goal against Egypt, was the defensive sweeper the squad petitioned Robson to play, after the defender had missed the 1986 World Cup with a broken leg. He pointed out, as Steve Coppell had done in Ron Greenwood's England setup, that the team was full of characters and there were 'captains all over the pitch'.

One of them was Terry Butcher, who, as mentioned, Robson had managed at Ipswich Town. In a memorable image, Butcher played most of the World Cup qualifying game against Sweden in 1989 wearing a headband, his head having been cut open in a challenge. Here was the kind of player Daniel Storey called 'the bulldog, the hard-as-nails defender or midfielder who was prepared to run through walls for his country'.

More modestly, Steve Bull was named as a striking option, famously called up despite not playing in the English First Division. He came on as a substitute in the game against the Netherlands. 'There was a humility about the team,' John Barnes wrote of Robson's players, who 'never felt like we were the best' and thus sought to 'maximise the potential' they had. Brian Glanville suggested that Barnes was told by Robson to 'play too close to his own left-back', which caused his England performances to suffer and shows how club form often has little bearing on international success. At least Gary Lineker was able to play in the middle of the pitch, rather than out wide as he was forced to do when he played for Barcelona.

Barnes, the highest-profile black player in Robson's England squads, recalled how the press pack failed to write about how a group of supporters with a National Front flag refused to count his terrific goal against Brazil. A similar flag had been spotted at the 1986 World Cup, a depressing reminder that bigotry was still present among travelling fans whose support for the team was a disguise for nationalistic prejudice. Subsequent generations, with smartphones in their pockets, would be empowered to bypass the gatekeepers of the media, who themselves would be more diverse in appearance, and force them to report on such abuse.

Those who did travel for the right reasons were not served enjoyable matches, at least in 1988. Even with 'the best front four in Europe', as Robson termed them, that year's European Championship had been a disaster. Barnes and Beardsley had played too many games, and Waddle had just had a hernia operation. Lineker's body was incubating hepatitis, which caused his performances to be ineffective too. There was also hooliganism off the pitch, with fans rioting after the loss against the Republic of Ireland and trying to force entry into the match against the Netherlands.

All the same, the FA rejected Robson's resignation, as it had done in 1984 after a defeat at Wembley against Denmark which cost England a spot at that year's continental tournament. The manager also turned down an approach from Barcelona, keen to see out his deal until the 1990 World Cup. That was the year the FA allowed Robson to talk to PSV, which perversely made him a traitor to the same writers who had called on him to resign in 1988; *The Sun* had superimposed a dunce's cap on his head after the team were knocked out of the European Championship, calling him a 'bungling boss'.

Back in 1974, recalled Ted Croker, Alf Ramsey had been treated like 'a martyr' when he was sacked, with the FA deemed 'heartless' even though they had done exactly what the press had been demanding of them. There really was no way to win against the press pack, although this may also have been part of the trend of lambasting the FA whatever they did.

For Robson, there was 'no higher plane to play on' than at a World Cup. He was no longer trying to instil pride into an Ipswich fan but trying to bring joy to 'the young lad in Stockport, the old lady in Plymouth and the bloke selling petrol in Carlisle'. Barnes wrote that Robson 'endeared you to the idea of Englishness, of representing your country with pride and passion'. His team talks were filled with English leaders and war victories. Before the penalties against Germany, Robson likened himself to 'a First World War general asking for volunteers'.

The headline in *The Sun* before the Germany game had been 'Help our boys clout the Krauts', which Paul Hayward reckoned made the country seem 'paranoid, xenophobic, trapped in the past', much like the old chant of 'Two world wars and one World Cup'.

In *Farewell but Not Goodbye*, Robson wrote, 'Emotion, more than reason, determines the public's attitude to our England teams. Logic comes a remote second to passion and patriotism. Ours is a game of the heart, as well as the head.' This is not unique to English football – think of various European and South American nations – but it is nonetheless true. Supporters demand effort and commitment, and they are pleased when a well-timed tackle stops an attack. It has been noted that only in England do fans applaud the award of a corner.

Robson, who received a knighthood in 2002 while he was still managing Newcastle United, wrote of 'an upturn in the national mood' after the 1990 World Cup. This was visible to the team when thousands of people welcomed them home at Luton Airport, in a time before the proliferation of cheap flights, wearing T-shirts that read 'England pride restored'.

That pride had taken a knock. In his book *Two Tribes*, Tony Evans chronicled the problems in the city of Liverpool, 'Between 1966 and 1977, 350 factories closed or moved away from Merseyside. More than 40,000 jobs disappeared in the 15 years before 1985.' In that year, one in four people in the city were unemployed, including almost half of people between 16 and 24. All the same, Evans wrote, 'Everyone you knew went to the match. No one chose it. It was something everyone did.'

Fortunately, those supporters saw Liverpool and Everton win multiple league titles and domestic cups. The 1986 World Cup squad contained three players from the blue team on Merseyside – Gary Lineker, Peter Reid and Gary Stevens – but, oddly, none from Liverpool. In 1990 there were no Evertonians, with Lineker now at Tottenham, and three from the red team in town: John Barnes, Peter Beardsley and Steve McMahon. In fact, thanks to the ban on English clubs in European competition, there were more footballers in the latter squad who played in Glasgow – Terry Butcher, Trevor Steven, Gary Stevens and Chris Woods – than in Liverpool.

David Goldblatt wrote that football offered 'a parallel universe of success alongside the otherwise vertiginous urban decline'. There had been riots in the Toxteth area of Liverpool in 1981, and the city council included several members of the Militant Tendency, who were keen to overthrow the more moderate members of the Labour Party. Liverpool had set its own budget in the middle of the decade, with an illegal £30m deficit, which set it against the Tory government, who reluctantly released extra money to stop the city going bankrupt. Even the Labour leader Neil Kinnock had to fight the enemy within his own party.

Jamie Carragher also mentioned the city's football triumphalism when he was growing up. Liverpool's wins in European tournaments were 'the one area where Thatcher's Conservative government couldn't hurt us ... We wouldn't be trampled on.' Similarly, in the north-east, wrote Goldblatt, 'With no ships to build or metal to work, the collective celebration of Newcastle United had become the single remaining coordinate of an older masculine working-class culture that had otherwise disappeared.'

At this point, we must again mention the Hillsborough disaster at the FA Cup semi-final between Liverpool and Nottingham Forest, when a crush led to the deaths of 95 fans, later rising to 97. Following the recommendations of the Taylor Report, the all-seated stadium requirement was, to Goldblatt, 'the single most significant change in football's infrastructure, culture and economic model since the coming of professionalism'.

Such crowd control measures, he wrote, 'dampen the emotional tenor of the crowd' and they brought to an end the era when fans stood on the terraces, pushing and swaying and tumbling when a goal was scored. Seating was the only option after '30 years of accumulated problems' across society, which pointed to the stadium tragedy being in no way an exception to the rule; in the latter half of the decade, England had also mourned victims of sinking ferries, and fires at King's Cross station.

To bring their stadiums into the modern era, clubs used public money and then charged higher ticket prices afterwards that were well above the rate of inflation. To Goldblatt, this was an 'effective but vulgar' method that would be replicated in future by brand partnerships and stadium naming rights. Wembley Stadium gets around the latter by boasting of being 'powered by EE'. Often, when a stadium was rendered obsolete by the Taylor Report, new structures were built away from town centres, lessening the likelihood of fans walking up to the ground, and instead taking the bus or driving to the game. The old images of L.S. Lowry's matchstick men were ossified in the past.

From a football perspective, the European ban on English clubs in the aftermath of the Heysel disaster also served to disrupt the development of tactics and players' technical ability, given that no English team could test themselves against Italian or Spanish opposition. However, plenty of the 1990 World Cup squad went abroad for their football: Gary Lineker played for Barcelona, David Platt for Sampdoria and Chris Waddle for Marseille. Goldblatt also argued that, with English fans unable to follow their clubs in European competition, they simply switched to backing the national team.

Bobby Robson presented an informative package in January 1989 for ITN. 'No England manager should have to argue for more time to spend with his team before crucial games,' he said, thanking the clubs for allowing this before a game against Albania. 'We are a generation removed from Jack Charlton prioritising Leeds United over England.' Robson also noted that kids had the opportunity to choose from over a dozen sports to play at school, whereas he played cricket in the summer before football could start again.

Trevor Francis lamented how each First Division side played the same way, apart from his own Queens Park Rangers team, who sometimes played the sweeper system. 'Our players go into the national arena, and it's something new to them,' he said, requesting that club managers accustom players to dealing with these new formations. Robson, for his part, had to 'incorporate those players in the best system that they understand and get the best out of them'. Damningly, Robson added, 'If I tamper with a different style, I think we'll be up the creek.'

The package showed Robson at Lilleshall in his natural habitat, bellowing at young players and joining in the training exercise in a typically ebullient manner. Down at Tottenham's Centre of Excellence, coach Keith Waldon said that Germany didn't have a schools football system, which as a result enabled their continental counterparts to work on technique rather than placing prominence on the '11-a-side awareness' that young Englishmen experienced. Very soon, the clubs would take control of youth development and schools football would no longer be an avenue for youngsters to pursue.

The BBC's World Cup coverage, which included England's game with West Germany, was soundtracked by the Puccini aria 'Nessun Dorma'. Football might be theatre or television, but, thanks to its Italian setting, it was operatic too. The climax of the 1988/89 season, where Arsenal beat Liverpool to the title, had also been shown on TV, and it became the pivotal moment in Arsenal fanatic Nick Hornby's memoir *Fever Pitch*. David Goldblatt called the book, which arrived in 1992, 'an elegy for the old football', coinciding as it did with Sky Sports launching its coverage of the sparkly new Premier League.

Hornby wrote it for fans like him, and for 'anyone who has ever found themselves drifting off, in the middle of a working day or a film or a conversation, towards a left-foot volley into a top right-hand corner ten or 15 or 25 years ago'. Musing on the redevelopment of Highbury, and the steep increase in ticket prices to sit in the North Bank, he added, 'Middle-class families, the new target audience, will not only behave themselves, but pay much more to do so ... Who'll make the noise now?' Atmosphere was exchanged for affluence at the highest level of the English game, a dichotomy which is still fragile two decades after Arsenal moved into their new, more expensive stadium.

The same can be said of the new Wembley Stadium. Hornby went to the old one to watch England play the Netherlands in a friendly before Euro 88, remembering previous visits where fans 'gave drunken Nazi salutes during the national anthem'. His seat, when he reached it, was occupied by one of the 'crop-headed, thick-necked' fans who had forced their way into the ground; 'There was not a steward in sight,' Hornby sighed, although today there are hundreds on duty at a contemporary England game. He was forced to endure the sound of monkey chants aimed at Ruud Gullit, and he left the stadium before half-time. Following the 1990 World Cup, 'what with Gazzamania and Lineker charm', Hornby felt that the crowd was changing.

'There's an air of unreality about any World Cup,' wrote Lineker himself in his book *Behind Closed Doors*, 'a sense that you've crossed over into some kind of parallel universe.' He fondly remembered the team celebrating their wins, or commiserating on their semi-final defeat, with a blast of 'Do Re Mi' from *The Sound of Music*, a tournament 'propelled by Julie Andrews'.

Lineker recalled how, before the penalty shoot-out against West Germany, 'Waddle put his arm up, very reluctantly' and Robson's words of advice were, 'There's 30 million people watching this at home. Don't let me down!' Tony Evans called Robson 'the man who was too courageous for his own good', but it was clear that his deep patriotism was a force for good during the tournament.

Those fans in front of their TV sets had eschewed the cinema, where in 1990 *Dances with Wolves* put Kevin Costner in the American west and *The Krays* put Gary and Martin Kemp in postwar east London. There was also a filmed adaptation of Tom Stoppard's play *Rosencrantz & Guildenstern Are Dead*, which takes place offstage during a performance of *Hamlet*, whom Mel Gibson played that year. For something more romantic, Juliet Stevenson and Alan Rickman starred in *Truly, Madly, Deeply*.

In 2022, thanks to the Channel 4 documentary mentioned above, the 1990 World Cup had become the subject of its own film. In 1991 it had inspired the stage play *An Evening with Gary Lineker*, which was written by Chris England and Arthur Smith; three years later it was filmed for TV with Paul Merton and Clive Owen, who, alongside Martin Clunes's character Dan, watch England's semi-final against West Germany. After one emotional moment, Bill, played by Owen, stands up to correct his wife Monica's protestations by saying, 'It won't be Gary Lineker getting the trophy; Terry Butcher is the captain.'

A few moments later, Bill says, 'Men, when they get together, they never talk about the things they really care about, their emotions. They just talk about football.' Instantly, they segue into talking about Lineker's goal and walk out of the room to miss the shoot-out. England and Smith rewrite the result so that Pearce scores with his kick and Lineker, referred to as 'the Queen Mother of football', converts his second penalty. The striker then himself appears as a silent *deus ex machina* figure to the strains of 'Nessun Dorma', and kisses Monica.

Magical realism, inspired by true events.

1994

BOBBY MOORE, the captain of the 1966 England side, died of cancer in 1993. That same year, the national squad failed to qualify for the latest World Cup.

Just before the deciding qualifier with the Netherlands, the BBC debate show *On The Line* aired an edition about the state of football in the country, with the title 'Crisis! What crisis?' Even if England were to make it to the finals, presenter John Inverdale asked, would it 'paper over the cracks' of a nation whose team were 'gallant losers'? According to the latest, recently incepted FIFA rankings, Switzerland and the Scandinavian clubs were higher than them.

Steve Heighway, who managed Liverpool's youth teams, wanted to 'provide the philosophy' by cultivating the environment for players to thrive in and to win, especially with clubs' own Centres of Excellence taking the lead rather than schools. To John Cartwright, the man who left Lilleshall shaking his head in irritation, coaching was 'verging on a national disgrace. We have a system that is controlled by nobody ... The whole system is geared to winning rather than learning.'

To that end, Malcolm Allison reprised his outspoken punditry with a wish for 'teachers for the coaches ... Our training is pathetic.' He was keen for kids to have hour-long exercises, rather than full-sided games, to enable them to improve their ball skills, which explained why the Dutch, for instance, were so far ahead of the English. 'We think that great sportsmen are born and not made,' offered the ever-reliable Jimmy Hill, although he might have overlooked Kevin Keegan's hard work that helped him become European Footballer of the Year. Fans, too, were 'impatient' if teams weren't out on the attack, and the argument was for them to be 'educated' in how to watch football, as it was for the kids' parents.

Labour MP Kate Hoey, who seemed to be the only woman among the few dozen participants in the debate, blamed the 'lack of real leadership' shown by the FA who 'don't seem to be listening to the real supporters'; she argued that the rise of Monday night games meant fans could not travel to support their teams. The association, whose amateur ethos still endured over a century after the body had been established, also needed to be more representative of the 'money-led' professional game which was, as planned, becoming progressively more commercial in focus.

Management consultant Alex Fynn, who wrote a book called *Out of Time* about the changes in the game at the turn of the 1990s, pointed to how England squad members were 'knackered' after playing seven games for their clubs in a three-week period before the important match against the Netherlands. Arsenal chairman David Dein predicted that the England team would be more successful if the new Premier League was smaller; he was in favour of trimming the division from 22 to 18 clubs, and he would be granted his wish partially when it dropped to 20 for the 1995/96 season. Coincidentally, with the benefit of four fewer league games, at the end of that campaign England would host the 1996 European Championship. John Inverdale signed off with the wry comment, 'I just hope we're not having this same debate again in 20 years' time.'

The man who picked the team for that match against the Netherlands was Graham Taylor. In his memoir, published just after his death in 2017, Taylor recalled taking on 'the best job in football', and the biggest job of his or any English coach's career: 'Can you imagine how proud I was, walking my daughter down the aisle on her wedding day, knowing that I would be unveiled as my country's football manager two days later?'

The chapter of the book immediately following this statement is called 'A Lonely Job'; writing two decades after leaving the role, he still felt guilty for not qualifying for the 1994 World Cup. 'I don't think anyone was more disappointed than me,' he said. Bobby Robson, however, told Niall Edworthy that 'they threw away my experience overnight' when Taylor replaced him, something that would never have happened at 'a major corporation'.

This was slightly unfair, given that only five men had managed England permanently in 40 years and any new appointment was bound to be less experienced and forced to learn on the job, adapting to the international game just as Revie and Robson had done before. It took until 2012 for a man, Roy Hodgson, to be appointed to the England job who had previously managed a national side.

Taylor had, of course, gained experience at Watford and Aston Villa for over a decade, earning multiple promotions and high league finishes while Robson was steering England to two World Cup tournaments. To Taylor, though, being England manager 'felt more like steering an ocean liner and my job was to try to avoid the many icebergs'. At other times he felt like 'chief babysitter' who looked after players that saw playing for their country 'as an escape from their clubs'. These players would complain that 'there was a lot of time to kill', which would see them ordering drinks to their hotel room at a time when sports science was less of a concern to a professional footballer than it is today.

Taylor bemoaned the injuries that denied certain players the chance to play in his side, writing that 'the hardest thing was getting the best 11 players on the pitch at the same time'. He dedicated a chapter of his book to Paul Gascoigne, who made 11 appearances in his time as manager, which lasted for 38 matches. He was denied the use of the midfielder for two whole years due to two dreadful injuries. 'He could take your breath away one moment and have you tearing out your hair the next,' he wrote.

When he asked former managers of the national team how to approach the job, there was no consistency in their answers, because 'each person had done the job the way they felt was best'. Taylor's conversations with the agent who represented the England squad about payments for commercial activities, moreover, convinced him there was more to playing for the country than 'purely for the honour', although the inverse is true today when players are so well remunerated by their clubs.

Taylor's time in charge of England overlapped with the creation of the Premier League, which increased the size of the numbers on their employers' spreadsheets and, in turn, their wages. Unlike Don Revie, fighting for fair compensation for playing for England was less of a concern for Taylor. Much of his job, when he wasn't scouring for players, was spent 'on the telephone, leaving messages with people, waiting for them to call back'.

He grew to think that managers were not really interested in the health of the England team, noting that Alex Ferguson and George Graham saw it 'as an inconvenience'; coincidentally, both of those managers were Scottish, while he was sure he overheard a third

Scot, Graeme Souness, telling someone he wasn't there to take his call. Worse, during the run-in to the 1991/92 season, Ferguson pulled three players from an England squad before a game in Czechoslovakia. Glenn Hoddle also mentioned having angry phone calls with Ferguson 'ranting and raving ... I can't repeat what he called me'.

Above all, Taylor missed 'the bustle and the banter' of a club job. The new Premier League allowed for some free weekends for international football, but it was the start of the period which saw foreign talent shrinking the pool of English players from which the national team manager could pick. Worse was the apathy from England fans: in November 1992, two years after the team were welcomed home from the World Cup by thousands at Luton Airport, only 43,000 people watched the team beat Turkey at a half-empty Wembley, and this was one of the 11 games Gascoigne played in. The front pairing was Alan Shearer, who had moved to Blackburn Rovers for an English record transfer fee, and Ian Wright, who along with Tony Adams and Lee Dixon was one of three Arsenal players in the side.

Besides, Taylor continued, an international team 'is made up of a collection of individuals who are all used to doing things differently', on the pitch or off it. He would try to encourage them 'to be part of the group even if they weren't in the team', a sign of good management that was a change from the small squad he had had at his disposal at Watford.

History recalls Taylor more than most England managers, including Robson and Revie, because of *The Impossible Job*, a film the manager could have stopped or at least offered edits for; in his book, the only thing he apologised for was his language. The documentary, which preceded the wave of reality TV that led to the commissioning of shows like *Driving School* and *Airline*, also gave viewers the chance to watch footballers in their natural habitat. Sometimes they played along with the conceit: David Platt agreed to stage a shot for the cameras after Taylor told him that he would not be captain for the next game.

Assistant manager Lawrie McMenemy, however, was not happy with the cameras being in the workplace. Poor Phil Neal, who was also on the coaching staff, became a figure of fun because of his habit of blithely agreeing with the manager, which he claimed jeopardised his own coaching career. For the deciding match against the Netherlands, the camera crew were smuggled into the stadium, enabling them to film a match which pivoted on Ronald Koeman not being sent off for a professional foul.

Today, *The Impossible Job* would be an impossible job to film, since there would be too much control given to the participants and their representatives, who would be wary of the blowback and the effect on their client's reputation. They would also be more likely to release a documentary themselves, as the likes of Cristiano Ronaldo and Antoine Griezmann have done. Two England captains, David Beckham and Wayne Rooney, have also contributed to sanitised films about their lives and careers.

The film about the Three Lions' quest to qualify for the World Cup helped inspire Barney Ronay to describe the England manager's job as one that led to a 'public breakdown, a shared neurosis of blame and rejection'. Niall Edworthy wrote of the 'polite embarrassment' shown by his interviewees when Taylor was brought up, with 'a near universal reluctance to advance any form of criticism' of a man who was kicked enough in the failed qualifying campaign.

Even without a new manager in post, England were going through a period of transition; between 1990 and

1994 they were made to cope without Terry Butcher, Bryan Robson and Peter Shilton. Taylor named Stuart Pearce as his captain initially, but injury denied him several international call-ups during the period. 'I wanted England to do well,' he wrote in *Psycho*, 'because a lot of the players are my mates and I always want my country to do well.' Too many players, he added, 'pay lip service to playing for their country', whereas he followed the example of Trevor Brooking and Kevin Keegan, adding, 'I treasure every one of my caps.'

Pearce commended Taylor as 'proud and passionate', although 'he didn't wear it on his sleeve all of the time'. Taylor's fault was that 'he overdid it with his selection of honest, hard-working players'. The documentary made the Sheffield Wednesday midfielder Carlton Palmer an avatar of this sort of player. He was never picked for England by Taylor's successor, Terry Venables.

Taylor misjudged the media, preferring not to have favourites, which meant, as he wrote in his memoir, 'When the press turned against me, they all turned against me.' He recalled the impact on his family when TV crews disturbed his parents, walking in through their open back door, and they also accosted his wife Rita. Members of the public would feel chastened to approach him with criticism when he was with Rita in public, but he was nonetheless always 'on guard' when out and about. He once snapped and grabbed someone by the shirt when they called him 'an idiot', and he asked *The Sun* politely to stop referring to him as a turnip, a nickname given firstly to his players and then to him after England lost to Sweden.

Just as Bobby Robson found with the move from Ipswich to the national team, Taylor had to adjust to a job where he wasn't just making the people of a town happy or sad. After the overachievement at the 1990 World Cup, he was aware that people reckoned England 'should win every game they play', which is all well and good so long as it doesn't 'become a sense of arrogance or entitlement'. In the 1980s, however, other nations 'caught up' with England.

John Barnes recalled a game played in advance of the 1990 World Cup, against Tunisia, where the opponents had more of the ball, 'but we'd live with them because we were good in the air, and aggressive'. A few years later, referees were instructed by FIFA to be more strict with players, coming down harder on tackles from behind; this forced England to adapt their 'old up-and-at-'em spirit' and turn to the tactics that sides like Tunisia had been using for many years. 'We've lost time. We've fallen behind,' Barnes lamented in 2016, echoing what his old Watford manager also thought.

Deprived of Pearce as his captain, Taylor replaced him with Gary Lineker due to his 'quiet authority', but dropped the striker when he fell out of form. Taylor claimed he did not want 'a situation where a player is thought of as untouchable'; as we will see in the 2000s, with Sven-Göran Eriksson as manager, this was not always a policy adopted by the man in charge of England. For his part, Lineker saw himself as a fall guy for Taylor, because the discussion was about how the manager had taken him off at Euro 92 in a match against Sweden. 'If he'd kept me on, and I hadn't scored,' Lineker told Henry Winter, 'I'd have been hammered with the rest of the team. He made me a hero!'

All the same, Lineker has spoken of Taylor's lack of international football experience as a player, something which Bobby Robson, and later Fabio Capello and Gareth Southgate, did possess. He also told Paul Hayward that Taylor assembled, to play at the 1992 tournament, 'the least creative side I played in by a mile. We weren't very good.' Coming to his defence, Steve Coppell admired how Taylor had used a 3-5-2 formation to guide Aston Villa back to the upper reaches of the First Division, where significantly he had abandoned the direct football that had brought success to his Watford side.

Like his predecessor, Taylor gave plenty of good copy to journalists and even gave them his phone number for direct contact; after all, his dad had been a football reporter so he knew how to foster good relations with the men whose opinions could become a lightning rod for supporters. In a sign of the times, though, the FA only had one press officer, David Bloomfield, who would juggle requests from photographers, TV, radio and newspapers. Once again, the FA's amateur and amateurish ethos shone through at a time when they needed to be more front-footed and proactive.

Far from the current environment, where politicians are trained to answer a different question than the one asked of them, back in 1994 football managers had no such training. Thus Bloomfield was assisted, eventually and at Taylor's request, by David Teasdale, who used the expertise he had gained working for Margaret Thatcher. He had huge sympathy for the England manager, especially when he conducted interviews and press conferences immediately after a match.

'Alastair Campbell would never let Tony Blair face the press when he was so tired and unprepared,' Teasdale told Niall Edworthy for his book *The Second Most Important Job in the Country*. Unlike politicians, managers had to respond to questions 'when the adrenalin and the emotions are still swirling ... No wonder they trip up.'

In an interview with Hunter Davies for *The Independent*, headlined 'He's so nice but crikey they're mean', Taylor complained about how the media would take what he said and 'use it to abuse you. They take things out of context, twist my words so I appear to be criticising a player. You have little or no status as England manager, and receive little respect. After the royal family and the prime minister, the England manager has more words written about him than anyone else, most of them abusive ... In every country I get recognised.'

As Ramsey had done, Taylor prioritised the team over individual excellence, which perhaps meant that being deprived of Gascoigne benefitted the group, 'I'm trying to establish a squad ethos. The fewer problems there are, the better.' If only prime minister John Major, on whom more shortly, could have had the same luxury.

Teasdale let Taylor be Taylor, realising that there was little point in treating him like a political figure, because he could never be less than 'engagingly honest'. Just as the political press loves to create tribes and factions within a party, so the football reporter looks for cracks within a squad, 'a manager who will blame the players and players who will blame the manager'. This made it a surprise in Gareth Southgate's time as England coach that the squad were committed to a common cause, although this coincided with a time where there were many more media operatives within the FA ranks to keep players on message.

In the last few years, the Labour Party has had to mollify a minority of their 400 MPs. Several outspoken rebels made life so awkward for prime minister Keir Starmer that they had the whip removed before forming a new party, still as independent MPs. The Conservatives have also dealt with internecine warfare: in the 1980s, Margaret Thatcher had to deal with the so-called 'wets' who were not as zealous as her inner circle, while the thorns in Theresa May's side were always ready with a negative comment during her own premiership. It is a relief that professional footballers are not so Machiavellian and, instead of having to lose the whip or their seat, can be left out of an England squad or can choose to retire from the international scene.

Masochistically, Taylor watched the 1994 World Cup, mostly alone at home. 'It was almost like I was punishing myself,' he wrote. 'I felt it was part of the process of getting over it.' After every game, he would head out into the garden and kick a ball about. When the tournament finished he felt as if he could 'move on'. Within two years he was back in the Watford dugout, leading the side to back-to-back promotions for their first season in the Premier League.

He persuaded Ronny Rosenthal, who had played for Liverpool and Tottenham, to be around the squad even though he missed most of the 1998/99 season through injury. Taylor also got the most out of two strikers, Nick Wright and Allan Smart, whom he signed from Carlisle United. He was, after all, the man who had developed John Barnes into one of the club's only England internationals. He also knew how to deal with stars given that Watford's chairman was Elton John, and he had practice for Paul Gascoigne's errant ways after he helped Paul McGrath fight his addictions while he was at Aston Villa.

When Taylor died in 2017, Alex Ferguson commended him as 'approachable, open and honest'. Such a stance included his comment on the incoming Premier League as 'based on greed' rather than having been set up to help his England team. A generation after the home ownership revolution of the 1970s, this was an even greater time of enterprise and individuality. Kenneth Clarke delivered the Budget for the Conservatives in November 1994, where he sought 'to prevent the emergence of a deprived underclass, excluded from the opportunity to work and dependent on welfare'. The bill to create Jobseeker's Allowance (JSA) was brought as part of the 1994 Queen's Speech, as well as one to counter discrimination against disabled people.

JSA introduced a childcare allowance to help parents enter the job market, and Clarke dangled the promise of a rebate if a business took on someone who had been unemployed for over two years. An additional scheme enabled people to work for three weeks without losing their benefits, with no burden on the employer to hire them afterwards; this was in contrast to Labour's idea of creating a minimum wage, which even in 1994 was still yet to be introduced.

Pertinently for this investigation, Clarke compared the low levels of inflation with those 'that were last seen when England won the World Cup ... Before that game I had lived in a low-inflation economy.' He also took a swipe at the 'post-socialist resistance' to the government's policies that encouraged private finance into public health, prisons, education and transport projects, including the London Underground; this is commonly thought of being something the Blair government introduced. Clarke said a Venture Capital Trust would, in the language of management consultants of the time, set about 'generating equity investment in dynamic, innovative growing businesses'.

As per the focus on the environment, Clarke's Budget provided grants to everyone over 60 years old to insulate their homes and save on their bills, which to counter the rise in gas prices would also be reduced when the payment was made promptly. The government also set out the future introduction of a landfill tax, again keenly aware that waste was a modern watchword.

As well as mentioning that university attendance was up from one in eight in 1979 to one in three in 1994, the chancellor noted how it was strange that taxes should only apply to those arcade games which offered prizes. The Conservative government introduced the National

Lottery in 1994, which would help deliver funds to sport and the arts. As the BBC reported at the time, 'A £1 ticket gives you a one-in-14-million chance of striking lucky and guessing correctly the winning six out of 49 numbers.' You had more chance of becoming an international footballer than winning the jackpot.

Unlike Harold Wilson before him and like Tony Blair after him, prime minister John Major had followed the USA into conflict, taking British troops into the first Gulf War. Like Thatcher, he had to deal sensitively with the IRA, especially after Downing Street was attacked by bombs in February 1991 during a cabinet meeting. 'It's about time they learned that democracies cannot be intimidated by terrorism, and we treat them with contempt,' he said after the attack.

Major had won leadership of his party in November 1990, four months after Graham Taylor was appointed England manager, in a campaign which he said was 'based on substance and not personality'. Like Taylor, Major was a keen observer of newspaper commentary on how he and his government were doing, and he had to deal with enormous criticism, particularly about the relationship between the UK and Europe.

'Politely but firmly we shall say what we think,' Major told party members in his victory address. He spoke of his wish to 'build a truly open society' which was 'genuinely compassionate' as well as 'classless'. Excusing the disaster of the Poll Tax, he said that 'the government that never reviewed policies never made any'.

As they did with Gascoigne, the British media used political figures for stories and took some scalps in the form of resignations: David Mellor, who was pilloried with negative coverage of his extramarital affair, which included a fabricated story about wearing a Chelsea shirt in bed;

and Neil Hamilton, who took payments to ask questions in parliament in contravention of good conduct. He was one of several MPs to be accused of breaking the rules about lobbying, which tainted the Conservative Party led by Major.

Major had tried to deal with the rot within the party by launching a committee on standards in public life. This saw the introduction of the non-binding Nolan Principles, which were seven pointers towards good public service: selflessness, integrity, objectivity, accountability, openness, honesty and leadership. You can suggest which England managers best fitted these principles, although certainly Robson and Taylor were two of them.

Also like Taylor with his utterance of 'Do I not like that!', the most quotable line from *The Impossible Job*, the prime minister was caught on a microphone, in his case describing Eurosceptic members of his cabinet as 'bastards' who were 'causing all sorts of trouble'. Major had negotiated the Maastricht Treaty in 1992, which set in motion the single European currency of which Britain would not be part.

Major's time in office carries the mark of Black Wednesday, 16 September 1992, which saw the pound fall out of the European Exchange Rate Mechanism. Britain had only joined it two years earlier when Major had been chancellor, and his successor Norman Lamont had tried to rescue the value of the pound by inflating interest rates twice in a day. It was certainly a more expensive error than England not qualifying for the 1994 World Cup.

The treaty also made it easier for workers, including football players, to travel freely around the continent with European citizenship. The 1994 Beatles biopic, *Backbeat*, chronicled the early days of the band, including their own time in Hamburg. Danny Boyle's debut film *Shallow*

Grave contrasted with another, frothier British film, *Four Weddings and a Funeral*.

Contemporary football, meanwhile, was to David Goldblatt 'drenched in nostalgic affection for the social formation that had just passed into history, for a world where large numbers of people would gather under one roof or in one industrial place'. This is a reference to the demise of heavy industry, and the closure of steelworks and coal pits.

As Jeremy Paxman wrote in his book *Black Gold*, coal mining was the only industry that the government had left to divest in. Already in private hands were 'aerospace companies, airlines and airports, bus and car companies, electricity, steel and water companies, gas and oil concerns, ports and railway firms'. It would soon be the case that the contract to provide coal to the privatised electricity firms would expire and, now that there was natural gas extraction as another form of energy, it would be easier to close down some of the coal mines.

By the 1990s, England's main industries were of service rather than of manufacturing. Writing in Iain Dale's book *The Prime Ministers*, Julian Glover thought that Major 'understood that to survive, public services had to treat the people who used them as customers with rights, not lucky supplicants'. This led to the rise of customer services, call centres and the dead hand of user feedback which proliferates to this day.

The England football team, of course, were accustomed to enjoying instant feedback in the form of boos or cheers, or a half-empty national stadium.

1998

IN 1995, the Labour leader Tony Blair was in Brighton for his party's conference. The day before his speech, he met Newcastle United manager Kevin Keegan. In a few years, Blair would lead the country and Keegan the England football team, with the former having a much better time of it than the latter.

In his diary, Blair's adviser Alastair Campbell wrote that his boss 'wasn't bad with a ball' and overcame objections from other members of staff that any interaction with a football risked embarrassing Blair, referred to as TB. 'It was a fantastic success and provided the best pictures of the week,' Campbell added. 'I asked Keegan to throw the ball at TB and get him to head it back. Then they just kept going, I think for 28 consecutive headers. TB said he had never been able to do that in his entire life.'

These days, Campbell presents a blockbuster political podcast, leaning on the decade he spent steering Labour back into power. He and Blair attended the Euro 96 game between England and Scotland, where Campbell noted 'how much of a feelgood factor you could get going' with the football team doing well. 'There was part of me that did not want a great nationalist football fervour,' Campbell wrote, 'that could let the Tories win back a bit of a lift.' In 1970, Labour had feared an England defeat; now they were wary of an England victory.

At the semi-final against Germany, Campbell commiserated with Denis Howell, the man whom Harold Wilson asked whose fault it was that England had lost their match against West Germany at the 1970 World Cup. Howell had told Campbell that, as with the Falklands victory in 1982, an election would soon follow, although after watching England struggle against Switzerland Campbell was 'pretty confident' that England would fail to win the tournament.

As *Titanic* dominated cinemas with a ship-sinking love story, Guy Ritchie offered *Lock, Stock and Two Smoking Barrels* and Jane Horrocks was *Little Voice*. The reign of Queen Elizabeth I was seen through Cate Blanchett's performance, while the England of 1998 was still coming to terms with the previous year's death of Diana, Princess of Wales. Blair inserted himself into the narrative by calling her 'the people's princess', while normal TV programming was interrupted and her funeral was broadcast on TV. Images of thousands of bouquets of flowers laid outside Buckingham Palace were matched by mourners throwing them on to her funeral procession.

Over the summer, England took part in the 1998 World Cup just across the Channel in France. Terry Venables left the manager's role in 1996 after guiding England to the semi-finals of the home European Championship, when they were a few penalties away from a final. Sportswriter Mihir Bose thought Venables was 'the first manager to realise you could go into a press conference and shape the next day's reporting', which was akin to how Campbell would manage the media grid for Blair.

Before Euro 96, the England squad had been photographed drinking in Hong Kong. In bygone days, the incident would not have been reported because of the aforementioned omertà between player and journalist. Now, the rise in tabloid kiss-and-tell stories, with members of the public being paid for gossip and tattle, risked lowering the privacy of the squad, and gave the press another line of attack away from performances on the pitch. As Stuart Pearce's bulgy-eyed celebration of scoring his penalty at Euro 96 showed, the power of the image could set the tone for how a footballer was viewed.

In 1998 Venables was banned from being a company director for seven years by the Department of Trade and Industry. As one government minister correctly said, 'Even our national heroes cannot be allowed to fall below accepted standards of probity when they enter the business world.'

In his place came 38-year-old former England international Glenn Hoddle. In his memoir *Playmaker*, Hoddle recalled how he was sounded out, meeting selector and former England international Jimmy Armfield in a Hyde Park car park. 'It felt like we were in a spy film,' he said.

Hoddle gave the captaincy to Alan Shearer because he would 'command instant respect'. Players had 'a responsibility to their talent', and Hoddle would be annoyed if they dropped their standards or failed to concentrate in training sessions. Striker Michael Owen wrote that Hoddle's big weakness was that 'he thought everyone should be as good as he was', while journalist Brian Glanville noted that Gareth Southgate would criticise Hoddle's 'self-indulgence' in training. As a rule, English people do not like tall poppies, and are keen to cut them down to size so they do not get above their station. Trying too hard is also more a fault than an asset.

Writing in his book *Safe Hands*, goalkeeper David Seaman was annoyed that Hoddle 'wanted to know what you were doing in your own time'; he limited the time Seaman could go fishing close to a game, forbade the players from drinking alcohol so that the body's lactic acid levels would not be affected, and once ordered new mattresses for the squad so they could sleep better. 'His attention to detail became a little over the top,' Seaman said, although these all seemed practical decisions to optimise the players' performance. His Arsenal team-mate Tony Adams believed the England job came 'too early' for Hoddle.

Hoddle also changed the team's formation from what he termed the 'bland' and 'painfully rigid' 4-4-2 that forced them to play 'in straight lines, making them far too predictable'. Worse, he followed the writer Hunter Davies in thinking England were ossified for many years by the World Cup victory of 1966, which he termed 'our nemesis ... We never moved on from that summer. We became stuck in our ways, arrogantly and blindly clinging to 4-4-2.' This was satirised in the 2001 movie *Mike Bassett: England Manager*, where Ricky Tomlinson played an old-fashioned manager who announced his cherished formation to the media after intoning 'If', the poem by Rudyard Kipling.

Hoddle, however, switched to 3-5-2, giving his team an extra man in midfield and, he wrote, making them more solid, even though he could only pick one attacking wide player so as not to be 'cavalier'. A five-man defence also risked 'inviting pressure' but 'an unshakeable confidence' led him to think England would qualify for the World Cup so long as the players would 'trust in the process'. He sought to balance control with flair.

'He had a crystal clear vision of how he wanted us to play,' wrote defender Rio Ferdinand, 'with purpose, with a real focus on being flexible and tactically creative.' The West Ham academy graduate would play the role of 'a creative centre-back', similar to how Pep Guardiola would use Javier Mascherano or John Stones, and the new formation suited him given that two defenders would remain back while he pressed forward.

You can see an invisible smile on Hoddle's face, even off the page, as you read his recollections of his first game in charge, the 3-0 win over Moldova in September 1996. 'A 1-0 win would have led to a few grumbles, while a thrashing would have sent expectations through the roof,' he wrote. This tallies with something Gary Lineker wrote about the national team in 2019, 'Things are either entirely brilliant or entirely terrible and very rarely anywhere in between.'

That game saw David Beckham make his debut. Beckham claimed that he found out he'd been called up for the squad when his mum noticed it on Teletext, the rolling news service which was made redundant, first by the red button on a TV remote control and then by smartphone internet use. At the time, still a young player who used to watch England Schoolboys games but never the men's team, Beckham got his manager to sign one of his England shirts, writing in *My Side* that 'the intensity never dropped' with Hoddle.

Against Poland for his first match at Wembley, Hoddle 'wanted to be bold'. He wrote that following Euro 96 it was his 'job to lift the mood … Every player had talent, pride and a burning desire to succeed.' He called starlet Michael Owen 'ruthless … He had so much belief in himself.' Perhaps Hoddle saw something of himself in Owen.

As Graham Taylor and Don Revie had found, the long gaps between international fixtures were hard for Hoddle. 'I almost had too much time to prepare for games,' he added, and there was the risk 'of overloading my players with information'. He used an excellent metaphor when he noted that, as England manager, 'you're only leasing the car', which Roy Hodgson spelled out more clearly in a conversation with Henry Winter in 2016, 'They are the clubs' players, paid by the clubs, belonging to the clubs.'

Hoddle's main motivation was 'always about how to get the best out of them', and he placed as much importance on the team that finished the game as on the starting XI. At the end of the away qualifying against Italy, having broken out into a sweat, he had an atrial fibrillation and was put on heart medication. It pays to recall how involved he used to be with England matches even as a child, crying when they lost. His enthusiasm for the team had not dimmed with age and experience.

Before the squad headed off for the 1998 World Cup, they went to see a musical in London's West End. Hoddle recalled how fans 'spilled out of pubs' to cheer them en route, 'The patriotic fervour gave me a greater appreciation of the responsibility on my shoulders … I was going to be as important as the prime minister.'

By 1998, Tony Blair had settled into his role as the actual PM. Three years previously he had written an article for the *Mail on Sunday* on the occasion of a speech at a dinner for the Football Writers' Association in honour of Stanley Matthews. It is plausible that football fanatic Alastair Campbell had written it for him.

Headlined 'How Our Soccer Idols Are Betraying Britain', Blair's article included several worrying aspects of the modern game, including the transfer fee exchanged to take Andy Cole to Manchester United from Newcastle United. 'I worry that the game in which one individual is deemed to be worth £7m and whose club must raise the money with ever more lucrative and exclusive TV deals, merchandising and expensive seats is a game which may lose touch with its roots,' he wrote.

Replica strips, meanwhile, had not gone the way of the hula hoop, as that Conservative MP had wished in the

1970s. Now, with regular updates that coaxed fans into buying one for each new season, such items crossed the line 'between marketing and exploitation', a commercial focus which points to 'sporting and social decline'. Blair also lamented the individualism which was rife in society, 'the get-rich-quick, something-for-nothing philosophy', as well as the lack of shame from players who were sent off.

Stanley Matthews, meanwhile, stood and still stands for 'fair play, the role of the individual within a team or community, honesty and romance'. It is always easy to turn figures from the past into totems and signifiers of a more innocent time, but a more materialistic age demands that footballers participate in it. As we shall see, one particular England player became a billboard for brands, in turn morphing into a brand himself. David Beckham followed in Matthews's own footsteps.

In his memoir *The Way It Was*, the older winger recalled signing a deal with the Co-op, 'to my knowledge the first ever commercial deal struck by a footballer (unless you count Denis Compton)', to wear lightweight football boots, an arrangement which was worth more than his weekly wage at Blackpool. He also made public appearances in stores on matchdays where he would sign photos of himself. Perhaps the number of noughts on the end of a modern endorsement deal was what appalled Blair. Can a modern player not represent their community or their profession and pick up some sponsorship?

Rupert Murdoch and his media empire supported Blair as much as it did the televising of Premier League football, which helped to fund the commercial boom of English football that saw it overtake the England team in esteem. The Murdoch-owned *Sun* had staunchly favoured the Conservative Party in the 1980s and persuaded voters not to back Labour at the 1992 election; 'If Kinnock wins today will the last person to leave Britain please turn out the lights' read its splash at that time. The paper came out for New Labour in 1997, calling Blair, who is godfather to one of Murdoch's children, 'a leader with vision, purpose and courage who can inspire them and fire their imaginations'; the Conservatives, meanwhile, were 'tired, divided and rudderless'.

To Steve Richards, Blair 'chose to stress that there would be no turning back. His vision was defined by his constant urge to prove his party had changed.' This is why they were called New Labour, a rebranding from the old entity which had been ejected from power in 1979. Their election manifesto of 1997 complained that, as 2000 approached, the old political struggles, including 'public versus private, bosses versus workers, middle class versus working class', were irrelevant.

Blair and his party decided to eradicate a line of opposition attack and stick rigidly to what the Conservatives had announced they would spend from 1997 to 1999, with no change either to the planned income tax rates. Labour were at pains to be competent with the economy in order to counteract the received wisdom that they were not to be trusted with running the country. As Samuel Earle later outlined in an excellent book, Britain was really a Tory nation; the Conservatives saw it as natural that they would be the ones in charge, just like the England football team saw themselves in 1950 and 1973.

In previous Queen's Speeches, international concerns were placed before domestic ones, but the system was reversed in 1998. This announced the creation of the Financial Services Authority to regulate markets, at a time when the government was also keen to promote e-commerce, referred to as 'electronic commerce'. Teachers are a common feature of many speeches, and here there was a plan for 'the most far-reaching reforms of the teaching profession for 50 years'.

In the clause concerning benefits, widowers were to be compensated for the first time. A London mayor and assembly were to be established, and a congestion charge discussed, while MPs would be granted a vote on lowering the age of consent for homosexual activities from 18 to 16 (it would be, from 2000). They would not, however, be able to vote on the mandatory abolition of hereditary peers from the House of Lords, who took the role that the FA Council took in English football, a stuffy relic of a bygone age.

Gordon Brown delivered the 1998 Budget in March. 'We must build a national economic purpose around new ambitions for Britain,' he opened, 'to advance the ambition of all.' His buzzwords were 'stability and prudence', but this seems incompatible with the buccaneering tone, a few sentences later, of wanting to 'lift our productivity in each and every industry towards the levels of the world's best'. Key to this was to introduce tax reliefs for venture capitalists and to change how companies paid corporation tax, enabling them to do so in instalments rather than upfront and helping Britain become 'the best place in the industrialised world in which to invest'.

Building on the Conservative Budget of 1994, a landfill tax had been brought in, which Brown raised to £10 per tonne of active, rather than inert, waste. A total of £50m a year would be provided for rural bus services and £1.7bn earmarked for the NHS, a Labour invention of 1948. Brown's Budget outlined the welfare to work scheme where 'every young person unemployed for more than six months will have the offer of work or training'.

The big announcement was the tax credit for working families and disabled people in work, 'Your responsibility is to seek work. My guarantee is that if you work, work will pay.' There was an additional credit to give parents better access to childcare, a £2.50 rise in child benefit payments and a provision of unpaid parental leave. This acted in tandem with the Sure Start scheme, which helped half a million children in deprived areas across 250 programmes nationwide.

Brown's golden rule had been that governments should only borrow to invest, rather than to spend it. It was Blair, meanwhile, who decided not to join the European single currency, the Euro, more through scepticism that it would benefit Britain than protectionism.

Like contemporary football itself, Blair united the classes. He and his New Labour team knew the party needed to widen its base beyond the working person, so accordingly he had abolished Clause IV of the party's constitution. This removed the commitment to public ownership, which continued the enterprising spirit of the age ushered in by the Conservatives in the previous two decades.

New Labour and Manchester City Council both pushed 'municipal socialism', coming together to rebrand the city using the pull of its youth music scene to attract a workforce and investment. Hence why the city submitted an unsuccessful bid for the 2000 Olympics and a successful one to host the 2002 Commonwealth Games. At the time, wrote David Goldblatt, football clubs were a 'working model of the kind of collective action and social solidarity they would like to nurture', although Manchester United would soon broaden their ambitions beyond their home market.

The government wasted no time in setting up a Football Task Force in July 1997, two months into their term. Steered by future Mayor of Greater Manchester Andy Burnham, it collected evidence over the course of two years. It pushed for Premier League clubs and the FA to fence off five per cent of their TV income to the Football Foundation in order to propagate the grassroots game, and it also led to the creation of Supporters Direct, which helped fans of clubs including Exeter City take control of their club and which has since merged with the Football Supporters' Federation.

In contrast to this, Goldblatt concluded in *The Game of Our Lives* that: 'The neoliberal programme of deregulation and commercialisation in football produced a booming economic sector that delivered immense wealth to a small number of people.' This led to a resistance to regulation; like the banking sector, the football industry developed 'nonchalance, even disdain' for how things were, meaning that the task force was better for smaller clubs than the big beasts of English football. Clubs outside the top division would still be punished by the collapse of ITV Digital in 2002, another disaster for private enterprise.

Unfortunately, in 1999, hooliganism was back on the political agenda. Before the opening group game of the previous year's tournament against Tunisia, which England won 2-0, there were concerns about holding the game in Marseille. Sir Brian Hayes was a policeman who was taken on by the FA to advise on security. In 2018, he told the BBC that 'the whole climate was wrong'. This included the presence of a big screen on the beach, where England fans risked being provoked into violence.

Rioting had started the day before the match, with battles in the streets lasting seven hours, forcing French police to fire tear gas in a reprise of what their Italian equivalents had done back in 1990, the last time England fans had travelled to watch their team in a World Cup. It can only be wondered how American law enforcement officers would have dealt with them had England qualified for USA 94.

Blair was moved to condemn the rioters, while FA chief executive Graham Kelly criticised those '400 drunken English people' who went 'to sit in bars and drink for 24 hours'. Hayes said that the game had been a turning point in how to deal with these sorts of problems, with banning orders put in place and a keenness for 'identifying the troublemakers beforehand [and] getting passports withdrawn'.

Speaking in parliament, Home Office minister Kate Hoey – the same MP who had been present in the BBC debate of 1993 – brought up the violence in the context of the Football offences and disorder bill. Predictably, she emphasised the 'small but disproportionately high-profile minority' of violent England fans who 'tarnish our international reputation'. She sought to protect 'the safety and security of the decent law-abiding supporter', the kind who was part of the official England supporters' club.

Hoey continued, 'I said that hooliganism had not gone away. Those committed to breaking the law and using football as a platform for their activities know that violence or trouble inside grounds is likely to be prevented from happening and that when it occurs, it will be swiftly nipped in the bud. Hooligan behaviour is now more likely to occur some distance from the stadium, often some time before or after a match.'

As to the match itself, David Beckham had been dropped from the team that played Tunisia. He felt Hoddle was playing mind games with him, to which the manager told him that he lacked focus. Beckham attributed this charge to how he failed to participate in the team golf day to spend time with his girlfriend. His place on the right was taken by Darren Anderton of Tottenham, a player known as 'Sicknote' because of the long periods he spent injured.

'I found myself wishing that I wasn't there at all,' Beckham recalled, feeling like a failure and full of shame too. Fans chanted his name as he warmed up against Romania, when he came on for Paul Ince after half an hour. England lost 2-1 and needed to beat Colombia in the final group match, which was attended by Princes Charles and Harry. Handily, Beckham started and scored a direct free kick in another 2-0 win which set up a last-16 match against, once again, Argentina.

Graeme Le Saux, the England left-back, was married to a lady from Argentina, which caused him some aggravation from the newspapermen. The tabloids also printed pictures of Paul Scholes's house, continuing their old tactics that failed to add anything useful to the tournament coverage. As with Robson and Taylor before him, the relationship between Hoddle and the press pack was still poor, though this may have been the fault of the manager himself. The media had grown tired of the fabrications Hoddle had been telling them; at one stage he untruthfully denied Gareth Southgate was fit to play, and he also kept journalists off the team plane, reducing their opportunities to mix informally with the squad.

Hoddle wrote of the tie, which England lost on penalties, 'The pain was immense. I've never been able to watch that match back. It was an emotional rollercoaster.' As in 1966 and 1970, tears flowed, although this time around his son was there to remind him it was 'only a game'. Hoddle added that he 'wasn't defined by my job. There's more to life than football.' All the same, he forced himself to get it together before talking to the BBC 'with who knows how many millions of people watching me'. He was sure people were 'mourning' the exit, if it was anything like the England dressing room, which was 'an eerie place'.

Hoddle recalled in his World Cup diary, which was serialised in *The Sun*, that Alan Shearer was sat on the dressing-room floor 'for an unbelievable length of time. It was as if he couldn't actually bring himself to stand up and get on with his life.' In extra time, he was involved in a challenge where an Argentinean defender was not penalised for a handball in the penalty area, an incident which was overshadowed by a disallowed Sol Campbell goal. Shearer then scored his penalty in the shoot-out.

When Stuart Pearce was omitted from the tournament squad, he went on holiday. 'There was an empty feeling,' he wrote in *Psycho*, but even though he was 'very detached' from the tournament, he would watch England play on TV. He caught the Argentina game in an airport lounge. After Beckham was sent off for raising his foot and catching Diego Simeone, whose tumble to the floor convinced the referee to eject the Englishman, Pearce realised he could probably have done a job in a 'back-to-the-wall situation'.

Beckham himself endured months of catcalls around England as he became the latest scapegoat, in a far worse way than Pearce and Waddle had been in 1990. He and a friend would laugh about 'getting fitted up in bulletproof vests and crash helmets before we left the house'. He remembered playing at West Ham and seeing the hatred in the faces of their fans, which went 'way past anything to do with football'. People would hurl abuse at girlfriend Victoria too. 'Envy? Contempt? Nothing better to do?' he wondered in his memoir *My Side*.

Alex Ferguson wondered whether people 'had gone totally insane. He could hardly have been more vilified if he had committed murder or high treason.' In fact, an apt comparison is when Tony Blair chose to take England to war with Iraq and Afghanistan, a decision which also impacted the country and caused people to protest, though with far greater prominence than effigies and abuse in football stadiums.

'It doesn't seem to matter that football is a team game,' Beckham wrote. 'When things go wrong, someone always has to take the blame.' Beckham 'let us down, and I still hold some resentment about it today' was how Michael Owen put it in *Reboot*, but Beckham was not a fan of such scapegoating, which he felt held back the team. It didn't help that Beckham, thanks to his relationship, was a global celebrity. Paul Gascoigne's fame had mostly been confined to England.

Jermaine Jenas remembered how the squad would be in the hotel on away trips and tournaments, listening to people chanting outside the hotel for Beckham, making it 'like travelling with The Beatles'. Looking on, former England international Rodney Marsh was disdainful of how the FA were 'almost subservient' to the man who would soon be named England captain, behaving 'like fans in his company'.

To Marsh, the ranks of the governing body were full of 'commercial people' rather than football men in the C-suite positions. He also blamed them for enforcing that England wore, horror of horrors, an away shirt when playing away. 'The FA and the supporters are so far apart,' he wrote, 'gone in a commercial whirlpool of greed and money.'

In 1997, FA chairman Keith Wiseman noted in the report into its accounts that only his organisation could 'take a balanced and constructive overview' of English football. In Italy, in the match that secured qualification for the World Cup which caused Hoddle's heart rate to jump, 'we looked a genuinely world-class side'. Henry Winter recalled how 'cynical' England were, finally taking on the Europeans at their own game. 'They stayed down and wasted a bit of time when they were tackled,' he wrote.

The means justified the end, and England had set aside 'the English way' which they had been keen to adopt against Argentina in 1986.

Accordingly, Wiseman wrote, 'Payments to players should substantially reflect performance. This is the way it is in commerce, the arts and many other branches of life. If too much is paid for too little return, then I believe that way lies the alienation of the fan and ultimately a loss of support for the game.' This is sensible advice, and prescient, too, given that wages would increase at a rate well above an ordinary fan's.

In the report, Tony Blair was pictured at the launch event for Let's Kick Racism Out of Football, while there was also a mention of how Lottery money helps to fund all-weather pitches. In 1997 the FA announced that it was bidding to host the 2006 World Cup, with helpful mentions of both upgraded club stadia and the new national stadium, as well as 'leading British companies' which could support the proposal with private finance.

'Commercialisation in football has been mentioned in pejorative terms by some commentators,' the report continued, 'but the funds made available by sponsors have been the lifeblood of many of the game's most valuable initiatives.' In any case, the FA 'does not pay dividends' and was grateful for any financial support from, among others, Walkers crisps.

Just as the Labour government looked to the future, so too did those who were custodians of English football. In 1997 the FA commissioned the Charter for Quality 'to lift standards' and develop players, with importance placed on under-tens playing on smaller pitches. 'The charter is a unified and integrated plan for action with many dimensions and objectives,' the jargon read, with emphasis placed 'on the education of the "whole" individual, socially and physically as well as technically ... Football will be viewed as a profession rather than a job.'

The England manager at the time of the charter's publication, Glenn Hoddle, would be out of work by the middle of 1999. To Gary Neville, the FA had what he called 'a rubber dinghy management system: they chuck you overboard and look after their own'. History remembers Eileen Drewery, the faith healer Hoddle employed around the England camp, whose presence he justifies by showing concern for the players rather than 'the public reaction ... football is a macho environment and some things simply aren't accepted'.

By deviating against the norm, it became an eccentricity, although doubtless Drewery would have become a far more important figure if England had progressed further in the 1998 tournament. Stuart Pearce wrote of the press reaction to the Argentina defeat, 'All those chinks in your armour are overlooked when you are successful, but once you start losing they all come to the fore.'

As with Graham Taylor, Hoddle felt he 'wasn't canny enough' with the media, mentioning how 'the game didn't start and end on the referee's whistle'. Worse, he told journalist Matt Dickinson about some general views on reincarnation and disabled people, which he maintained in his book *Playmaker* were not ones he held himself. Two dozen Labour MPs submitted an Early Day Motion in parliament calling on Hoddle to resign, and Tony Blair was moved to comment on the story in a TV appearance with Richard and Judy, which in turn made Conservative leader William Hague accuse Blair in parliament of meddling in the issue.

'There is a limit to the number of things politicians should poke their noses into,' Hague said, 'and lecturing football associations on who they should sack is beyond that limit.' Niall Edworthy thought the incident was testament to how 'at the drop of a quote, the British media has the power to whip up the country into a frenzy of moral outrage'.

Hoddle also regretted not spending enough time speaking to players individually 'to build those human connections', which would have made him a more emotionally intelligent manager. In his book *Hooked*, Paul Merson wrote that Hoddle had 'an aura about him, really soothing, an inner serenity that oozes belief'. He recalled how positive Hoddle was when Merson was about to take a penalty against Argentina; his advice of 'You. Will. Not. Miss.' helped him convert it, with Paul Ince and David Batty failing to score theirs. The latter had never taken a penalty before. This did, however, seem to be a better piece of advice than Bobby Robson reminding the taker how many people were watching back in England.

On playing for his country, Merson continued, 'All anyone expects of you is to give everything you've got – that's because the people back home, even though they can't play, would assure you ... they would give their all. They love people working hard because that's what they would do if they were in the team.' David Seaman, who played with Merson at Arsenal, got goosebumps simply by walking out of the tunnel before the game against Tunisia. 'I really felt the responsibility, the expectation back in England,' he wrote, so much so that he couldn't even sing the national anthem.

David Beckham and Gary Neville both professed to prefer having success as a Manchester United player. 'As a kid England meant very little,' wrote the latter; for him, the England team stood for Bryan Robson, the United captain. He was one of many 'fantastic professionals' at the club to whom Neville and Beckham were exposed as teenagers. 'You have no excuse as a young kid not to have that intensity,' the former wrote in his book *Red*.

The 'patriotic' Neville nonetheless considered playing for his country as 'a bonus', something which was a long way from how Ian Wright treated the opportunity, the striker always one to sing the national anthem boisterously. 'I felt like I wanted to belong, be part of it ... do something for my country. I don't know what a soldier must feel like but I feel that patriotism,' he told Henry Winter in 2016. 'It's modern-day war ... Wherever we went, England were big news.' Injured in a World Cup warm-up game, he stepped into the pundit's chair, 'literally draped in the flag' as David Goldblatt recalled. Having briefly taken on jobs as a light entertainment host, Wright has instead become an avatar for not just black footballers but black English people, even at a time when there were MPs of African and Caribbean descent.

The man who presided over the English legislature, Tony Blair, was continuing the work John Major had done to bring peace to Northern Ireland. It was in 1995 that, when England played the Republic of Ireland, neo-Nazi chants from the hooligan group Combat 18 were heard. The seats that they threw into the lower block of Lansdowne Road, where Irish fans were sitting, caused the game to be abandoned. Defender Gary Pallister, in the England team that night, recalled in 2013 ahead of the sides' first meeting since the abandonment, 'I'd felt more disappointed than frightened.'

Nationalist factions were still committing acts of terrorism on English soil. The Arndale Centre in Manchester was bombed in 1996, on the same day that England beat Scotland at Wembley, and a few months after the IRA attacked London's Docklands. The following year's Grand National was postponed after a bomb threat.

This makes it all the more incredible that, on 10 April 1998, Unionist and Republican politicians signed the Good Friday Agreement in Belfast and agreed to share power in their own devolved parliament.

One European court case concerning a football player had an impact on both the game and freedom of movement. Jean-Marc Bosman's long fight for justice went all the way to the European Court of Justice, where it was declared that it was a restraint of trade when he was unable to move clubs after the expiration of his contract. UEFA's rule which limited the number of foreign players a club could have in their matchday squad during a European competition was also rendered void, allowing clubs to fill their rosters with as much international talent as they could afford. For English teams, the trickle became a flood.

When England returned home on their Concorde flight to Heathrow, they were met by thousands of people. Hoddle looked at his diary. 'The pages were blank,' he wrote. He and his players had brought the country together, with several mums at his son's school sports day telling him that they had been enraptured by football for the first time. The treatment of David Beckham had created a 'test' in how to show players 'compassion and forgiveness'.

Alex Ferguson wrote in his autobiography *Managing My Life* that taking on the national coaching role was 'an impossible job' unless you were an experienced manager, something Hoddle lacked even though he did have plenty of ability. Ferguson was concerned when he made Beckham take part in a press conference having been left out of the Tunisia game. 'Being questioned by a roomful of reporters was not my idea of the best means of focusing his mind on battling to regain his place,' wrote the very experienced Manchester United manager, whom Hoddle had criticised for speaking out against another coach's decisions.

Ferguson was a staunch Labour supporter, and was in regular conversation with Alastair Campbell, as we learn in the latter's diaries. In February 1997, before the announcement of the general election, he told Campbell Labour were '2-0 up, and now we had to sit back'. In words that would console any England manager, good leadership was about appearing calm and 'cutting out everything that didn't matter'. One of his key rules was to 'never let outsiders sense that you're not in control'.

'If you fall out too badly with your chairman, you're finished,' Ferguson also told Campbell, words that Alf Ramsey and Don Revie would certainly concur with. In October 1996, there was a less famous episode involving football and Tony Blair than the Keegan one that began this chapter: Blair kicked some penalties alongside Ferguson on a school trip, in which Campbell noted the manager's shock at the size of player sponsorship deals. Perhaps this informed Blair's words in that *Mail on Sunday* article referred to earlier in this chapter.

Ferguson mentioned to Campbell in the autumn of 1999 that he was going to fine Beckham for 'being away ... at some fashion event'; he said the player 'was losing the plot'. The following year, he and Campbell were complaining about the press; 'All they could do with success is knock it' was Ferguson's wisdom on the subject, although it had been easy to knock the England football team in the previous 30 years.

As for Hoddle, whom Campbell met in 1997 to discuss England bidding for the 2006 World Cup, he thought he 'seemed quite a nice guy, and he was a lot more articulate in real conversation than he was on the box'. As with Graham Taylor before him, it is one's words, more than one's character, by which an England manager is judged, and it is the *World Cup Diaries*, ghostwritten by the FA's

David Davies, that are recalled as often as how its writer's team reached and performed at the finals.

'Only in England,' wrote Paul Hayward in his biography of the England team, 'would the director of communications be ghosting an intimate inside account by the manager from inside the camp, with Concorde the mode of transport home' from the 1998 tournament. Such are the highs and lows of the England football team after another glorious defeat.

2002

'JUST THINKING about the 2002 World Cup upsets me now,' admitted Michael Owen. 'That was our World Cup.'

It was hosted jointly by South Korea and Japan, and England were drawn in a group against Sweden, Nigeria and, them again, Argentina. Two draws and a famous win against the South Americans thanks to a David Beckham penalty brought a last-16 game against Denmark, whom England defeated 3-0. Then came a quarter-final against Brazil.

Kieron Dyer called the World Cup 'the last great football dream I had to fulfil', but when the midfielder came on against Brazil he was half fit. Poor Rio Ferdinand remembered needing 'vigorous treatment sessions just to get fit for a game', while Jamie Carragher missed the tournament to have knee surgery and Steven Gerrard was also ruled out with an injury in the weeks before he was due to travel. Was it bad luck or a heavy workload that had contributed to these injuries and fitness troubles?

In his memoir *Carra*, the Liverpool defender wrote that Sven-Göran Eriksson was either 'an international manager or international playboy' who became more of 'a Casanova' the longer he managed England. The Swede led the team 'to its rightful level' and did 'a good job rather than an extraordinary one'.

Kevin Keegan's disappointing spell as manager, despite his 'spirit and enthusiasm', still led to failure at Euro

2000, which Carragher felt caused the FA to 'lose faith completely' in Englishmen. To Tony Adams, 'At a time when we should have been coaching the coaches, we simply hired a foreign manager.' It would seem strange for Adams to look askance at an experienced, league-winning Swedish manager taking charge of the national team. After all, he had been captain of an Arsenal side with Dutch attackers and a French central midfielder, and which was managed by a Frenchman, but this set a new precedent in defiance of English exceptionalism.

It took until 1990 for England to adopt a sweeper system, so we ought not to be surprised that it took until 2001, after the arrival of Arsène Wenger into English football, for the FA to look beyond the English coaching system for the best in class. Gary Neville thought an English manager might be preferable 'but the best man for the job is the priority'.

Eriksson 'inherited a team with its chin on the floor' and turned it around with 'sensible decisions about team selection and simple but effective communication. He gave us a sense that everything was under control.' Like the English prime minister, who won a second term of office in 2001, the England football manager had to be a communicator and line manager who was capable of managing upwards and downwards.

'We were treated like men, given respect and, at the same time, expected to take responsibility for ourselves,' noted David Beckham, adding that Eriksson fostered a great team spirit with 'a real mutual respect' between him and the players. Ferdinand remembered a manager who was 'very unimaginative' in terms of tactics but for whom 'we always wanted to play'. Bobby Robson inspired similar feelings in his players, and nobody ever marvelled at how England played football under Eriksson, only at the results.

He also shared some of Alf Ramsey's traits, uniting the cool Swede and the Englishman who managed the national team four decades apart. According to Jermaine Jenas, 'You never got that emotion out of him, never got that anger or happiness. It was just still.' Unlike Eriksson, however, Ramsey was described as taciturn and terse.

Jenas was another player to thrive when representing England, 'I stepped on the pitch realising the whole nation is watching me. I absolutely loved it. The shirt didn't weigh me down ... I'm a fan.' To his fellow midfielder Frank Lampard, 'Being a young Englishman playing for your country is the most exciting, nervous thing you can do. I never lost that excitement at hearing the roar of the crowd, and that pride of playing for my country.' Lampard told Henry Winter for his book *Fifty Years of Hurt* that such games were 'an intense cauldron that I have to play well [in] because everyone's watching'. He added that he became more patriotic as he gained more caps for his country.

'Playing for England was something I adored doing,' wrote a third player, Emile Heskey. 'I gave my all every time.' Under Eriksson 'everything was relaxed', although Heskey couldn't recall players talking about what he euphemistically termed his 'off-field antics'. Naturally, the English press were concerned with this soap opera aspect of the manager's life, knowing that chronicles of his relationships would sell newspapers in a time when they still enjoyed a near monopoly on gossip. Men's magazines like *Zoo* and *Loaded*, as well as the female-targeted *Heat*, sold thousands of copies every month. David Beckham, meanwhile, was on the cover of *Attitude*, whose audience comprised gay men.

It was Beckham who jumped out of a tackle, which led to Brazil's first goal, something the captain rationalised in *My Side* by claiming the ball was going out of play. Brazil won 2-1 with ten men on the field, with a free kick from Ronaldinho sailing over the ponytailed head of David Seaman, who was not expecting an attempted shot from well outside the penalty area.

This time around, there was an easy excuse for England's failure to win the World Cup, as David Lacey wrote in *The Guardian*, 'Among the leading English clubs most goals are either scored or made by foreigners, the best passers are foreigners and with the exception of Rio Ferdinand the best defenders are foreigners.' Furthermore, it was argued that Englishmen played too much football with no winter break, and the games themselves were too intense, which accounted for the team dropping off in intensity in the second half of every match during the tournament.

'Most of my experiences were tinged with the feeling that we could have been doing so much better,' Ferdinand wrote, cursing a lack of 'top-level players'. This is a point Graeme Souness addressed in 2017: England only had five or six players who could get into most teams, rather than the 'seven, eight or nine top men you need to win a World Cup'. This led to 'disenchantment with international football ... because it ends in disappointment'.

Peter Shilton agreed, writing in his own autobiography that you need not just 'top-class' but also 'world-class' players; in 1990, the latter category included Paul Gascoigne and Gary Lineker, if not the goalkeeper himself. He also advocated for peaking at the right time during a tournament, like Olympic athletes, although this is harder to achieve when it is a team of 11 doing so rather than one sportsperson.

Souness argued against the grain that the reason for this apathy with the England team was not the rise of domestic or European football, or that there were too many non-English players in the Premier League – instead, he referenced the then recent success of the home nations at Euro 2016, which served to galvanise the respective fanbases. It was England's turn in the 2002 World Cup, which followed closely on from the famous 5-1 win against Germany and a nail-biter of a final qualifying game against Greece.

By the 2000s, helped by modern-day stewarding and Home Office bans for troublemakers, England supporters were surprised to see East Asian football fans take the nation and the team to heart. They formed a celebratory conga after one game with the England band providing the soundtrack; in South Africa in 2010 they would organise a trip to Robben Island. Reporting for BBC Sport in 2002, Chris Slegg noticed that 'few supporters display club colours at matches, a trend which has so often plagued international games at home. Individual loyalties have been put aside, with every venue visited so far awash with a sea of red and white.'

After hooliganism in Belgium at Euro 2000, with over 900 arrests, parliament debated whether stronger powers, including international banning orders, could be brought in to deter similar violence. Home secretary Jack Straw, in a time-honoured fashion, called the rioters 'a boorish minority' which had placed the country 'on a yellow card'. The situation at home, he continued, had improved due to 'a combination of increasingly effective police action, better design and security in the grounds, and a greater acceptance of responsibility by the clubs'.

When England fans travelled abroad, Straw said, the violence 'is not organised, and nor is much of it specifically premeditated'. The Blair government had brought in the Football (Offences and Disorder) Act in 1999, which prevented 1,000 England supporters from heading to East

Asia, but they wanted to go further to encompass people with previous convictions who travel without matchday tickets just to experience the atmosphere of an away match. It had been noted that a lot of violence happened outside the stadium, and this was a precautionary measure.

Problems off the pitch included those in several English football boardrooms. The introduction of ITV Digital had prompted clubs to play matches on Thursday and Sunday evenings in an attempt to maximise eyeballs which never arrived. The service had collapsed in 2002 after clubs had spent the money that would be promised to them, forcing 11 league clubs to go into administration in the same year. They included Leicester City, Bradford City and Ipswich Town. Burnley sold their ground Turf Moor to a bank and could not buy it back for a decade.

Elsewhere, Wimbledon FC relocated to Milton Keynes, which so distressed existing fans that they formed a phoenix club, AFC Wimbledon, as detailed by the club accountant Erik Samuelson in his book *All Together Now*. The book's first sentence describes the story's heroes as 'a group of very resilient, determined people and how they reacted to and overcame adversity'. It is as if Samuelson is describing an England football team, but here the FA were in opposition to them; their attempts to form a new club were, they said, 'not in the wider interests of football'. In 1991, Wimbledon's Plough Lane ground had been a victim of the Taylor Report, since it could not meet the new suggestions on how to make it safe in the new climate, and the Dons were forced to play at Crystal Palace's ground, Selhurst Park.

Having legally administered for stadium safety a decade previously, hunting with dogs and antisocial behaviour were in the government's vision, as per the 2002 Queen's Speech, including a tightening up of licences for shops selling alcohol. In the justice system, 'Sentencing will be reformed to ensure that the punishment is appropriate for the offender.' This suited the Labour agenda to be 'tough on crime, tough on the causes of crime'. Conversely, in 2000 they had also permitted a greater right to roam in the English countryside.

In health, NHS Direct was put in place to allow patients to phone a number for non-emergency issues. In 1999, in a bid to shift responsibility for healthcare away from government, they created the arm's-length body NICE, the National Institute for Clinical Excellence, although they still stepped in, for example, when there were limits on the prescription of Herceptin, a breast cancer drug.

The Labour government was also keen to continue the Private Finance Initiative that the Conservatives had launched, enabling private money to build hospitals and creating multi-year mortgages for the health service to repay those costs. As Isabel Hardman noted in her book *Fighting for Life*, 34 hospitals were constructed in the first six years of the Labour government; during the 18 years of Conservative rule, there had only been seven.

Gordon Brown delivered the Budget in April 2002, with much to boast about in the opening statement. 'Britain has experienced the lowest inflation and the lowest interest rates for 40 years,' he said, adding that 'unemployment in Britain is lower than in America'. The now independent Bank of England was able to cut interest rates seven times in 2001 alone, testament to the strength of the economy.

As with previous Budgets, Brown compared the UK economy to other developed nations, with net debt far lower than in the US, Japan and across Europe. 'We will never compromise our commitment to meet our fiscal rules and disciplines' was as strong a statement as Eriksson continuing to play David Beckham wherever he could fit into the team.

Brown also wanted 'a culture of entrepreneurship in every community', with helpful measures for small businesses to lure global enterprises to the country and make their VAT returns far easier to compile. Employers could access funds so their staff could gain new skills, a sort of personal development programme. 'In the mid-1980s,' Brown said, '350,000 young people aged 18 to 24 had been unemployed for more than a year. Today, the figure is just 4,700.' This shows the enormous success of the welfare to work scheme, and a judicious use of statistics.

As a useful mechanism to explain how much the government spent on its health budget, Brown offered this statistic from 2001, 'We invested £2,370 for the average household in the NHS. By 2007/08 we will be investing £4,060 per household.' It was, Brown concluded, 'the best insurance policy in the world ... a British ideal ... fairness and enterprise together'.

Building on the 1998 announcements for mothers, the 2002 Budget extended maternity pay to 28 weeks. Three decades after North Sea oil was first mentioned in a Budget, Brown still made room to mention the 'stable long-term framework' (note again the management consultancy speak) for its use. Another liquid, beer, benefitted from a halving of duty for small brewers, which Brown noted were 'often village pubs, some two centuries old'. He was delighted to announce the cut 'in time for the World Cup'.

Blair once bypassed Brown with an announcement to raise spending, because he knew the chancellor would baulk at it. Not for the first time, in either British politics or the England football team, it was a challenge to pair differing personalities. Much has been written about the Blairite and Brownite factions within the party, with reporters and pundits commentating on it much as how football reporters try to explain the goings-on of the England team.

Both men were football fans, Blair of Newcastle United and Brown of Raith Rovers, the team from Kirkcaldy in Fife. He sold programmes as a boy and owned shares in the club. When Raith beat Celtic on penalties in the Scottish League Cup Final in 1994, Brown was unable to watch and had to listen to a radio commentary over the phone. He wrote in *The Observer* in 2000, 'People sometimes ask why politicians talk about skills and training all the time. I tell them they would too if they had to go and watch Raith every week.'

Figures from outside the football world were enriching the culture of the game. Down in Brighton, Attila the Stockbroker was poet in residence, following the example of Ian McMillan at Barnsley. Attila, whose given name is John Baine, had been a punk poet in the days of Margaret Thatcher and was at the forefront of the fan protests against his club's owner, who wanted to sell the land that housed their stadium.

'One way that we got a lot of favourable publicity,' Baine told the Poetry Foundation, 'was by completely inverting the normal concept of football fans. "Football fan" to the middle-class equals hooligan, beer, violence. So what do we do? Poetry.' His poem about the Goldstone Ground, which encapsulated the importance of supporting your team even through the 'inexorable decline' of the bad times, was one that 'even the most hooliganesque Brighton lads don't slag off'.

At the cinema, Danny Boyle returned with the apocalyptic *28 Days Later*, as did Shane Meadows with *Once Upon a Time in the Midlands*. Steve Coogan played one-off Mancunian motivator Tony Wilson in *24 Hour Party People*. Films with a South Asian theme included

Anita & Me, *The Guru* and *Bend It Like Beckham*. Bond was back in *Die Another Day*, and the second Harry Potter book, *The Chamber of Secrets*, was adapted to continue the screen version of the saga. The Second World War gave us *Two Men Went to War*, based on a true story of two dental corps soldiers who went off on an unofficial adventure.

England, meanwhile, were without a home thanks to the redevelopment of Wembley Stadium, which would now, significantly, lack an athletics track. It would one day become the home of the FA, who at the time moved to Soho Square and were, belatedly, beefed up with press officers and commercial executives to bring them into a new century. Chief executive Adam Crozier had been drafted in from the world of advertising but he found himself in disagreement with the Premier League, who wanted English football to be run differently, as well as over various commercial deals the FA signed with England players.

BBC Sport reporter Phil McNulty called him 'too good at his job, a high-profile victim of his own success' who had turned the FA into 'a slick and modern organisation'. It was Crozier who appointed Eriksson. *When Saturday Comes* compared Crozier to Blair, since the pair were both seen as modernisers, and saw Crozier as a victim of 'a battle between powerful brands' where the top clubs trumped the FA. He went on to work for Royal Mail, ITV and Whitbread, but is only known outside of the business world from his time involved with English football, once again showing the sport's importance to life in the country which makes household names of CEOs.

Chris Smith, the culture, media and sport secretary, told parliament in May 2001 that the cost estimate of the Wembley Stadium project had doubled from £300m to £650m. Banks had been reluctant to fund it, and the

FA wanted the government to provide that shortfall, on top of the £120m of lottery money. Smith said this was 'simply not on', given that the stadium had to be 'affordable and sustainable'. The Conservative MP Peter Ainsworth tried to make this into a 'humiliation' for the minister and the country, 'a fiasco and a byword for government incompetence'.

'On my calculation, this is the 39th time that the honourable gentleman has called for my resignation,' Smith replied. 'I refer him to my first 38 answers.' In any case, it had been the Conservative government that had mooted the idea before Labour got into power.

The following year, as part of a report into the project, there was mention of 'self-inflicted injuries' from an 'overconfident and overambitious' company running the redevelopment plan. Smith, who remembered how it had been 'flawed, tainted and unsustainable', spoke of wanting things to be 'cleansed', after allegations of procurement and tendering, and that it was now 'the last chance for Wembley'. One member of the House of Lords compared the situation to *Groundhog Day*, while others likened the stadium to London Zoo or, in the case of Bob Russell, to 'a McDonald's arch'.

It is interesting to remember that England's second city had also put in a bid to be the site of the new stadium. The Lord Bishop of Birmingham argued that his city would complete the project on time, while another lord harked back to the Great Exhibition of 1924, which prompted the construction of what was then the Empire Stadium. 'The nation felt pride and was given a great uplift,' said Lord Anthony Clarke, who advised the interested parties to 'get on with it'.

The new secretary of sport, Tessa Jowell, was insistent that Wembley would be 'the home of English football again', which would have been in jeopardy had the rebuild been cancelled. She reminded the house that it was 'not a government project but an FA project' which nonetheless needed public financing. What Jowell did not say was that the stadium, with its dozens of annual events and busy surrounding area, would bring local revenue and international esteem, even as the Premier League surpassed international football in the eyes of many English football fans.

Here's another Conservative MP, Gregory Barker, speaking in June 2002 with the old Wembley still standing, linking the performance of the football team to that of the government, 'Sadly, on this occasion, despite the heroic efforts of our team, the World Cup will not be coming home. However, if the same level of risible skill and effort had been displayed by our England team that has been characteristic of the government's handling of the national stadium, it would not have made it even to Japan!'

The sniping continued in a select committee hearing in 2003. Labour MP Gerry Steinberg wondered why, by subsidising the project, the taxpayer should contribute to a stadium that hosted 'sportsmen who run around swearing and snarling and spitting at each other'. And why, he continued, was there a need for a national football stadium at all when the team could travel the country 'without having to be dragged down to London'?

The qualifiers for the 2002 tournament were played at Anfield, St James' Park and Old Trafford, which is why the decisive match against Greece took place in Manchester. This made the equalising goal, direct from a free kick, by David Beckham even more emphatic for the Manchester United player. The following year, after the Argentina game at the World Cup, the city's Deansgate thoroughfare was clogged with revellers stopping the traffic. There was the same party atmosphere in Trafalgar Square in London too.

'I'm patriotic,' Beckham wrote in *My Side*, but 'pressure sometimes makes players scared to try things, makes them nervous about taking risks and really expressing themselves'. Contrast this with Ronaldo having a joke with the referee in England's game against Brazil, something which Beckham felt had something to do with Brazilians playing their domestic football away from their country of birth. 'England players know what kind of stick they can get,' he added, knowingly.

At very short order, Beckham replaced Paul Gascoigne and Diana, Princess of Wales as the most regular and bankable face in tabloid newspapers and celebrity magazines. The description of his home as 'Beckingham Palace' contributed to his pseudo-regal status, and his role of England captain under Eriksson meant he engaged with the press in a way he could not do under the eye of his club manager. In 2002, Kevin Mitchell of *The Observer* called him 'a pop star in shorts' who 'emits an aura', with his colleague Richard Williams seeing him as 'an ordinary man thrust into an extraordinary situation'. Beckham was also far more photogenic than the mavericks of the 1970s who kickstarted this footballer-as-popstar trend.

Perhaps it was also a matter of social mobility, which Beckham exhibited more starkly than any other footballer before him in becoming a working-class kid made extremely wealthy. In previous generations, players either had their earnings capped at £20 a week or were less inclined for their wages to be of a distorted multiple to the man or woman on the terraces. With their names and images now scattered across newspapers and magazines, as well as the World Wide Web, they could earn salaries that made them akin to movie stars, forcing them to live in mansions within gated communities.

Other players of Beckham's celebrity had been more talented, but the lad from Leytonstone had surrounded himself with a team which included Simon Fuller, the man who had helped launch the Spice Girls. Thanks to his relationship, his haircut and his ability to bend a ball into the box or the goal, Beckham was the most visible star of the Premier League era. He became an internationally marketed brand who could be trusted to attach himself to other brands in a manner that George Best or Paul Gascoigne could not be. Brylcreem, Pepsi, H&M, Boss and Sainsbury's all drafted Beckham in to help advertise their wares, which also served to advertise Beckham himself.

Even though Michael Owen's goalscoring abilities would best assist England at the 2002 World Cup, Beckham was a far starrier presence. There was an element of drama in the build-up to the tournament after the midfielder injured a bone in his foot while playing for his club. *The Sun* tapped into the public mood by printing a photo and asking readers to think good thoughts on his behalf. As ever, Tony Blair was on hand to lead the well-wishes.

Beckham was passed fit for the World Cup, and the penalty he scored against Argentina was part of a storyline which began in France in the summer of 1998, when he was the 'callow youth' of Williams's description. In the ensuing decades, England has watched Beckham grow up and his fame expand. As the face of Hugo Boss he adorns the walls of stores across Asia, and his involvement in the Inter Miami franchise is excellent for the city and also for Major League Soccer. It is also useful for Brand Beckham, just as how other sporting stars and actors have invested in sports teams.

2002

As of 2025, he is followed by 88m people on Instagram, a social media platform that emerged in the early 2010s while he was signed to Los Angeles Galaxy. His marriage, his children and his knighthood all lead traditional news coverage, which remains in thrall to him three decades after his breakthrough. He is a figure of the celebrity age which promised to make ordinary people stars, too, thanks to TV shows like *Big Brother* and *Castaway*.

Beckham, of course, was in many ways a TV star too. The Premier League highlights programme had switched from the BBC to ITV in 2001. At the time, Deloitte reported that the league would earn the 20 clubs a total of £1bn in turnover, roughly half coming from broadcasting rights, which according to a BBC report would 'outstrip takings from ticket offices'. In spite of the TV money, higher wage bills only made seven clubs profitable in the 1999/2000 season. In November 2000, Manchester United announced a 13-year, £300m contract with Nike, testament to their commercial acumen; they were selling over £20m of merchandise a year at the time.

Professionalisation also came to refereeing in 2001, with the introduction of the Professional Game Match Officials Board, now Professional Game Match Officials Limited. Having previously fitted games in around their existing day jobs, be they schoolteachers like David Elleray or police officers like Howard Webb, full-time referees would now be part of an elite group with coaching and fitness sessions on top of their matchday duties.

This pleased David Seaman, who was a year ahead of the curve when he proposed this in his 2000 memoir. He also pointed to limited opportunities for young English players due to the surfeit of foreign talent in the top division, something the FA was keen to tackle too. Seaman was also pleased that the cash injection in the game had rejuvenated the 'tatty, rundown stadia' in which he used to play, as well as the pitches he played on and the training grounds he practised in.

Arsenal's swimming pool had a floor that could be moved to accommodate injured players, something that would have been beyond the reach of the FA. Such were the benefits of the side winning the double of Premier League and FA Cup in 1997/98. Manager Arsène Wenger, whom the FA would unsuccessfully approach in 2000 and again 2016, had brought his methods, including a focus on sports science and nutrition, to English football.

His teams synthesised an English back line, including Seaman and defender Lee Dixon, with continental imports like Marc Overmars and Patrick Vieira. Englishmen often failed to feature in the Arsenal starting XI entirely, although Wenger would give players like Theo Walcott and Jack Wilshere useful experience in European competitions which would prepare them to step up to the senior England team.

'The national team is not purely football,' Wenger said in 2006 of turning down the England job before Eriksson's appointment. 'People identify with national culture and pride.' When Thomas Tuchel, another foreign coach, was hired in 2024, Wenger reiterated his stance by saying that a manager should not be in a position where he could not sing his own national anthem in a game against his home nation.

At a time when bankers and lawyers were able to move freely to the UK from elsewhere in Europe thanks to the Bosman ruling, the opposition to a non-English manager of the England football team seemed perverse. The prime minister might have to be British, and players who wore the Three Lions might have to have a strong connection with their country, but if a marginal gain could be sought off the pitch, why not follow the modern trend?

2006

BEFORE THE 2006 World Cup, which took place in Germany, *The Telegraph* headlined a piece '14,560 days since Bobby Moore lifted the World Cup', while the *Daily Mail* superimposed a scarf around a picture of Admiral Nelson. The FA went as far as hiring actor Ray Winstone as an ambassador to mix with fans, with *The Sun* having him record messages of support.

Handily for the newspapers, their journalists were in the same hotel as the players' wives and girlfriends, which made up for the fact that the team were sequestered away in their own bubble. Referencing lifestyle magazines, Gary Neville lambasted 'the whole *OK* and *Hello* culture' which drove the coverage of the England side. This was boosted by the glamour of Ashley Cole's popstar partner Cheryl, and Victoria Beckham at whose wedding Neville was the groom's best man. Following the success of the Sky soap opera *Dream Team*, ITV screened *Footballers' Wives* from 2002 to 2006, so there was a fictional precedent for the real-life reporting.

The players themselves were nicknamed the 'Golden Generation', in the latest iteration of press-driven hype that journalists could later knock down to size once they failed to achieve the hard task of winning a World Cup. Tony Adams thought the term was 'a bit of a myth and couldn't see that the new crop were any better' than those of previous tournaments. 'You always found out who was an England international from training,' added Jermaine Jenas.

Neville suggested that he and his fellow England players never 'felt they'd made it ... That's the trick. Never believe you've done it.' As they had done at the 2002 World Cup, they also went above and beyond for the team in 2006: in the game against Ecuador, David Beckham was not fully fit but still scored a free kick. Michael Owen limped off in the opening minutes against Sweden; although he and Wayne Rooney were both unfit going into the tournament, Sven-Göran Eriksson left Jermain Defoe out of the squad, instead picking a wildcard in 17-year-old Theo Walcott, who had yet to play for Arsenal after a move from Southampton during the 2005/06 season.

Walcott was 'a kid I'd barely heard of', Gary Neville admitted in his memoir *Red*, and 'at training it was clear that he was still just a kid'. It was as if a new government had a newly elected 20-something as a minister based purely on the potential for them to master their brief and support the secretary of state. Fortunately for Walcott, the fuss made over older, starrier players kept the spotlight off him. It included the concern over Rooney's injury, which was a sequel to Beckham's of 2002.

The group games pitted England against Paraguay, Trinidad and Tobago, and Sweden. They won the first two without conceding and drew 2-2 with the Swedes, with a superb goal from Joe Cole, to set up the last-16 tie against Ecuador. Yet for Richard Williams, writing in *The Guardian*, that victory served to 'lack personality either as a team or, except insofar as some of them have achieved celebrity status, as individuals ... Sluggish in thought and movement, they appear to be making their games up as they go along.'

Bookings incurred for time-wasting were, to Williams, 'thoroughly embarrassing'. Without an injured Rooney at the start of the tournament, England were 'nothing more than football tourists, travelling first class'. By selecting the Manchester United striker, Eriksson had defied Alex Ferguson, who had bellowed at him for overruling the club doctor about the state of Rooney's foot. Every England manager, it seems, had their run-in with the United boss.

One member of the World Cup squad was a Canadian-born midfielder who was the child of British emigrants, a Welsh mum and a Bolton-supporting English dad. Owen Hargreaves played for Bayern Munich between 2000 and 2007 before joining Ferguson at Manchester United, and he chose to use his heritage to play for England's senior team. At least he had closer ties than Australia-born Tony Dorigo had when he travelled to Italy for the 1990 World Cup: neither of Dorigo's parents was English and he gained citizenship before the FA adopted new rules in 1993.

Hargreaves told *FourFourTwo* magazine in 2025 that the reaction to his decision was 'lazy ... People made a big deal over my accent.' A 2004 *Guardian* profile called him 'a perpetual outsider', especially since he first met his international team-mates at an England training camp. Tony Blair's wife Cherie asked him at a reception why he played for England if he had been born in Canada.

'Nobody ever bothered to look into my background and realise what it meant to me to pull on that shirt with the Three Lions, and the pride that my dad and my family felt in seeing me wear it,' Hargreaves said. Writing in his column for the BBC Sport website, Hargreaves remarked on how the media coverage in England was 'more intense' than it was in Germany: 'In some countries you are famous for being an athlete so they write only about that, not who you are dating or what you are wearing ... In England you are a public person and everything you do will be spoken about.'

As for the manager's role, with some hyperbole Hargreaves called it 'one of the most difficult jobs in the world'. He revealed that the players each had their own hotel room, rather than having to share as Dorigo and the rest of the squad had to do in 1990. Back then, Chris Waddle was the poor soul who looked after Paul Gascoigne, which would have made for a gripping series of social media videos should the opportunity have arisen (and had the FA's media team been brave enough to commission it).

At the 2006 tournament, in his role as a perpetual impact substitute, Hargreaves was booed by England fans when he came on against Paraguay, which appalled England captains past and present. Terry Butcher thought you were not 'a true England fan' if you jeered a player, while David Beckham praised how he was an 'honest player doing his best for his country'. It is hard to believe that, at the time, the Bundesliga was seldom screened in England, making Hargreaves an unknown quantity to most fans. Coming to his defence was Tony Woodcock, another England international who had played his domestic football in Germany.

For the quarter-final against Portugal, Gary Neville noted that Frank Lampard and Steven Gerrard were 'in poor form and not in great moods' yet big names like them 'were guaranteed to play rather than the best team … They all wanted to be match-winners.' Gerrard labelled the 2006 England side the best he had played in, but his Liverpool team-mate Jamie Carragher admitted in his 2008 book *Carra*, 'I can't recall a game where we played to our potential.'

It was Carragher who missed a decisive penalty in the quarter-final shoot-out, having been brought on at the end of extra time specifically to take one. He had scored it at the first attempt but was ordered to retake it. As in 1990 and 1998, penalties had defeated England, who had to do without Owen, Beckham and Rooney for the shoot-out, in which Hargreaves was the only successful taker; Beckham had gone off injured, while Rooney had been sent off for a stamp.

Much like Ray Wilkins in 1986, it was more in frustration with a previous refereeing decision than in malice. Writing for the *Sunday Times* in 2020, Rooney admitted he should not have gone to the tournament because of his injury and that the senior pros should have taken the lead from the England squad of 1990 and campaigned to play the 4-3-3 formation that would have suited their midfield.

Famously, manager Eriksson told the nation to go easy on the striker. 'Don't kill Rooney,' he said, 'kill me.' Rooney himself wrote of the sending-off, 'You don't want people to think you're mentally weak so you keep it inside and bottle it up and get to the point where it boils over.' Doubtless a team psychologist would have helped him there, and Eriksson later admitted that he regretted not taking one to the World Cup, in particular to cope with penalties. Rooney did add in his piece that Roy Hodgson took one to tournaments in 2014 and 2016, which were low points in the recent years of the national team.

After the Portugal game, however, Carragher lacked 'the same emptiness' as other players did, repeating his neutral reaction to watching England lose as a fan. 'At least it wasn't Liverpool' was the thought that would often underline his experiences as a pro, similar to how his future foil as a pundit, Gary Neville, viewed playing for England in comparison with Manchester United. To Carragher, who would not 'bellow out' the national anthem before a game, it was 'an extra honour ... I saw wearing a white shirt as a chance to represent my city and district as much as my country'.

Losing with England 'felt like a disappointment rather than a calamity. The Liver Bird mauled the three lions in the fight for my loyalties ... The clubs represent the lottery numbers and the country is a bonus ball.' Playing for the national team was like 'colliding with a different culture', given the quotient of Londoners in the squad; 'If you're born near Wembley,' he wrote, 'it's bred into you' to follow England, whereas it was rare to travel to the stadium, at least to follow the national team, if you were from Merseyside. Perhaps Carragher was reflecting what Francis Lee said about picking a goalkeeper who played for Chelsea in 1970 in order to satisfy newspapers in London.

To Carragher, the England side were akin to a London club; 11 of the 23 squad members played for Chelsea, Arsenal or Tottenham at the 2006 World Cup, whereas he was one of four Liverpool players. For Rio Ferdinand of Manchester United, speaking in an interview with *The Times* in 2018, club rivalries impacted the unity of the national squad. Given that he 'considered the Premier League to be my title', he was reluctant to open up to the Chelsea or Liverpool players in the squad, 'because of the fear that they would then take something back to their club and use it against us'. This shows how far we had come from the team spirit which Don Revie and Graham Taylor tried to conjure, as well as the individualism common to the era in which Ferdinand played.

The period which encompassed the 2002 and 2006 World Cups, wrote Paul Wilson in *The Observer*, 'will go down as a decadent period of wild over-optimism and blatant self-delusion'. It cannot be coincidence that, away from football, these were the years before the credit crisis revealed itself, as England burdened itself with future promises to pay for things they wanted but could not afford.

David Goldblatt later wrote that England under Eriksson looked 'bereft of an alternative plan, unable to react to adversity; skilled and committed but without any innovatory capacity'. This is slightly unfair, given that the tall striker Peter Crouch complained of being a 'last resort' when England were chasing a game under Eriksson and his successor Fabio Capello.

In an encomium of Eriksson for *The Times*, James Gheerbrant called him 'a luckless general and a perfect gentleman' who 'failed in a way that was endearing'. Prior to travelling to Germany, it had already been agreed that his contract would be terminated after the 2006 tournament, following a *News of the World* sting where a reporter, in the guise of a sheikh, led the manager to ponder aloud about future job opportunities. This sort of stunt, where an England boss was recorded and caught off-guard, was repeated a decade later with Sam Allardyce. It would have been the sort which would have caused the defenestration of honest men like Bobby Robson and Graham Taylor.

Writing in his memoir *Sven*, Eriksson spoke of wanting to sit down with England fans in a pub and talk football with them, in an acknowledgement of how hungry for the game they were. Sharing Owen Hargreaves's hyperbole, he said, 'It was the biggest job in the world. Everyone in England was a fan of the team that I managed. It was an amazing feeling. The passion for the game in England was unrivalled.' Bear in mind that he had managed in Italy, which is also known for its enthusiasm for football.

Passion of another sort was something David Dein, Arsenal chairman and FA International Committee member who helped to appoint Eriksson, recalled in his own book *Calling the Shots*: he remembered being told that Eriksson's only weakness was women. He added that the 'serene and calm' Swede often looked 'like a man heading off on holiday', which was especially helpful before England's famous victory over Germany in 2001. To Dein, Eriksson 'put oxygen into a body that was comatose'.

Eriksson himself recounted similar tales to his predecessors. As with Bobby Robson, he had taken a pay cut in spite of being paid far more than Glenn Hoddle had been. As with Graham Taylor, he had to wait months between competitive fixtures, filling time with watching matches to scout for players. As with Hoddle, negotiations were done in secret, in his case in Rome while he was manager of Lazio. In common with other tournaments, the squad 'lived in total seclusion' in 2006, with only an activity room with video games and table tennis to keep them busy.

As soon as Eriksson was announced as Kevin Keegan's replacement, the English press flew over to Italy to spy on his training sessions, and at his first press conference one journalist asked him who played left-back for Sunderland, to try to expose his lack of knowledge of the English game. They then, of course, published photos of his London apartment. Unlike the direct line they had to Graham Taylor, the only way the media could get in touch with Eriksson was to arrange an interview with the FA and its by now populous team who handled press enquiries.

The Swede exchanged pleasantries with Tony Blair, who won a third term as prime minister in 2005 and who wondered which of them would be in their job longer. After one of many front-page stories about his private life, the press bombarded Eriksson with questions; as had happened with Robson, these were news journalists who were far less interested in the game he was notionally talking about. 'It was embarrassing for the real sports journalists,' he wrote.

'I was almost treated like a criminal.' He apologised to the players, who merely laughed and welcomed him to the gauntlet of the English press.

Eriksson preferred not to shout and swear, because 'you could not let emotions govern you'. His main goal, similar to the one Gareth Southgate would later adopt, was to inculcate a 'good atmosphere in the team', and he treated players with respect and trusted them as 'grown men'. He was nonetheless perturbed when some of the squad overstepped the mark and partied too hard during the World Cup qualification matches in March 2005.

Eriksson was impressed with how they switched on for instructions at half-time, in contrast to his teams in Italy who would need to 'calm down' before a team talk. His guiding hand helped England qualify for three tournaments, with his first loss in a competitive match coming against Northern Ireland in 2005. This was viewed by the media as a disaster, even though England were still in a good position to qualify for the finals, but it meant the manager could not go and watch the England cricket team take part in an Ashes test. Fifty reporters were stationed outside his house, in a measure of how much scrutiny his job was placed under and how newspaper editors believed the England manager would, all these victims on, still help sell copies to the public.

Similar attention greeted a photograph of him discussing a possible appointment at Chelsea. 'As the England manager, you were expected to sit politely and wait for the day you got fired,' he wrote. His planned replacement, Luiz Felipe Scolari, was scared off by the extreme tabloid interest in his life. Eriksson himself told of his sadness that he could not attend his daughter's graduation at the University of East Anglia, three years after the 2006 World Cup, because she remembered the paparazzi who had attended her high school graduation.

Managing England, as was well known by 2006, affected every facet of your life. This also applied to being the prime minister, as Tony Blair found out when various stories involving his family became public knowledge. Eriksson, like Paul Gascoigne and David Beckham, was public property, and even his girlfriends became tabloid characters and punchlines on TV chat shows. The England football team were part of a shared, common culture, something that millions of people knew about; like the Premier League in which the players regularly appeared, playing for England made you a member of a soap opera cast in a white or red shirt.

In his job, Eriksson also learned of the hierarchy of English football, with the Premier League now above the FA in importance. He had no luck arguing for a winter break because, he noted sombrely, 'The English had their traditions,' and he was blindsided by the FA when he wanted longer to prepare for the World Cup after the end of the season. He had initially asked FIFA to force the Premier League to fall into line, but the FA sought an exemption on the league's behalf. 'The whole mess exposed the weakness of the leadership at the FA,' Eriksson wrote, adding that he had a very poor relationship with FA chairman Geoff Thompson.

Like Alf Ramsey and Don Revie with Sir Harold Thompson all those years ago, Eriksson was no fan of the man in the FA blazer. In 2005, Lord Burns conducted a report on those suits at the FA in which he prompted them to become 'the parliament of football'. He wanted them to open up the organisation to diverse voices, with fewer committees and more non-executive directors. Times were, very slowly, changing, as was evident in 2004 when another former manager lost a high-profile job.

2006

Ron Atkinson was sacked as a TV pundit for using racial language that showed both his insensitivity to the current moment and how much language had moved on. By referring in a derogatory manner to Marcel Desailly, he provided English football with another chance to show it had, unlike Atkinson, modernised in an acceptable manner. 'I can't believe I did it,' Atkinson said, especially because he had been unafraid to play black players in his West Bromwich Albion team.

Also in the 2000s, Liverpool hired top European talent and very good managers from France and Spain; Gérard Houllier and Rafael Benítez respectively spearheaded their victories in European competitions, with teams full of English talent like Danny Murphy, Michael Owen and Emile Heskey, as well as future England captain Steven Gerrard. After decades of promoting from within their celebrated Boot Room, they were looking further afield at the right time, just like Chelsea had with Ruud Gullit and the England team had with Eriksson. Manchester United had been all set to appoint the Swedish coach had Alex Ferguson not reneged on his retirement in 2002.

Meanwhile, American owners also took over the two domestic club rivals, Malcolm Glazer at Manchester United and Tom Hicks and George Gillett at Liverpool. Both parties had taken huge loans to buy the clubs, but when the latter pair failed to make good their promise to build a new stadium, they sold it on to other Americans in 2010.

The Spirit of Shankly protest group followed a decade after the Independent Manchester United Supporters' Association, who were keen to press upon fans the importance of buying shares in the club and keeping up a dialogue with the directors to prevent ticket prices becoming unaffordable. David Beckham was pictured with a green and gold scarf around his neck, exhibiting the colours of protest club FC United of Manchester and once again consolidating his own brand. The England Supporters' Club had no such vetoing power, although they could always vote with their feet and stop attending matches, which was difficult when the chance to see multiple top players in action was such a strong draw.

Roman Abramovich, meanwhile, had alighted upon Chelsea as a place to park the money he had been given as part of the post-Soviet state asset sell-off. While Arsenal were patiently constructing a new stadium, Chelsea bought an entire team, hired José Mourinho as manager and ran away with several Premier League titles. To David Goldblatt, their success proved that 'rational business practices, even when conducted with care and caution', simply did not work in English football; and this was before Manchester City were bought by the ruling family of Abu Dhabi. As Abramovich's millions were helping Chelsea to multiple trophies, workers in the financial sector were gambling with irrational and opaque products, a state of affairs which would not reveal itself until 2008.

The Chelsea captain was John Terry, who stayed with the club for almost his entire career. Born in Barking, Essex, he was the sort of defender whom Daniel Storey may have had in mind when he contrasted him with Paul Gascoigne, subject of his book *Gazza in Italy*: 'The British footballing stereotype is that only the hardest will survive, and strength can only be displayed through passionate commitment rather than through skill,' he wrote, with fans preferring 'perspiration over inspiration'.

Terry was another centre-back in the tradition of Terry Butcher, a vocal and committed defender. As if to prove the point, his biography on the official Chelsea website has a picture of Terry taking a boot in the face from an

Arsenal defender. To his left, for country as with club, is Ashley Cole, who despite his off-field scrapes and tabloid infamy was one of the world-class members of England's national side.

Writing in his 2004 memoir, Peter Shilton was sad that football had become 'more intense' in the modern era of Cole and Terry, and how it was less about fans being entertained than allowing them to exhibit 'anxiety and angst'. On top of this, players were less funny than they used to be, although Cole was unconsciously funny when he wrote of nearly swerving off the road when Arsenal offered him too little money for a new contract. Peter Crouch celebrated goals with a robot dance and infamously said he would have been 'a virgin' had he not been a footballer, while Jamie Vardy was always ready with a quip or a catchphrase.

Among entertainment products on the movie screen, Daniel Craig was introduced in 2006 as the latest James Bond, in *Casino Royale*. The Victorian tale of Tristram Shandy inspired *A Cock and Bull Story*, while the David Nicholls novel *Starter for Ten* and Alan Bennett's play *The History Boys* also enjoyed movie adaptations that were particularly English; the former was centred around *University Challenge* contestants, the latter on sixth-formers in their seventh term as they tried to pass the Oxford and Cambridge entrance exams. More recent history was documented in *The Queen*, which saw Helen Mirren play Queen Elizabeth II in the days following the death of the Princess of Wales.

The same monarch announced the Labour Party agenda in the 2006 Queen's Speech. It included the development of ID cards and an increased border patrol, as well as mechanisms 'to make it easier to deport those who break the law'. There was a bill on climate change as part of the government's policy to protect the environment, which was consistent with the need to secure long-term energy supplies. There were also measures to regulate both human embryology and estate agents, as well as an announcement of free off-peak local bus travel for pensioners and disabled people.

The 2006 Budget was once again delivered by Gordon Brown, who was delighted to report the tenth year of economic growth in a row as part of 'a culture of stability ... We lead in opportunity and fairness.' In Labour's decade in power, investment in schools had gone up tenfold to £6bn; this time around, they wanted to recruit 3,000 science teachers and to fund after-school science clubs. Mothers could shortly enjoy nine months of paid maternity leave, while whiskey drinkers would not pay any more duty on a bottle than they did in 1996.

Amid announcements about the 2012 Olympics, Brown found room to mention an English bid for the 2018 World Cup in the context of improving sporting facilities across the country. He would also fund an initiative, at the cost of £2m, to offer sporting opportunities to young people in a collaboration between community groups, the police and Premier League clubs.

It seemed the FA was confident that it would have a better shot at hosting that World Cup in 2018 than when it launched one for the 2006 tournament. A select committee report of April 2001 concluded that 'the politics of international sport' had put the kibosh on things. 'The Football Association was also required to take sides in the contest for the FIFA presidency and made enemies as well as friends in the process,' read the report. Nor was it a good look for the men's coach, the chairman and the chief executive to all leave their posts in rapid succession. Keith Wiseman, the FA chairman, resigned after a £3m loan to the Welsh FA was revealed to be in exchange for a vote for an English candidate for the FIFA executive committee.

The FA also pointed to the 'relative lack of influence' that it possessed as it sought to champion the English cause around the globe. This was in spite of Bobby Charlton's presence as part of the bidding team 'personifying English football', and his cameo coaching youth sides at each place the team visited during their tour of countries who had a vote on the tournament's host.

The FA submitted a memorandum to the select committee in the form of a diary of the bid. The amount of diplomacy and glad-handing over the three-year period is mind-boggling. When FIFA inspectors visited England in October 1999, the team were given motorcycle police escorts around London and were set down on the Wembley pitch by helicopter, where 'the Wembley roar greeted them over the tannoy'. For an extra sprinkling of stardust, Hugh Grant made a cameo appearance at a banquet at Hampton Court Palace.

There is also mention of 'the gentlemen's agreement' between England and Germany, after the latter promised to support England's wish to host Euro 96 with the quid pro quo that England would do the same come the 2006 World Cup. UEFA favoured Germany's bid even as England still pushed ahead with its own, denying any written confirmation of their word. Infamously, to help curry FIFA's favour, Manchester United were told to play in the 2000 Club World Cup, which meant they had to withdraw from the FA Cup, and there was also violence in Copenhagen before the UEFA Cup Final between Galatasaray and Arsenal.

Then came the hooliganism at Euro 2000, the month before FIFA voted; 'it was the England bid's worst nightmare come true' and it was, accordingly, 'in tatters'. One BBC report in 2000 summarised one of England's arguments as 'in effect "Give us the bid, because otherwise our hooligans might come and destroy your cities"'.

Outlining the final weeks of the bidding process, the document makes them resemble the end of a war. 'Emotionally, we wanted to fight on, but cold thinking suggested that dignified withdrawal was preferable,' the submission read, 'and to put a brave face on defeat.' The FA would learn the lessons of the 2006 bid when it sought to host the 2018 World Cup, so long as England could 'overcome its hooligan problems and improve its standing in European football'.

One of 12 suggestions for such a future attempt to host the finals looked towards 'the active commitment to the bid of the sport's national authority, recognising that it may have to make considerable sacrifices, at the expense of the domestic game, to satisfy international expectations and win support'. This comes across as wishful thinking, given the dominance of the internationally marketed Premier League and the sums involved in club football. The FA could never regain its former importance when it was up against such a juggernaut.

In 2004, tuition fees were introduced for university students at a maximum of £3,000 per year, and civil partnerships were permitted for gay couples, though they were not yet termed 'marriage'. Tony Blair's second term as prime minister was dominated by Britain's response to the 11 September 2001 attacks on American soil, where he pledged that his country would stand alongside US president George W. Bush in the wars in Iraq and Afghanistan.

Steve Richards, in his book *Turning Points*, referred to Saddam Hussein's weapons of mass destruction, which were allegedly able to be deployed within 45 minutes, writing that Blair 'placed a preposterously excessive weight on intelligence that was obviously unreliable' where he was 'guided by evangelical belief irrespective of popularity'. This prompted a million people to march against the invasion of Iraq in 2003, and to this day Blair is still forced to defend going to war as the right thing to do. In 2016, he apologised again. 'We underestimated profoundly the forces that were at work in the region and would take advantage of change once you topple the regime,' he said.

In 2005, after the England squad had visited the Auschwitz concentration camp, Sven-Göran Eriksson helped mark the memory of another war, with Blair and the Queen in attendance. Some things are far more important to remember than how to qualify for an international tournament.

2010

'BOY, COULD he shout, sometimes just for the sake of it,' wrote Emile Heskey of Fabio Capello, the Italian who managed England at the 2010 World Cup in South Africa. Rio Ferdinand put forward similar thoughts about a man who ordered players to 'do what you're told or you're out', which is more or less what Alan Mullery said of Alf Ramsey. Ferdinand added that there was 'never much warmth' with Capello, who was 'so aggressive sometimes it was just ridiculous'.

This was the inverse of Sven-Göran Eriksson, who found it pointless to shout. Capello had a sartorial focus too: Jermaine Jenas recalled how every player had to wear the same clothes, even down to the collar on the shirt. Interestingly, this difference in dynamic extended to Tony Blair and his successor Gordon Brown. Whereas the laid-back style of Blair was described as 'government by sofa', Brown was infamous for his volatile temper, which included raised voices and items being thrown across his office.

Capello set out his England side in the kind of 4-4-2 formation that Glenn Hoddle had thought was outdated a decade before. This made the team look 'predictable and out of date' to Gary Neville, and weak in midfield to Ferdinand. 'Rubbish teams were passing the ball around us,' the latter complained, but fortunately for the defender, he was not a participant but a spectator for the tournament. He engaged with fans on social media as a very early adopter of Twitter, which explains the hashtag in the title of his book: *#2Sides*.

Sometimes, players realise that their jobs are not as important as the sports journalists would make it appear. Ferdinand wrote that no sooner had he found out that an injury would probably make him miss out, he watched a man who had been involved in a car accident come into the hospital he was being assessed at, which offered him enormous perspective on his inability to play for England that summer.

Writing in his own book *I Was Born a Loose Cannon*, Rodney Marsh boasted, 'There is no one more passionate and patriotic towards England than me.' He thus felt 'betrayed' when the Italian, Capello, was appointed. 'What next, a manager from Germany?' he wondered, admitting that he sounds like 'an old dinosaur'. Marsh played nine times for England and 'was ready to hand back all my England caps' because the manager had not been English. He then rather undercut himself by saying he accepted Eriksson, although this may have been because Capello needed a translator when he took the job. He reserved his judgement on Thomas Tuchel, who took over in 2024, 'until England play a quality football country'.

'I believe that wearing the England shirt should be a matter of pride,' Capello said in his first press conference, to mark his unveiling. 'I want to see all players playing for England like they do for their clubs,' he continued, which seemed a sombre thing to remind them of but was necessary at a time of regular matches in European competitions like the Champions League with the attendant, attractive win bonuses. In his 2010 World Cup squad, Capello picked four Chelsea players and five from Tottenham, with only two from Manchester United in Wayne Rooney and Michael Carrick.

Marsh made a much less contentious point about how often the Wembley pitch was relaid, 'ten times in four years' since the stadium opened in 2007; it should be 'the best surface in the world', he complained with more English exceptionalism. In common with the old stadium, the new one would host music gigs and rugby league finals, but it also welcomed American football sides.

This was not the first time it had done so: in the 1980s it had hosted non-competitive matches, and the London Monarchs franchise played there in the early 1990s. Starting in 2007, the NFL brought over competitive fixtures, with teams like San Francisco 49ers, New York Giants and New England Patriots among those who won games away from their home continent. Just as the Premier League sought to be an internationally targeted competition, so the NFL wanted to expand its brand, with Wembley a willing host and the FA attracted by their share of the revenues.

Brian Glanville, whose book *England Managers* ends with the appointment of Capello, asked 'which Englishman' should get the job, if not a foreigner. Glenn Hoddle, who played under Arsène Wenger at Monaco before the Frenchman moved to Arsenal, thought foreign coaches 'brought a completely different technical side to the game and outlook. Back then, everyone was a British manager and everyone was thinking too much the same way. It got staid, bogged down, played in a 40-by-60 box.'

'If our best isn't good enough, tough,' wrote Jamie Carragher in 2008, although he saw it as 'practical' to choose an English coach rather than 'stealing the expertise' of another country. Partly because he had been played out of position by Steve McClaren, Carragher had retired from international duty, 'a huge weight lifting' from him when he did so, but he soon reversed his decision and travelled to South Africa for the 2010 tournament. To him, Capello was 'my idea of a proper football manager'.

Given that he was so far down the list of centre-backs, Carragher recalled 'those long dreary afternoons in hotels' which were 'purgatory for me'. Happily, he started against Algeria and came on against the USA; less happily for the team, both ended in a draw. After the first of those games, Wayne Rooney looked down the lens of the TV camera and commented on how nice it was 'to hear your own fans booing you'.

'The fans were entitled to let us know that it wasn't good enough,' wrote Emile Heskey, who was 'ridiculed, almost to the point of being bullied' by the media when he was recalled in 2007 by Capello's predecessor McClaren. Similar teasing was given out to lanky striker Peter Crouch, who wore the number nine shirt at the 2010 tournament. He was winningly self-effacing enough to enjoy a post-playing career as a pundit and podcaster; like Owen Hargreaves before him, he was barracked by England fans. 'I'm an easy target,' he told the *Sunday Times* in 2006, admitting to ignoring media coverage when on a goal drought.

As part of the press pack who reported on the 2010 World Cup, Paul Hayward sensed 'rigidity, fear, inhibition' in the England camp, where the manager adopted 'pre-emptive control' of any given situation, with limited opportunities for the players to enjoy themselves. Eventually, the players protested and Capello allowed them to have a night with plenty of beer to drink. To Hayward, there was 'always a fine line between remoteness and disdain' when it came to how the Italian viewed English culture and team building. He never had the sort of run-ins with the media that Eriksson had about his personal life, although the biggest mistake he made was to put his name to an index of player ratings.

In the lead-up to the tournament, two England players' private lives became a matter of public interest. The court overturned a super-injunction which had previously forbidden any mention of an affair John Terry had had with the former girlfriend of Wayne Bridge, or even the knowledge of that super-injunction. The judge who lifted it referred to the sponsors who associated themselves with the pair, a reminder that they were commercial as well as sporting figures. In the end, Capello selected Terry but not Bridge for the World Cup squad.

Back on the pitch, in common with how Graham Taylor's wife was besieged by members of the press, the sister of goalkeeper Rob Green, who let the ball slip through his hands for the USA goal in the 1-1 draw, was the target of tabloid attention. 'I'm sure there's 50-odd million people disappointed with me this evening,' Green said after the game, though he had no wish to blame the aerodynamic ball that was being used during the tournament. When Green and Carragher were in conversation on Sky Sports in 2021, the defender remembered how his goalkeeper 'saved my bacon' after he made an error himself. Despite the propensity to find individual heroes, football remains a team game.

'My parents would go out for a walk, and then you get back to your house and there's 20, 30 people from the press there waiting for you,' Green recalled. Perversely, they were also camped outside his own, empty flat. David Beckham, who travelled to South Africa as part of the England coaching staff, was a confidant for Green, although the mistake meant he was dropped for the game against Slovenia, where Jermain Defoe scored the only goal.

The last-16 match against Germany ended in a 4-1 defeat, with Frank Lampard's shot that went over the line not given as a goal. The 5-1 victory of 2001 was painfully reversed, even if the absence of goal-line technology gave England an easy excuse for their loss, sparing the search for a scapegoat. Nor were there any headlines akin to the one that, back in 1996, screamed at the Germans 'Achtung! Surrender.'

Coincidentally, new prime minister David Cameron watched the game in Toronto with his German counterpart, chancellor Angela Merkel. 'At least with a scoreline like that we can't say we were robbed,' he said. 'We weren't. We were beaten.' He did, however, compare football's lack of technology with the Hawk-Eye system that was used in tennis and cricket.

Reporting for *The Guardian*, Kevin McCarra pointed England towards 'a museum of football history'. Just as in 1953 and 1973, they looked like a team who needed to catch up with modern tactics. After the USA game, Franz Beckenbauer thought England had 'gone backwards into the bad old days of kick and rush', adding that the Premier League's many foreign players were at fault for blocking the emergence of English talent. They also needed an injection of youth, as the experience of the squad melted away in the face of a youthful German XI. Goalkeeper David James was soon to turn 40, with Terry and Gareth Barry (both 29), Steven Gerrard (30) and Matthew Upson (31) all in the side.

In the stands, the St George's Cross was once again the flag of choice for England fans. When they had played Beckenbauer's West Germany in 1966, the mascot World Cup Willie was adorned in a Union Jack waistcoat, while fans flew that flag too. Ditto at the 1990 World Cup, but by 1998, helped by shops selling the cross rather than the Union Flag after its visibility at the home European Championship, the red and white one became a fixture on car aerials.

The 2000s had also seen the rise of data in football, with Opta providing possession statistics that were used during Premier League coverage and Arsenal buying StatDNA in 2012. Coupled with the popularity of the *Football Manager* simulation game, supporters were more aware of the numbers behind football. Soon the expected goals metric, which gave Rory Smith the title of his 2022 book, had made its way into the conversational lexicon. Anything that provided marginal gains for a football team, be it in statistics or sports science, was approved of.

David Goldblatt called football 'a highly reflexive game, in which participants are analysing their own and their opponent's actions with greater detail and intensity' in the 2010s than they previously did, at least outside of Don Revie and his dossiers. The ball would stay in the middle of the pitch a lot more than it used to and, with more attention paid to strength and conditioning, players were given warnings when they were in the so-called red zone from covering far more ground in lighter footwear. Ian Graham's book *How to Win the Premier League*, based on his work with Tottenham and Liverpool, is an essential primer about the modern data-led tactical approach to the game.

By 2019, England were using data to prepare for matches, although manager Gareth Southgate sought 'the bit that makes a difference'. It was particularly crucial when preparing the players to be fit enough for a match and when analysing penalties during shoot-outs, as well as monitoring their club performances.

While data has improved the game, so has the international composition of what Brian Glanville called the 'Greed is Good League'. Son Heung-min became Korea's most famous footballer in his role captaining Tottenham. Manchester City had been owned by Thaksin

Shinawatra, the Thai PM whose face was beamed back home, before Abu Dhabi's ruling family decided to buy the club. Leicester City won the title under Thai ownership in 2016. All three helped develop the talents of players who travelled to World Cups with England and grew familiar with international footballers whom they might encounter at a tournament.

'The labour market in football is full of hyper-competitive, over-optimistic buyers motivated by winning rather than profit, a guarantee of massive wage inflation,' noted Goldblatt of something that had become eradicated in the international game, where it was the might of the football association and the investment it was able to plough into the game that helped a national team do well. Such success, however, was also dependent on the fitness of a group of players, or the presence of a superlative talent who galvanised the team.

There was also a sort of homegrown premium that club owners had to pay to sign English players, since they contributed towards a quota in the squad they had to register every season. Andy Carroll, who wore the number nine shirt at Euro 2012, was signed by Liverpool in 2011 as a 22-year-old for £35m in a transfer which worked out far less well than that of Luis Suárez, who joined the club on the same day. Later on, Jadon Sancho would move to Manchester United for £73m, and Ben White to Arsenal for £50m.

Alex Ferguson baulked at the sum he would have had to pay to sign Lucas Moura, a promising Brazilian midfielder, in 2012; that same year, he convinced Robin van Persie to move from Arsenal to deliver him one more league title before retirement, which at least distracted Manchester United supporters from overly complaining about their American owners.

Three years before the emergency rescue of the English financial system, Malcolm Glazer and his family had purchased United by means of a leveraged buyout, borrowing money to load the club with half a billion pounds of debt, with the assets as collateral for the loans. United had risen in value because of their success in the Premier League, which had become an international product. In 2008 the league proposed a 39th game of the season to be held at five venues around the world, replicating the introduction of international fixtures in the NFL.

Premier League chief executive Richard Scudamore referred in his proposal to 'globalisation', but the FA was concerned about fixture congestion and the plan was knocked back. Post- and pre-season tours are a non-competitive replacement for the extra game, while it can be argued that the Club World Cup is FIFA's attempt to capture the market by including clubs from each continent. When it threatened to arrive back on the agenda in 2014, *Times* journalist Oliver Kay recalled how the 39th game was not about connecting with overseas fans but a matter of 'pure greed' and a threat to 'sell the English game's soul'. No wonder the FA was so concerned by its introduction.

Kay's colleague Henry Winter wrote about the proposal in 2019, which broadened the Premier League's ambitions by recognising that it was competing with other sporting leagues like the NBA or NFL. 'It would be two fingers to the real supporters,' Winter said, aware of the friction between acknowledging these long-term fans and attracting the new breed raised on TV coverage. The special atmosphere of the domestic game, which was by now far removed from the hooliganism of the pre-Premier League era, was attractive to tourists who would serve to dilute that atmosphere when they attended those matches, which was more prevalent in the 2010s and beyond. Nick

Hornby's warnings back in 1992 about the new kind of Arsenal fans had been prescient.

To match the 24/7 globalised world and to accommodate European games staged across three midweek evenings, Premier League kick-off times and dates vary enormously, so that a domestic match round is often spread across three or four days. Football therefore falls into line with other entertainment products, be it the BBC iPlayer or Netflix, giving viewers the option to watch live and follow the drama as it happens, or to catch the highlights afterwards.

Alongside the popularity of the domestic league, the national team, who play friendlies that enable Premier League players to be watched in the stadia of different countries without the need for a 39th game of the season, must compete for attention and esteem. In 2008, Jamie Carragher wrote that the England team mattered more for supporters of teams in lower leagues. 'It's their only chance to travel to Europe,' he suggested, something that helped people feel 'empowered by their opportunity to tell the stars what they really think of them'.

As Bryan Robson had said a generation previously, Carragher felt that with England, 'There's a demand to play in one robust 100mph style. We're always looking for the killer pass. The supporters demand it goes forward as quickly as possible.' Instead, he argued that they should 'bestir a flawed team' with their cheers, aware that coming up against Brazil or Portugal is far different from a qualifying game against a lesser nation. Two years later, with Carragher in the team and with some (mutually exclusive) justification, those same England fans were booing the side.

Speaking to *The Guardian* in 2020, Fabio Capello said that England came to tournaments 'tired'. During the early part of the season they would be a match for the best teams, but they would struggle in the summer. 'Your culture is fight, fight, fight, never stop,' he said, 'even if you're four down. I liked that.' Another continental onlooker, Michel Platini, reckoned the English to be 'lions in the winter and lambs in the summer'. Although many England players have diagnosed the problem with the international side, these two outsiders also got to the nub of things.

Football was by now a marketplace where the customer demanded success, both at international and domestic level. Thanks to the work they had done to win trophies and exploit their commercial potential, by the early 2010s Manchester United and Arsenal were bringing in total matchday incomes of around £100m, 20 times more than, for instance, Blackburn Rovers. Had prices risen with inflation, David Goldblatt explained, a United season ticket that cost £96 in 1989 would only cost £170; instead, it set fans back over £500. Fans who chose to form FC United of Manchester were merely replaced by far-flung visitors who would spend more at the megastore.

The Premier League was, to Goldblatt, 'essentially a branding machine and TV rights-selling business', one that had to open itself up to more channels after it was ruled unlawful that only the BBC and Sky could have those rights. This precipitated the variety that followed: ITV Digital, Setanta, BT Sport and now TNT and DAZN. The sums of those TV deals increased with every new agreement, and the numbers showed no signs of peaking or decreasing, moving the game further away from the one enjoyed by Alf Ramsey and Don Revie.

Outside of the big clubs, some of them were unluckier in their ownership. In 2007, Mike Ashley bought Newcastle United and plastered their stadium with branding of his own business, Sports Direct. He took on £100m of debt and endeared himself to supporters by standing among the crowd in a game against Sunderland, but the club were relegated twice during a decade where Ashley was accused of heading up a 'Cockney Mafia' alongside the director of football, former England international Dennis Wise.

Portsmouth went through several pairs of hands in the seasons after winning the FA Cup in 2008, eventually being owned by their fans who sold it on to Michael Eisner and Disney. This showed the attractiveness of the English game to American investors, much as how Silicon Valley start-ups and New York banks would also have bases across the Atlantic. England's 2010 World Cup squad included Portsmouth goalkeeper David James, as well as former players Peter Crouch, Jermain Defoe and Glen Johnson.

The FA, meanwhile, continued to protect the grassroots of the game. It had launched two schools programmes after the 2006 World Cup: FA Skills, which went into primary schools between 2007 and 2018; and Respect, which sought to foster a good environment in which to play football via the We Only Do Positive campaign. Parents were threatened with education courses or suspensions, and they were encouraged to 'celebrate effort and good play from both sides'.

Despite its best efforts, some politicians were keen to highlight the FA's shortcomings. In a Westminster Hall debate on football governance in September 2010, Conservative MP Robert Halfon suggested 'a democratic revolution, led by the fans' which would stop the FA board being 'a Byzantine court, with decisions being made like puffs of white smoke appearing from the Vatican rooftops'. His solution was to enable supporters of the England team to decide who was on the board, the rights for which would be given by an annual subscription. 'If England are to win a major tournament, we cannot go on as we are,' Halfon said.

Some England fans took the initiative themselves. A few weeks before the start of the 2010 World Cup, Kick It Out helped launch the I Am England campaign. Writing for *The Guardian* website, Mark Perryman contrasted the 'alternative English citizenship' of football with the worries about globalisation and immigration that would dominate conversation during the upcoming general election. Just as all one needed was a voting slip to feel part of the democratic process, an England football fan only required 'the shirt and the will to believe'.

Perryman wanted to work towards an idealised 'rainbow nation' in the form of 'jerk chicken and pork pies on the half-time menu', with none of the prejudices from politically charged fans getting in the way of supporting the team. The presence of more black players in the England teams of recent years, including goalkeeper James, defender Ferdinand and striker Defoe, was coupled with a more diverse fanbase which followed England to biennial tournaments.

At the time, Perryman followed England home and away, writing the book *Ingerland* about his experiences; its eye-catching cover was of a man with a red St George's Cross shaved into his head. Before the Euro 2020 tournament, again for *The Guardian* website, he remembered launching the Raise the Flag movement, with the FA's support: fans held up cards that formed the cross while they sang the national anthem. The ultimate goal was for fans to be treated as 'equal partners in creating this backdrop of Englishness' during World Cup finals, and key to this was a better relationship between the England fans and the FA.

In advance of the 2002 World Cup, Perryman had organised a series of forums held in London pubs, which the media also reported on. He held the view that dialogue, and 'the act of simply listening to one another', could break down barriers. Next came matches involving fans and school visits, as well as wreath-laying ceremonies at Holocaust memorials in Poland. This all contributed to giving fans agency in 'reinventing what England away might mean ... open, welcoming, friendly Englishness'. The challenge is still acute in 2026, especially with populism and rancour lined up against inclusivity and tolerance.

Knocking aside worries about immigration, which have never gone away entirely, was the global financial crash of 2008, which spread from the US markets around the world. It was Gordon Brown, Tony Blair's successor as prime minister, who ordered public stakes in three British banks in return for £37bn, with HBOS and Lloyds to be merged.

Brown had set up the Financial Services Authority to regulate the banking sector in 1997 and deal with individual banks. However, much as how hooliganism was a problem without a solution in the 1980s, the banking sector of the 2000s had issues which were systemic and embedded within the industry. Casino banking was far riskier, and more rewarding, than traditional methods, and new products were offered for homeowners, with debt parcelled up and sold on to investors.

Labour were blamed for the crisis and, accordingly, were voted out of government in 2010. The Liberal Democrats became the kingmakers and went into coalition with the Conservatives, who as with Labour in the first general election of 1974 had not achieved an overall majority. It was entirely possible that Labour could have remained in power if they had convinced the Lib Dems, led by Nick Clegg, to form a government with them.

In the manner of a young full-back, Clegg had burst on to the scene during the general election campaign, appearing in TV debates which saw Brown and Conservative leader

David Cameron repeatedly 'agreeing with Nick'. It was as if they knew they would have to seek common ground with the third party after an inevitable hung parliament which, as had happened in 1974, would deliver no overall majority for either of them. The Lib Dem manifesto included a wish to 'hardwire fairness back into national life'. Significantly, they wanted to 'scrap unfair university tuition fees', which was a pledge they abandoned during the coalition talks.

As per another part of their manifesto, the 2010 Queen's Speech outlined a referendum on the Alternative Vote system, to which the electorate said no, as well as investment in new high-speed broadband internet connections. In education the coalition government would also support academy schools which would 'give teachers greater freedom over the curriculum'.

Alongside the promise to spend 0.7 per cent of GDP on foreign aid, the government would limit the number of non-European Union economic migrants. Parliament would also be fixed at a five-year term. The speech also introduced recall petitions which would allow voters to more easily remove their MP after 'serious wrongdoing'. There would be sanctions for unemployed people who refused jobs that brought them back into employment, and ID cards were to be abolished. The latter announcement was one of many instant reversals of Labour policies.

The government also introduced a bill to devolve greater powers to councils and neighbourhoods and give local communities control over housing and planning decisions, pointing to the Big Society agenda that allowed people more of a say in their lives. This was a return to small-state government.

In June 2010, three months after the Labour government's final Budget and five days before England were knocked out of the World Cup, chancellor George

Osborne delivered his first Budget. It was a so-called 'emergency' one which was given seven weeks after the new government was installed. 'Yes, it is tough, but it is also fair,' argued Osborne at the outset. With an eye on the game against Germany, the announcement not to put up the duty on cider came 'just in time to celebrate England's progress to the quarter-finals, or else to drown our sorrows'.

They may well have done so in pubs, where from 2007 it was forbidden to smoke. Public health and the freedom to choose to harm oneself were constantly at odds in England and the rest of Britain. The smoking ban, which Harold Wilson's Labour government had first proposed in the 1970s, sought to lessen the burden on the health service and prevent deaths through cancer. There was already a ban on tobacco advertising, although we shall see that another illicit pleasure would be advertised heavily and would dominate English life.

Since 1986, light-touch regulation had enabled banks to take huge risks for massive reward, but the bailout of the banking sector, including £3bn to Northern Rock, which sponsored Newcastle United, had led to 'record debts'. The borrowing level had reached £1 of every £4 Britain spent, so the country, Osborne said, had been 'living beyond its means when the recession came'. His solution was a pay freeze for public sector workers until 2012 and a trimming of the £192bn spent on welfare, 'one of the reasons why there is no money left'. This is a reference to a notorious note to Osborne left by the outgoing Labour minister Liam Byrne in 2010.

An economy 'built on debt' would be transformed into one of 'private endeavour', as you would expect from a Conservative-led coalition. There would, Osborne also announced, be private funding into the Royal Mail and a selling-off of the shares in the air traffic control service

NATS. 'I want a sign to go up over the British economy that says "Open for business",' he continued, and he also followed Brown's example of slashing corporation tax to help drive enterprise.

Financial services, which were deemed too big to fail in spite of the damage they did to the UK's own finances, would not prop up the British economy. In an early mention of the government's buzzwords, Osborne said, 'We are all in this together.' This was also the first Budget to be overseen by the Office for Budget Responsibility, an independent body which would be 'immune to the temptations of the political cycle'. As Brown had done when he made the Bank of England independent, Osborne was creating a layer of oversight that would remain constant and offer checks and balances to government business. This is precisely what the FA board did when it put the kibosh on the Premier League's plans for a 39th game, even though the association is more than a century older than the top division.

Acknowledging the disparity of investment between the north and south of England, the government would invest in transport links for the big cities north of London extending the Manchester tram, refreshing Birmingham New Street station and upgrading the Tyne and Wear metro. They would also strive to make it more affordable to set up new businesses in certain parts of the country, some areas of which had put their trust in the Conservatives at the general election.

Osborne noted that, since the introduction of disability living allowances two decades previously, three times as many people were claiming it. Britain's spending on housing benefit exceeded the combined spend on universities and the police. This seems like a criticism of the previous government's support for the poorest. The opposition complained audibly when Osborne raised VAT to 20 per cent, which meant his hands were tied when it came to taxing alcohol, fuel or cigarettes, which remained a quick and easy way to support the public purse. Responding for Labour, Harriet Harman called the VAT rise a broken promise and the Budget itself 'driven by ideology, their commitment to a smaller state'.

At the cinema, Graham Greene's *Brighton Rock* and the epic *Clash of the Titans* were both rebooted. Chris Morris's satire *Four Lions* tried to make comic figures out of domestic terrorists, while *Jackboots on Whitehall* headed back to the 1940s where, in a parallel history, the Nazis had captured London. In a true-to-life retelling, *The King's Speech* reminded audiences of the personal struggles of King George VI as he conquered a stammer to address his subjects during wartime.

Andy Serkis played songwriter Ian Dury in *Sex & Drugs & Rock & Roll*, continuing the focus on famous English figures from the 1960s and 1970s. Released a week apart in October 2010, *Made in Dagenham* and *Mr Nice* also documented characters in British history, in the form of striking factory workers or notorious drug smugglers.

Labour were out of power, and the financial crisis of the end of their time in government was still affecting policy decisions, but English football was richer and more visible than ever before. In South Africa, the national team failed to reach the semi-final stage for a fourth consecutive tournament, but at least there was not a reprise of the media circus of wives and girlfriends. Wayne Rooney's memorable criticism after the Algeria game did not help relations between player and supporter, for which he apologised, blaming 'frustration of our performance'.

'This is not the England that I know,' said Fabio Capello, who was concerned at how often Rooney gave the ball away. 'The problem is in the mind,' he believed.

Looking on, Alex Ferguson blamed the lack of a winter break for England's players and the weakness of the teams in the group stage, which magnified the importance of the Germany game. Even without Lampard's non-given goal, which was rendered moot by a 4-1 defeat, there always seemed to be a way to explain away England's lack of success, including 'the burden of expectation' which Ferguson believed had unsettled Rooney. When would they be able to handle it?

The 1970 England World Cup squad topped the charts with their tournament song, the militaristic 'Back Home'. Adding their vocals here, from left to right, are Bobby Moore, Alan Ball, Emlyn Hughes, Norman Hunter, Peter Bonetti and Martin Peters. Hughes was the only one of those six not to have been part of the England squad of 1966.

Labour Chancellor Denis Healey delivered several budgets during his party's time in power. He is pictured here in November 1974, at the end of a turbulent year which saw his party win two general elections.

Kevin Keegan was England captain when Don Revie, who is stood to his right, was in charge. The manager set up a kit sponsorship deal with Admiral, which helped to move the England team into the commercial era.

Glenn Hoddle complained about how he was badly used by successive managers in his playing days, when the England side he played in did not qualify for the 1978 World Cup. He would manage the team at the 1998 tournament and use his favoured 3-5-2 formation.

Nigel Lawson gave several budgets for the Conservative party during the 1980s, at a time when the government pursued policies that were kind to the financial sector, following the decline of industries like coalmining.

Goalkeeper Peter Shilton and defender Terry Butcher were important players in England's teams of the 1980s, and also at the 1990 World Cup, where the side came a penalty shoot-out away from reaching the final.

During much of his time as England manager, Graham Taylor was deprived of Paul Gascoigne, the gifted playmaker who was turned into a celebrity at a time when football was broadening its audience in England.

When he scored with a direct free kick against Colombia at the 1998 World Cup, David Beckham made a positive contribution to the England team which he would later captain. He would become a scapegoat for the team's tournament exit before scoring another free kick to take them to the 2002 World Cup.

Prime Minister Tony Blair backed the unsuccessful bid for England to host the 2006 World Cup. Here, he welcomes manager Sven-Göran Eriksson and players David Beckham, Gareth Southgate and David Seaman to 10 Downing Street in 2002.

Gordon Brown, the chancellor who would succeed Tony Blair as prime minister, shakes the hand of World Cup-winning midfielder Alan Ball, with Sven-Göran Eriksson looking on alongside sports minister Richard Caborn and FA executives Brian Barwick.

Like Peter Bonetti in 1970, goalkeeper Rob Green is doomed to be remembered for his error at a World Cup, in his case in a group stage game against the USA in 2010. England went on to lose to Germany in the round of 16.

Conservative Chancellor George Osborne sits beside World Cup winner Bobby Charlton in 2015, the year Osborne was working towards what he called a 'long-term economic plan' for the country. Charlton had been an ambassador for England's bid to host the 2006 World Cup.

Prime Minister Rishi Sunak, another former Conservative chancellor, visits England's training complex St George's Park in 2023. He is pictured with captain Harry Kane and manager Gareth Southgate, who travelled to Russia and Qatar at successive World Cups.

Following the penalty shoot-out defeat at the final of the delayed EURO 2020 tournament, a digital mural celebrated Bukayo Saka, Marcus Rashford and Jadon Sancho, the three black players who missed their penalties and received online abuse.

Prime Minister Keir Starmer poses for a team photo with the England women's squad, again at St George's Park. The team successfully defended the European Championship in 2025, at a time when more investment was being poured into women's football in England.

Bobby Moore was immortalised in a statue at Wembley Stadium in 2007. As of the publication of this book, he remains the only English player to captain a side to a World Cup victory. The St George's cross behind him, which has been claimed by various groups of patriotic English people, was not a symbol of the football team in 1966, but it has been adopted as such.

2014

IN AN essay for the book *Saturday's Boys*, published in 1990, the then Labour deputy leader Roy Hattersley wrote that football 'does more than provide unrivalled pleasure on a Saturday afternoon. It keeps us in romantic association with our individual and collective past.' He and thousands of others felt 'an irrational loyalty' towards their club, in his case Sheffield Wednesday, and this loyalty also affected fans of the national side.

The past of this national sport once again inspired a piece of creative writing, this time to celebrate 150 years of the FA, in 2013.

Musa Okwonga's poem 'Ode to England' painted the game as 'that war of rival scarves', recalling 'Sir Geoff Hurst on Wembley's turf in destiny's pursuit' and the 'Gazza-needs-a-hanky' moment of 1990. These incidents had become folk stories and shared histories passed down from one generation to the next, to inspire and comfort England's fans when things went less well. So, incidentally, in certain corners of Britain had various protests between miners and policemen.

Isles of Wonder remains one of the most magnificent depictions of England, and Britain, on stage. On 27 July 2012 at the Olympic Stadium, a cast of thousands tried to put across what the country stood for: Victorian engineering, Mary Poppins and Tim Berners-Lee's creation of the World Wide Web 'for everyone'. David Beckham, naturally, was on a boat with the Olympic flame as it proceeded down the River Thames to the stadium.

There was an extended sequence on the National Health Service, free at the point of use and set up in 1948, two years before England played at their first World Cup finals. In 2012, the coalition government introduced a series of reforms to the NHS which allowed for less government control and more targets to hit. In 2025, these were totally reversed by the Labour government.

In spite of the nation's football team competing in Euro 2012, it was the turn of Olympic athletes – cyclists, rowers, runners and jumpers – to provide England with a warm glow over summer, which was shared with the other British nations. As part of the conditions of being the host nation, Great Britain had to send a team to compete in every sport. For the first time since the 1960 Olympics this included football, where aside from three overage players the squad would comprise players under the age of 23 from all four home nations.

Daniel Sturridge and Danny Rose, who would both play at a World Cup, were part of a mostly English team. Wins against the UAE and Uruguay, and a draw against Senegal were followed by a loss on penalties to South Korea, and focus turned to the start of the domestic season.

Speaking during a debate in March 2009, SNP MP Pete Wishart was critical of what was to be 'a meaningless competition'; no Scottish player was picked for the squad. Prime minister Gordon Brown had, bizarrely in Wishart's view, named Paul Gascoigne's goal against Scotland, Brown's country of birth, in Euro 96 as his favourite sporting moment. Any wish to send a united team to the London Olympics was seen to be part of Brown's 'Britishness agenda'. Wishart's party were still seeking a referendum on Scottish independence, so bringing up the

Olympic football team was another way to separate their interests from English ones. Conservative MP Mark Field worried that the team would set a precedent that might lead to a similar British team competing in the World Cup.

It was in 2014 that English Heritage, which runs 400 sites of historic interest around the country, became a charity, having been a government body. There was a precedent for this in the Canal & River Trust, which formed from British Waterways. Along with the new Historic England, English Heritage was responsible for the blue plaques that celebrate significant people in the country's history. One of them is dedicated to pioneering former West Brom player Laurie Cunningham, affixed to his old house in Stroud Green, north London.

The Queen's Speech of 2014 brought forward measures for a married couple's allowance, which would recognise marriage in the tax system, as well as a continued promise to promote the Help to Buy and Right to Buy schemes to support home ownership. Employers would suffer higher penalties if they failed to pay staff the minimum wage, which for adults was £6.50 an hour, while the focus on the environment prompted a reduction in the use of cheap plastic carrier bags. All infants would receive a free school meal, while there was also a measure to consider heroic acts, or those for the benefit of others, when judging court cases.

George Osborne's 2014 Budget opened with a declaration that 'we held our nerve' and a repetition of his new slogan which reminded people he was adopting 'a long-term economic plan' rather than a short-term fix. As we shall see, in a similar manner the FA was thinking more of 2022 than of 2016. The sum borrowed to decrease the deficit had been lowered from £157bn in 2009 to an expected £108bn in 2014. The round pound coins, approximately one in 30 of which in circulation was fake, were to be phased out in favour of one that was harder to counterfeit.

Osborne would direct the fines paid by banks who fixed currency rates to charities like St John Ambulance and, recalling the attention given to arcade machines in previous Budgets, fixed-odds betting terminals would now be taxed at 25 per cent. The chancellor noted that these had replaced bingo halls as a likely place for gambling, making the exercise less social and more solo.

In a globalised economy, he continued, Britain needed to export to expanding markets like China, India and Brazil, while there was another push for investing in science and engineering. When it came to big data, with the construction of The Alan Turing Institute, Osborne said he was 'determined that our country is going to outcompete, outsmart and outdo the rest of the world'. The discovery of graphene would, thanks to being developed in the UK, 'break the habit of a lifetime'; to give one example, the way football was played had been improved outside of the country before its on-field talent was combined with commercial acumen off it to create the Premier League.

Speaking at the Conservative Party Conference in 2013, David Cameron included the league among his list of ways Britain punched above its weight, fighting off the derision of being referred to as a 'small island'. There were also 300,000 new businesses since the coalition government began its time in office in 2010, and 4,000 cars were being produced in Britain every day. Cameron also pledged an in-out referendum on British membership of the European Union, which would dominate political debate for the next decade.

By 2014, David Goldblatt wrote in *The Game of Our Lives*, football had 'outstripped the real estate market' in its revenues and even after the global economic recession it was continuing to expand, with TV audiences growing around the world. This had served to help 'reshape and reinvent' football, making it 'an increasingly managed and commercialised experience' of the kind that the Chester Report suggested in the early 1980s. As well as checking that the goalkeepers were ready for the game to start, referees now had to wait for a touchline signal from someone from the TV company which was airing the game around the world.

Goldblatt was keen to note that foreign businessmen owned five of the major Premier League clubs, while an English billionaire who was based in the Caribbean owned the sixth, Tottenham. That man was Joe Lewis, who had made 'a big chunk of his money speculating against the pound' in the early 1990s. West Ham's Terry Brown, who owned holiday resorts, sold the club on to a consortium from Iceland, who in turn soon divested of their investment to English businessmen David Gold and David Sullivan.

West Ham moved into the Olympic Stadium, which became known as the London Stadium, adopting the same move that allowed Manchester City to play in the Commonwealth Games arena. Tottenham also bid for the rights to inherit the tenancy, in collaboration with the events group AEG. Their offer was conditional on demolishing most of the stadium because it had been designed for athletics, not for football.

West Ham suggested no such alterations and won the bid unanimously, although Tottenham challenged the award, which delayed the confirmation until 2013. West Ham moved in as tenants three years later. As had been the case with Wembley Stadium, public money was used, this time to convert the roof and install retractable seats so, again as with Wembley, it could be used for concerts and athletics events.

The FA was, at the time, still paying back some of the money that had been used to construct the stadium, although it only comprised £11m of the governing body's record turnover of £332m, £115m of which was invested back into the game. Corporate sponsors now included Carlsberg, Lucozade and Vauxhall, while the FA's annual report looked forward to rock shows by AC/DC and Foo Fighters.

Unfortunately, for a second time, the FA was unsuccessful in a bid to bring the World Cup to the so-called home of the game. Even though it tried to dazzle FIFA delegates with Prince William and David Beckham, it found the same difficulties they had experienced in 2006. And then there were the on-pitch struggles.

'By the time we get to the quarter-finals of a tournament, we're on our last legs,' Rio Ferdinand complained in his 2014 memoir *#2Sides*. Fortunately, England didn't make it that far in Brazil. 'We've wasted a generation or two,' he concluded of a time when the England philosophy was 'running about 100 miles an hour and working hard', picking up on something Jamie Carragher had written in his book. England, Ferdinand thought, needed 'hard work within a good structure'.

As a kid he would hear about 'hard work and tackling', rather than being demanded to show his skill; he wrote that Wayne Rooney had been fortunate not to have had those skills drilled out of him, and that he had taken the initiative in insisting he should play in attack rather than have coaches experiment with playing him in new positions. The excitement of young players like Ross Barkley, Daniel Sturridge and Raheem Sterling 'playing without fear' was not enough to dislodge Ferdinand's conviction that the focus must be on 'the under-14s and 15s'.

Added to this, the Premier League 'is completely detached from the ideas and vision of the FA and vice versa,' he wrote. 'All they care about is what benefits them', which is money. This precisely echoes the complaints of Kate Hoey MP in 1993, meaning that just as John Inverdale had feared, the conversation around English football had not moved on in 20 years. The result of this stasis, Ferdinand predicted, would be that 'we muddle along, tweaking a few things here and there'. And why, he wondered, did England have so few all-weather pitches or qualified coaches? Why were those coaches not remunerated as well as they were on the continent?

Why, indeed, just before the 2014 tournament, did Sol Campbell publicly say he could have been England captain for a decade had he not been black, reminding people that race was still an issue with the England football team even as more players represented Premier League clubs and various age groups of the national team.

In a *Times* interview in 2013, Dan Ashworth summarised his job specification as being to 'put the man on the moon'. The man who helped concoct the England DNA for the FA, Ashworth is one of the key architects of English football who is not a qualified coach. In another sign that the association was no longer amateur, he had the job title of director of elite development. This saw him work with the coaching staff to bring through players who could help England win the World Cup; in 2012, the job had been offered to Gareth Southgate. Ashworth returned to the FA, after working with Brighton & Hove Albion, Newcastle United and Manchester United, in 2025, this time to help bring through English coaches.

Ashworth's initial role was desperately needed even before England performed badly out in Brazil. In conversation with Henry Winter at the end of his investigation into why we 'never stop believing' that England can end, as per the book's title, *Fifty Years of Hurt*, new head coach Roy Hodgson lamented how 'once upon a time to play for England you had to be the first name on your club team sheet'.

'There's no doubt we're going to miss a lot of players if we're not careful because they're going to reach a certain level and then not play,' he added. Andros Townsend is an instant example, forced to leave Tottenham for first-team football and not picked for the 2014 World Cup squad; nor indeed were any Spurs players. 'Just because a league that is stocked with brilliant foreign players is strong,' Kieron Dyer had written, 'it doesn't mean our national team will be strong, too.'

There were brief thoughts about how the national team could replicate the way in which the English cricket team allowed foreign-born players to be selected. This would be done through FIFA's five-year residency requirement, of which all four British nations had opted out. Instead, a player born abroad could only represent England or any of the other three countries after five years of schooling.

To give two examples: Diego Costa was born in Brazil but, having been capped by their senior team, he decided to play for Spain at the 2014 World Cup after gaining citizenship there. Conversely, young prodigy Adnan Januzaj had broken into the Manchester United team and could have elected to play for England once those five years had elapsed, forsaking the four other nations for whom he was eligible through parentage and heritage.

Jack Wilshere contributed to this debate by cleaving to national characteristics. 'We are English. We tackle hard, are tough on the pitch and are hard to beat. The only people who should play for England are English people,' he said. 'If you live in England for five years, it doesn't make you English.'

The Canada-born Owen Hargreaves and Jamaica-born John Barnes were ignored in his argument, as was

Tony Dorigo, who had been born in Australia and was able to play for England at the 1990 World Cup via the residency rule. Raheem Sterling, who was also born in Jamaica, would be part of the 2014 squad, having been picked initially for the under-21 side managed by Gareth Southgate. 'The world is changing,' Southgate himself said, in how 'people move and work abroad'. The 2026 World Cup will see dozens of players take advantage of residency rules or family passports to choose their international team.

Back in 2013, Alan Shearer and Arsène Wenger agreed with Wilshere, the former sighing that the country did not boast enough world-class talent. Wenger looked to politics to resolve the issue. 'Some people feel differently to their passport,' he said. 'Do they have to be educated in a country to feel they love this country?' Mo Farah was born in what is now Somaliland and was trafficked to Britain at the age of nine. He became the most visible gold medal winner at the 2012 Olympics, telling one interviewer 'this is my country' when asked if he would have preferred to have raced for his nation of birth.

At the far less successful 2014 World Cup, in spite of England being managed by Croydon-born Hodgson, Barney Ronay was perplexed over why the England team needed to apologise, for their early exit. If anyone had to apologise it was the fans themselves, whom Ronay refers to as 'empowered component parts of a society that continues to produce game but under-skilled footballers'. We should also say sorry for 'the disappearance of our vital inner-city and suburban green spaces' and 'for standing by while the shared national treasure that is state-school sport atrophies into underfunded inactivity'.

This was a problem which could be blamed on successive governments. In the Conservative period of government between 1979 and 1997, 10,000 playing fields were sold off, with another 187 in the decade after Labour's promise not to do so. Holland Park School in west London, a well-funded state school, had to withdraw its application to fund a redevelopment which would use revenue gained from selling off its open spaces.

Ronay also expressed concern about the demands placed on young players, 'the disorientating effects of early overexposure, from too much concussive big-game football, a gruelling celebrity culture, to vast windfalls of disorientating lucre offered at an early age'. Several members of the 2014 World Cup squad, including Luke Shaw and Phil Jones, would be affected by horrible injuries, which in their case would greatly impact their playing time at Manchester United and for England. In 2025, after an unsuccessful season on loan at Arsenal, Sterling would be frozen out at Chelsea and made to train away from the first team. Wilshere was forced to retire years earlier than he should have done thanks to a spate of bad injuries.

Gary Neville, the United one-club man who was part of the England coaching staff at the tournament, curses the rise of agents snapping up teenage talent, 'hoarding them like sticklebacks in a net out of a pond' and treating them as assets. In my book *From Kids to Champions*, I chronicled the way in which Chelsea stockpiled young talent who helped them secure many FA Youth Cup triumphs, loaning them out for several seasons to lower-league clubs and holding back their development at the club they were contracted to.

Perversely, Chelsea now prefer to buy in young international-class talent, some of whom have been trained at other English clubs, not least Cole Palmer and Liam Delap, who both came through at Manchester City. They raise funds by selling youth-team players who often go on to become full England internationals. That includes Lewis Hall, who moved to Newcastle, and Marc Guéhi, who captained Crystal Palace to their FA Cup win in 2025.

For all the array of global stars at Premier League sides, the national team still has a large pull for a football fan. 'This is a big country, 60 million people,' Hodgson said, 'and many haven't got a top-class team within 50 miles, and even if they did they wouldn't be able to afford to buy a ticket to go and watch them play, so internationals are important.'

David Goldblatt wrote that, as England manager, Hodgson brought 'a welcome degree of moderation and calm to the circus'. He could speak several languages, having managed in Italy, Switzerland and, most successfully, Sweden, and he possessed the sort of hinterland that Alf Ramsey lacked. He was, as mentioned earlier, the first England manager to have previously led another international side. Rio Ferdinand, whose time as an England international ended when Hodgson was appointed, felt he served to 'lower the expectations to a more modest and manageable level', but he still 'got it wrong in his approach to mixing youth and experience'.

Nor did it help, in his view, that he burdened Steven Gerrard with too much responsibility as team captain. Gerrard gave a pen pic of Hodgson in his memoir, published after the 2014 World Cup, as 'a dogged manager' and 'very organised, very compact', adding that 'honesty shines out of him' and praising how, like Sven-Göran Eriksson, he treated the squad 'like adults'. Yet Gerrard, who during the tournament had in mind the busy pubs back home which were staying open late to allow England fans to support the team, was conscious of 'much more realism' among the fanbase this time around. 'Most people realised that we did not have the players to win,' he wrote.

As it had done in Mexico in 1970, the climate also acted against their efforts, as it did against Italy in the jungle of Manaus. Gerrard wrote that he 'mouthed the words to "God Save the Queen" but I just wanted to start playing'. He wondered why England were playing so aggressively, in common with what Ferdinand and Bryan Robson had also said of the national side. 'This was not a Premier League match. We were a little gung-ho instead of showing patience and concentration.' England lost 2-1, with the bizarre spectacle of physio Gary Lewin injuring himself while he celebrated Sturridge's equalising goal.

After the decisive defeat against Uruguay, which meant that England could not advance to the knockout round after only playing two matches, Gerrard had 'black circles under my eyes. I had hardly slept the last three nights ... I cared so much it tore me to pieces.' This brings to mind Martin Peters's description of the dressing room after the loss to West Germany in 1970, as well as Alan Shearer staring into space after the defeat to Argentina in 1998. It was still devastating to be knocked out of a World Cup, although not every player wanted to take the risk of falling on their face for their country.

Fronting up as captain, Gerrard attended a press conference before the Costa Rica game. This was where he asked journalists for the names of Tottenham players who felt England was, as Harry Redknapp said, 'too much aggro'. Remember that no Spurs player was picked by Hodgson, who instead went with three Southampton players in Luke Shaw, Rickie Lambert and Adam Lallana. Fraser Forster was about to join the club from Glasgow Celtic.

For Lambert, selection for the tournament was the culmination of a career working his way up the football pyramid. Having been released by Liverpool before he could sign youth terms, he played for four clubs in the north-west: Blackpool, Macclesfield Town, Stockport County and Rochdale. The last of these were in the fourth tier, and when he joined Southampton from Bristol Rovers in 2009, the south coast club had fallen into League One. Three seasons before being picked for England, he was helping Southampton gain promotion back into the Championship.

Hodgson called Lambert's ascent to international football 'almost fairytale-like', especially because he scored on his debut with his first touch in a win against Scotland. Hodgson was impressed with what Gareth Southgate would refer to as his resilience: 'If you look into his past, to suffer that many knock-backs, then surely he hasn't suddenly become a talented footballer who has got good touch on the ball, works hard for his team and has got a good understanding.' Perhaps only Jamie Vardy, who played non-league football for Fleetwood Town before his performances for Leicester City led to international appearances of his own, could boast a more astonishing rise.

After the stardust wears off, however, playing for England can also breed contempt. Jamie Carragher had revealed in his book that some players would deliberately pick up suspensions to get out of 'the next unattractive foreign trip', whereas he would cancel summer plans to join the England squad and inevitably sit on the bench. Even David Beckham was not immune to such ploys, earning a yellow card to get himself out of a game against Azerbaijan.

Michael Carrick, who was injured for the 2014 World Cup, admitted in 2018 to asking not to be picked for England, overwhelmed by the responsibility in a way he did not feel when playing for Manchester United. He recalled to *FourFourTwo* that his 'heart sank' when he was included in the squad for the 2010 tournament in South Africa, following, in his view, a bad season for his club.

As for Gerrard, he wrote that he could withstand any criticism and abuse 'because I also remember how much unearned adulation we received for so long', inferring the 'Golden Generation' label with which the team were tagged. He suggested that the media and the players needed 'to be more balanced', and to forget about the 'hysteria' surrounding the Premier League where he made his name. 'Such manufactured fame does no favours to anyone outside the kid's agent and his sponsors.' This, however, is what drives the player's brand and makes him a more commercially attractive prospect. Hype is the cousin of potential.

Among the 2014 squad, Hodgson picked the young Arsenal pair Jack Wilshere and Alex Oxlade-Chamberlain, who had just helped their team to an FA Cup victory. Both of them have, like Shaw and Jones, suffered from serious injuries, backing up Barney Ronay's point about the dangers of going straight into the men's game as teenagers. Wilshere missed three entire seasons of his Arsenal career, but he was fortunate that 2013/14 was not among them. 'I lived a kid's dream of playing for their country,' he said in 2021, when he was not yet 30 years old.

In a manner that was lacking in the time of Ron Greenwood and Bobby Robson, Gerrard continued, 'Our players are often told they're superstars even before their first England call-up.' He also mentioned the 'constant soul-searching' that accompanies 'countless mistakes and bad decisions to add to the confusion and disappointment' of a tournament exit. While Germany finds solutions and plans ahead by planting the seeds of a coaching programme which eventually led to the national team's 2014 World Cup victory, England 'specialise in hype and criticism'. We are back to where we were in 1974, with 'emotion rather than thought' as a guide, as Henry Winter wrote in *Fifty Years of Hurt*.

Parliament, in its role of guarding the guards of the game, was looking at ways to reform the FA in 2011 through the select committee into Digital, Culture, Media and Sport (DCMS), in the aftermath of England's 2010 World Cup performance. The introduction to the report included a remark that the sport 'generates strong emotional attachments that are hard to convey in statistics', but that the commercialisation of football served to emphasise how it could deliver benefits to that passionate community.

The committee had in mind sports minister Hugh Robertson's point that 'football is the worst governed sport in this country', given that the FA board and its separate council were of a different composition from that of every other sport's governing body, including the Premier League, of which the FA itself has a share. The FA had 'ceded considerable authority' to the league in the 18 years since its inception. It also showed weakness in changing Fabio Capello's contract without seeking approval from the board; 'There remains a lack of clarity as to who actually took the decision to amend the contract,' the committee wrote of a decision that looked better before the World Cup than after it.

In order to benefit the national team, the FA needed to examine youth development and coaching education. On the former topic, there was 'a lack of common purpose' between the FA, the Premier League and the Football League, although the Elite Player Performance Plan would be rolled out in 2012 to better compensate smaller clubs when a larger one poached their promising talent. Payments would be included should a player make an international appearance. The establishment of St George's Park, meanwhile, would help train thousands of coaches.

FA chief executive Ian Watmore spoke of the 'unholy alliance' between the FA and the clubs, who sought 'not to tread on each other's patch', frustration over which led to his resignation. Often, there were conflicts of interest which affected how certain board members, like Manchester United chief executive David Gill, could discuss financial issues or player call-ups. 'People from various sectors of the game would sit in meetings of the FA and talk about the FA as though it was a third party,' Watmore complained, something which could have been remedied by putting independent directors on the board. Lord Burns had recommended this in 2006 but it had not yet been put in place.

The committee emphasised that legislation would not be necessary except 'as a last resort' but the people who had given evidence to the committee were 'sceptical that change from within the game' would be possible. However, 'Putting the FA's authority on a statutory basis might have the unintended consequence of rendering the FA's decisions susceptible to challenge through the courts.' Parliament was damned if it did, and damned if it didn't.

Because the stakeholders had yet again failed to engage with their recommendations, there was a follow-up report commissioned in 2013, which now threatened to introduce legislation 'as soon as practicable' if nothing was done within a year. In 2011, something was done to change the complexion of the FA board when Heather Rabbatts was appointed as the first woman to serve on it. However, in 2013 she was aghast that the FA had set up a commission to improve the England team that had no ethnic minority or female member.

It did include former international players Glenn Hoddle and Danny Mills, as well as former England caretaker manager Howard Wilkinson, who remains the last English manager to win the top domestic league, the First Division with Leeds United in 1992 (no Englishman has won the Premier League). Led by FA chair Greg Dyke, the commission was keen to look at how to widen the pool of elite players who were qualified to play for England, something Dan Ashworth would make his role within the association.

The top division had seen numbers fall 'by more than a half ... We fear for the future of the England team.' Financially, English clubs were spending vast sums of money developing young players but only receiving 'a very limited return on their investment'. In an environment where TV shows *The Apprentice* and *Dragons' Den* showcased the importance of enterprise, this was simply bad, wasteful business.

Domestic clubs were not helping the national team as much as their European counterparts, as the data samples make clear: whereas 75 Spaniards and 54 Germans played in the Champions League during the 2012/13 season, only 22 English players did so. Of those playing more than half the games for a top-six team in a major European league, 24 out of 42 Spanish and German players were picked for their national team, which dropped to 13 of 18 in England. Added to this, Jermain Defoe was the only player under consideration for the 2014 World Cup squad who was playing outside the UK, in his case Toronto, whereas there were plenty of Germans and Spaniards in the Premier League.

The commission reported a few weeks before the start of the tournament, at which it was 'in the public interest' for the international team to have some measure of success. Mimicking George Osborne's focus on a 'long-term economic plan', Dyke had famously insisted that England would win the 2022 World Cup and installed a clock at

St George's Park to remind staff of his strategy. His report noted the 'duty of care' the FA had to English football 'and not just to football played in England', with a clear pathway needing to be available to the national side.

Ironically, in his role as a TV executive, Dyke was instrumental in making the Premier League more popular in the decades before taking on his job at the FA. At the time it was thought this would help the national team, given that English players would learn from their foreign counterparts, although in mitigation the Bosman ruling had not been made until 1995, three years into the existence of the breakaway league. This brought far more non-English talent into all levels of English football and had directly led to the alarming state of affairs in 2014.

Part of the problem with English football, exacerbated by the poor performance at the World Cup, was the paucity of opportunities for young professionals between 18 and 21 to play first-team football. Again, England fell well behind in comparison with Spain and Germany, with only 124 players under 21 forming part of various English first teams, compared with three times as many in the other countries; this makes importing players, either under the Bosman ruling or paying a transfer fee, a more attractive option for coaches of English clubs, perpetuating a cycle Dyke was keen to end for the sake of the national team.

His and the FA's proposed solution was, unsurprisingly, to follow what was happening in those other countries. The top clubs would be allowed to introduce B teams to play competitive matches against lower-league opponents in an additional division, League Three, within the football pyramid. This would solve the problem of players not having enough serious games as they were developing; at the time, an under-21 league had replaced the reserve league, but it had a focus that was less on results and more on game time.

This would mean that a young professional could still play for their own club, and use their facilities, rather than having the option of going on loan to a lower-league side, as Harry Kane did with Leyton Orient and Leicester City. In the end, although no new league was established, B teams were able to play in cup competitions and Brentford converted their youth academy into Brentford B.

Such a radical and disruptive idea was always going to be met with opposition from league clubs; 'We do not underestimate the sensitivities,' the report read. Clubs were mollified, however, by another proposal to encourage Strategic Loan Partnerships: the club which loaned the player had a greater role in their development, which would avoid cases where they were played out of position or not regularly enough. This was especially troublesome if the manager who had originally asked for a player left their post and the new coach did not see a way to use them in his own system. This could stunt his development and contribute to him being released from the club who were trying to bring him through.

Perhaps related to this, in recent years loan managers have been employed by top clubs to ease young players into the professional game in a similar manner to what the FA was proposing. This may, however, just as easily be down to how to better manage an asset who could be sold on after exhibiting his skills at another club, sometimes without even pulling on the shirt of the club who owned him. Club A could loan Club B eight players every season, with a limit to including only five of those in a match, which would boost the pool from which an England coach could be assured that they were testing themselves competitively.

Danny Welbeck, who travelled to Brazil in 2014, is given as an example of a player who made use of loans, in his case at Preston North End and Sunderland, before starring for Manchester United, the club that had developed him. The same could be said for all three England goalkeepers in the squad: Joe Hart had a useful period as Birmingham City's number one in 2009/10 in preparation for stepping up to take the role at Manchester City; Welbeck's old United team-mate Ben Foster enjoyed two seasons on loan at Watford before seeking regular football as Hart's replacement at Birmingham; and Fraser Forster never played for Newcastle United but was Norwich City's goalkeeper in 2009/10 before an initial two-year loan spell at Celtic, which was eventually made permanent.

Two members of the 2022 World Cup squad benefitted from loan moves early in their career. James Maddison spent a few months of the 2016/17 season at Aberdeen after Norwich City had signed him from Coventry City, and he travelled to the tournament after starring for Leicester City. Conor Gallagher also went to Qatar after four different loan spells between 2019 and 2022, where he tested himself in the Championship at Charlton Athletic and Swansea City before stepping up to the Premier League with West Bromwich Albion and Crystal Palace. He had never played for his parent club, Chelsea, before the start of the 2022/23 season.

Dyke's commission reiterated the point that too many players were coming into English football who would never be qualified to represent the national team and were blocking the pathway of those who could; the FA, of course, was pro-English, not anti-foreign. The report suggested that only elite clubs could sign such 'exceptional' talent, which would in turn promote young Englishmen playing further down the football pyramid. Interestingly, the FA dismissed the creation of an England under-21 side to play in the second tier, given that there was a clear separation between domestic clubs and the national team. There is little likelihood of such a team being set up anyhow, given that league clubs owned the players in the first place.

The FA also ignored thoughts of any quota system, which would further risk accusations of nativism and taking a 'little Englander' approach. In any case, speaking in 2015, Richard Scudamore of the Premier League agreed with the FA's concerns, proposing that England players were selected from across dozens of clubs rather than just concentrated within the top ten.

Of the 2014 World Cup squad, only two of the three goalkeepers – Foster of West Bromwich Albion and Fraser Forster, then at Celtic but soon to be at Southampton – played for a club outside those who had finished in the top ten of the 2013/14 Premier League season. After all, Scudamore said, Costa Rica drew with England at the World Cup and none of their players were at Manchester United or Chelsea.

The report is evidence that the FA was unafraid to suggest ideas, however far-fetched, that might improve English football, even though ultimately it could only propose and not enforce. After its publication, however, Tony Evans had written in *The Times*, 'The bitter truth is that the FA cannot revive grassroots football. The Premier League can, if it chooses to.' In the *Sunday Times* in 2025, the day of the final of the Women's European Championship, Jonathan Northcroft nonetheless praised Dyke for introducing 'ambition' to the FA and giving it 'a core purpose, which is to produce winning national sides'.

The association was beginning to at last look like the country whose football it represents, and 15 years on from Heather Rabbatts's appointment, the FA board of 2026 includes both women and people of an ethnic minority. Social media companies continue to be held to account for enabling people to post racist messages to footballers, on which the media stoically reports in a head-shaking manner. John Barnes is keen to argue, just as members of parliament did in the 1980s, that society is to blame, and that football is just a voluble place for it.

In 2021, in a *Guardian* interview promoting his book *The Uncomfortable Truth about Racism*, he called football 'probably the least racist industry, not in terms of the abuse you get on Twitter but the fact that so many black players can be worse than white players and earn more money. In what other industry does that happen?' Racism was as much a reason for turning people away from a career in the game as the tough tackling which affected skilful players.

Barnes expanded on this in a *Sunday Times* interview, 'I always say racism in football isn't real, because all those fans who racially abuse a black player will cheer for their own black players when they score a goal … Racism isn't personal. It's not personal to me. It's about a particular group.'

The number of black players in the top four divisions had doubled in the years between 1985 and 1992, with Arsenal fielding Paul Davis and David Rocastle, and Manchester United playing Paul Parker and Ryan Giggs, the son of a black father. The England squad of 2014 included Glen Johnson, Daniel Sturridge, Raheem Sterling, Ross Barkley, Danny Welbeck and Alex Oxlade-Chamberlain; in 2010, Johnson and seven entirely different black players had been picked.

In between the two tournaments, racism had been a hot-button topic, this time shown by one player to another. John Terry's racially abusive comments to Anton Ferdinand led to him losing the England captaincy, which was a resignation matter for Fabio Capello. Once again, an England manager had fallen foul of FA interference into how he sought to do his job, and Terry also chose not to fight the FA edict despite being cleared by the courts. Although he was picked for Euro 2012 weeks after Hodgson was appointed, Terry was not included in the same manager's 2014 World Cup squad. 'England was everything to me,' he lamented to *The Times* in 2021.

Writing for *The Guardian* website, Mark Perryman thought the FA's 'indecisive action', where after the initial incident four months elapsed before Terry lost the captaincy, showed how exceptional footballers were. They ought to be treated in the same way as any other 'public servant' such as a nurse or teacher, Perryman felt. In an environment where only two black managers took charge of clubs in the top four divisions, Perryman added that the FA could also have shown stronger leadership, which reminds us that football can be a weathervane in how to treat matters of social importance.

David Goldblatt pointed to the Stephen Lawrence inquiry, an investigation that reported in 1999 and found that the Metropolitan Police were 'institutionally racist', as reshaping race in England. The Kick It Out campaign to 'kick racism out of football' was rapidly given prominence in the mid-1990s. Clubs would pledge to cancel the season tickets of any fans who chanted abuse, although it took the response of a white player in Eric Cantona to catapult the campaign on to news bulletins. Ironically, in 2012, black players including Ferdinand and his brother Rio chose not to wear a Kick It Out T-shirt, because they thought Terry had not been punished severely enough.

Commenting on the incident in a newspaper with a wide readership, David Cameron put his name to an article for *The Sun* in which he said he would 'not let recent events drag us back to the bad old days of the past'. He wrote the piece as a concerned parent who had taken his son to watch Aston Villa and was worried that footballers would set a bad example for children with their 'foul, racist or violent behaviour'. He had convened interested parties to 'reaffirm our vigilance' against discrimination, part of which was to encourage the promotion of black coaches via St George's Park, the new hub for English coaching whose pitch was laid to match the one at Wembley.

In August 2011, there had been riots in Tottenham after the shooting of Mark Duggan by police, with arson and looting a by-product of the anger against the treatment of young people. Then, speaking in response to the events, Cameron had contrasted 'the worst of the British people' with those who cleaned up after the looters as 'riot Wombles'. As in John Terry's case, the vandals 'do not represent' England, and would not 'drag us down' with their 'complete absence of self-restraint'.

Cameron complained of a 'broken society', which he and his government would fix by making police and crime commissioners directly electable, and by introducing a National Citizen Service for 16-year-olds, some of whom would be able to coach football as part of their service in the community. He also, at the conclusion of his speech, mentioned that 'moral decline' has also happened in politics, the media and the financial industry, not just among the rioters. 'There is no "them" and "us" – there is us,' he said.

After England's friendly against the Netherlands was postponed due to the violence, newspapers picked up social media messages from Rio Ferdinand and Wayne Rooney. Ferdinand asked, 'What is all this in aid of? Innocent people, homes and livelihoods have gone up in smoke.' Rooney called the riots 'embarrassing for our country', mimicking the language of a politician in his role of England captain.

Writing in *The Guardian*, Kevin McCarra suggested that the match would have provided 'a place of calm' had it gone ahead, which sounded like a bizarre thing to conclude given the violence the team had attracted in the past. It had taken a generation, but things had finally changed around the England football team.

The obligatory war movie of 2014 was *The Imitation Game*, where Benedict Cumberbatch played codebreaker Alan Turing. There was also *Frank*, a filmed telling of the life of cult comic performer Frank Sidebottom, and *Mr Turner*, starring Timothy Spall as the landscape painter. With Bond absent, it fell to *Kingsman: The Secret Service* to document a fictional portrayal of British espionage. TV shows provided inspiration for *The Inbetweeners 2* and *Mrs. Brown's Boys D'Movie*, while the play *Posh* was turned into *The Riot Club*, documenting the indiscretions of a student dining society inspired by Oxford's Bullingdon Club.

Those Oxford students included the prime minister, chancellor and mayor of London. As Simon Kuper chronicled in his book *Chums*, the Oxford Union contingent of the late 1980s would grow up to turn the status of Britain in the European Union into a kind of moot, a jolly jape. One of them, David Cameron himself, asked MPs to join the Americans in another war, this time with Syria, a vote he lost in 2013. Opposition leader Ed Miliband referenced 'the lessons of Iraq' as a reason for his party going against the government's wishes. Just as the FA had learned from its mistakes over the inequitable treatment of black players, so had the Labour Party on even more serious matters.

As with plenty of political and football figures from the past, Miliband would be scorned by the tabloid press. In his case he was pictured while eating a sandwich and was called the son of a man 'who hated Britain'. Eager to pledge its support to the Conservative government, the *Daily Mail* had used diary entries from the late left-wing academic Ralph Miliband to tar Ed with the same brush. As a teenager in the 1940s, Ralph had imagined the typical Englishman as 'a rabid nationalist' who would see losing the British Empire as 'the worst possible humiliation'.

Deputy prime minister Nick Clegg used a sporting metaphor to discuss the story, saying, 'Politics should be about playing the ball, not the man.' Clegg had experienced the slings and arrows of politics himself after he went into government: he was once asked about how many women he had slept with in an interview with *GQ* magazine. The following year, Clegg's Liberal Democrats would be ejected from government as swiftly as England were knocked out of the 2014 World Cup.

2018

A FILMED adaptation of the Martin Amis novel *London Fields* came out in 2018, a year where cinema was dominated by the sequel to *Mamma Mia* and the Queen biopic *Bohemian Rhapsody*. Movie producers had realised that rock'n'roll, having been a success on the stage, could be adapted for the screen and marketed to a ready-made audience who had experienced ABBA and Queen the first time around, as well as their children and grandchildren.

Songs like 'Dancing Queen' and 'Bohemian Rhapsody' were music's version of England's World Cup victory, for ever in the air even though they emerged in the dim, distant past. In 2015, a musical version of *Bend It Like Beckham* had landed on the West End stage, a few years before a play about the England football team brought the sport and theatre together again.

The maverick Rodney Marsh wrote in 2011 that, back in the 1970s, the England team was 'the ultimate, the pinnacle of everything that football stood for', so when he was picked it was 'confirmation that I had arrived as a top player'. These days, 'the barometer for players is the Champions League … England football is now geared towards the club game'. That tournament, wrote David Goldblatt, is 'one of the very few areas of public life where membership of a wider European community is seen to be both practically advantageous and a source of status and pride'.

In June 2016, Britain left the European Union in a so-called 'Brexit' referendum called by prime minister David Cameron. The electorate were convinced by positive and negative reasons and the vote increased the tribal feeling among people who could call themselves Remainers or Brexiteers. Broadcaster James O'Brien called this the 'footballification' of British politics, with people forced to pick a side and tying a metaphorical scarf around one's neck that would prevent people from listening to points made by someone of the other side.

The Sheffield United squad that competed in the Championship in 2017/18 was, barring one Irishman, entirely UK-born, a point spotted by a Spanish journalist. Justifying this, their manager Chris Wilder said he had 'never once said about not signing foreign players. We're out there but we have to get value for money.' To Liverpool manager Jürgen Klopp, 'The choice was either you stay in Europe, which is not perfect, or you go out into something nobody has any idea how it will work.' Both quotations show that it was becoming normal for football managers to be asked about current affairs.

The decision to implement Brexit into the 2017 version of *Football Manager* aroused curiosity, given that players would be subjected to rules on free movement and work permits that the Bosman ruling had removed. Miles Jacobson, the director of the game's creator Sports Interactive, did mention his hope of a 'silver lining' that more British players would play for Premier League teams and graduate to their respective national teams.

But what, Marsh wrote scornfully, of the fair-weather fans who 'pack off to the pub for a knees-up' to watch England? Do they really 'care if England win or not?' They did in 2018 when England competed for the World

Cup in Russia, the tournament the FA bid for back in 2010. Sam Allardyce, who was appointed after England were knocked out by Iceland at Euro 2016, was moved to resign after one fixture of the qualifying group, stung by a newspaper journalist much as Sven-Göran Eriksson had been. Allardyce, by the way, had been in favour of Britain leaving the EU but, as West Brom manager in 2021, regretted that he could not sign three transfer targets because of work permit issues.

Accidental manager Gareth Southgate stepped up from the under-21 side, initially as caretaker. There would be no problems between manager and football association this time around. The FA's chief executive Martin Glenn called Southgate 'a great ambassador for what the FA stands for'. He also had the respect of his old England team-mates, with Ian Wright remembering how Southgate 'already looked like a first-team player at 15' and Stuart Pearce noting that, even as a player, Southgate was 'an old head on young shoulders [who] wants to learn and succeed'. Prophetically writing in 2000, Pearce thought himself 'very surprised if he didn't' go into coaching 'and if he wasn't very successful' at it.

Yet every supporter and journalist, as Southgate well knew, is allowed to have an opinion on the national team. 'Our fans and media exist in a state of habitual disappointment,' wrote Kieron Dyer in his autobiography; the midfielder nonetheless reckoned the England team never underachieved in the 2000s. 'Is it really a surprise they tend to go into their shell?' he asked of players when they were representing their country, some of whom notably froze in that Iceland game.

He added that 'the fear we play with' was the English disease. One game against Andorra took place in an atmosphere so 'poisonous' that England's defenders were barely able to 'play a five-yard pass ... The fear of getting a bad result and the humiliation that would follow crippled a lot of us.' There was not a great deal of focus on the mental side of the game, something Southgate would correct in his time as manager.

Writing in 2014, Rio Ferdinand concurred with Dyer, 'If a player's obsessed with what the papers will say about him, how is he ever going to go out and express himself?' Instead, he would play safe and take no risks. Ferdinand concluded that the atmosphere was 'just too intense', which is odd for someone who played for Manchester United, a club where the global fanbase expects results and which has existed in a panicked state for most of the last decade. Likewise, Gary Neville wrote in 2011, the modern England player was 'caught between these massive expectations and the reality of being good' but not good enough. This is what Alex Ferguson diagnosed of Wayne Rooney at the 2010 World Cup, even though Rooney was one of England's world-class players.

Part of what Southgate had to do was to remove that intensity and reset the culture of the team, taking a management consultant's view of things, to enable them to be good enough to progress to the latter stages of a World Cup and remove 'the 66 Overhang'. Coupled with this was his adherence to the England DNA, which Dan Ashworth had put into place in 2014 when Southgate was under-21 manager. It would force players to take 'ownership' for themselves, rather than respond to what the coaches dictated them to do, both with and without the ball.

An England team should have a definitive style with plenty of 'game intelligence', which updated but did not stray too far from what Southgate called their 'never-say-die attitude'. The plan sought to make players proud to represent their country, with a possession-focused playing style and consistency between each age group extending all the way up to the first team. Training sessions would include '70 per cent ball-rolling time', while off the pitch players would be supported by medical, nutritional and psychological staff. This coincided with England now being based at St George's Park in Burton upon Trent, Staffordshire.

Yet the FA, which supported the new centre with a government top-up of £6m, was the subject of some strong words from the government, as seemed customary at this point. In February 2017, in spite of the introduction of the England DNA programme, the MP Damian Collins raised the motion that the Conservatives had 'no confidence in the ability of the FA to comply fully with its duties as a governing body' and that the association needed to be reformed, which could only be done by enacting legislation. 'The FA cannot reform itself; turkeys will not vote for Christmas,' Collins said, and added that it was 'at the end of extra time'. Jack Straw had chosen the yellow card as a metaphor for a comment on English football, so this seemed far more urgent.

The 122 members of the FA Council, including 25 life presidents, only boasted eight women, which 'does not reflect modern society'. FA chair Greg Clarke had staked his job on reforming the organisation. Sports minister Tracey Crouch referred to the support the government gave to the Football Foundation charity via Sport England, which would be at risk if the FA held back on any reforms. Once more, it was time for the government to adopt the stick rather than the carrot.

'This government, and previous governments, intervened because we recognised the ambition that the FA had for football in this country,' Crouch said, adding, 'What right do we have to criticise the governance of FIFA if the nation's Football Association is not transparent in its own decision-making process?' Amazingly, one FA Council member thought women washed the kit, which surprised Crouch as a qualified coach 'and, oh, sports minister'.

Jason McCartney, a Conservative MP, wanted the England team to be successful to give the country 'the feelgood factor', and felt the FA should have been given access to some of the money accrued by the Premier League. Labour's Clive Efford reminded the house that there was one artificial pitch per 42,000 people and one coach per 38,000 people; the equivalent figures in Germany were one in 22,000 and one in 11,000.

'The enormous wealth that has come into the country has not been reflected in investment in grassroots football,' Efford said, due in part to the 'ancient' FA Council and the 'weak' FA board, who could step in and enforce a quota on homegrown players. This is something the FA had been disinclined to do when Greg Dyke launched his review in 2013.

Graham Jones began his speech by cheekily saying, 'It has been 50 years of hurt in the English game and we are all suffering, but at least we are not Scotland.' Nigel Huddlestone talked of the 'institutional inertia' at board level, while Andrew Bingham felt the £1m Sam Allardyce earned in his short stint as England manager, which the FA paid him, was 'destroying people's faith in football'.

More than one MP defended the FA for its work boosting women's football and acting on racism in the game, from which one can infer a reference to Kick It Out, as well as the £22m it invested in grassroots, even though Collins said it was only a quarter of Manchester United player Paul Pogba's transfer fee. Crouch added that the sum only represented 30 per cent of the total FA expenditure.

Bob Blackman pointed out that it was the Premier League, not the FA, who ran football, something which risked 'stagnation in our national game and our England football team being unable to win trophies'. He also thought it would be 'an abuse of our national stadium', in whose shadow Blackman grew up, if Tottenham were allowed to play their matches there while they were between stadiums. They did so in the 2017/18 season, with a squad containing Kieran Trippier, Eric Dier, Dele Alli and Harry Kane.

Speaking to a parliamentary select committee in July 2018, which was chaired by Damian Collins, FA chief executive Martin Glenn mentioned how he had allocated £30m towards hiring new personnel and reworking existing jobs within the organisation. 'I do not have the Premier League money,' he remembered telling a member of the FA, 'I have FA money.' It was no use waiting around for the government to tax the domestic clubs or the gambling industry, but to act in a more efficient manner and make the most of what they had.

This included mooting the idea of selling Wembley to Fulham owner Shahid Khan to free up some government money and allow the FA to fund the construction of more pitches; the stadium was never sold in the end. 'The England team is a national team,' Glenn added of his wish to play in grounds across the country. 'It is not a team of the M25.'

Collins expressed frustration at the 'Balkanised system' of football governance, coupled with how an FA chairman must harness all interested parties including local authorities, which he felt was 'one of the problems with funding sport in this country'. One can compare this to how an England manager must balance the competing interests of clubs, to whom the players are contracted, and various commercial organisations who sponsor the national side. It is easy to forget how many plates are being spun to help England win a World Cup, and how broad the objective is when it includes grassroots and kids' football right the way up to the globally successful clubs of the Premier League.

Under the England DNA plan, across all age groups, players had to involve themselves in tactical discussions. They would sometimes look at 'the stride pattern running into a shot', as Southgate said in an interview for the FA's coaching magazine *The Boot Room*. Southgate spoke of how he was keen for the players to 'write their own stories', something they were by now familiar with as individual brands with Instagram accounts. As he said when he delivered the Richard Dimbleby Lecture in 2025, Southgate spoke to members of his squad 'about their lives, their hopes and their fears' and sought to instil resilience into them.

In his desire to create a winning culture, he made Harry Kane his captain and Jordan Henderson vice-captain because they set an example when it came to 'their professionalism on the training pitch, in the gym, and in how they lived their lives away from football'. Most important of all for the manager was to 'protect the culture' when players misbehaved.

'We gave ourselves the best chance to succeed,' he added, a mentality he wanted to pass on to all English young men, regardless of whether they played football or not. It was clear that Southgate saw his job as a 'small "p"' political one, galvanising the country and going beyond merely winning football matches and putting a smile on the faces of English people. Whereas past England managers felt like politicians, Southgate embodied one.

In 2018, England were not locked in the sort of tournament bubble that disappointed Gary Lineker and David Beckham at previous World Cups. The players who travelled to Russia were conscious of what was going on in their lives back home. Fabian Delph excused himself from the England camp to be present at the birth of his child, returning in time for the quarter-final against Sweden. In 1998 goalkeeper Nigel Martyn had done the same, nipping back across the Channel when the World Cup was held in France. Bryan Robson, on the other hand, could not do this in 1982, even though the tournament was only in Spain.

Barney Ronay wrote in his World Cup diary *How Football (Nearly) Came Home* that there was 'a rebranding of expectation' under Southgate: the players were 'callow, unfancied … an object of uncertainty, angst and … hope' and were 'clearly un-golden, so [were] free of the burden of hype'. They were also open to the media. Danny Rose, the team's left-back, had spoken of his struggles with depression at a press conference, exacerbated by his own knee injury, the suicide of his uncle and racial abuse of his mum. 'England has been my salvation,' he said, grateful to his international manager for picking him. Ronay applauded the defender's 'emotional intelligence', a quality which was becoming as important to a footballer as his physical capability.

Such openness matched the way mental health was now a viable topic of public conversation. Prince William, who had been FA president since 2006, had launched the Heads Up campaign to counter the rise in male suicide and enable men to talk about their moods and anxieties. As a marker for the statistic that 125 people end their lives every week, the Campaign Against Living Miserably equates this to 'one every 90 minutes, the same amount of time as a football match'.

Within a generation, it was hoped that this statistic would decrease. There are few quick fixes, as shown by the amount of time that had elapsed for English hooligans to stop becoming a menace at World Cups. Those football banning orders introduced two decades previously had, by 2018, helped the authorities prevent 1,300 England fans travelling to the tournament.

It also took time to change things on the pitch: speaking to Henry Winter in the mid-2010s, Gary Lineker approved of how young players of the time were better on the ball. 'It's only now that we are just starting to get the benefits of teaching kids how to play properly,' he said. 'I don't think this will be such a problem in ten years because we're producing enough homegrown talents. There won't be this necessity to go out and get Joe Average.' Lineker also said that the longer the 1966 triumph recedes into the distance, 'the more the motivation should be'. He added, picking up on points raised earlier in this chapter by England internationals, 'Sometimes I can see there are too many nerves.'

Southgate would tell journalists he had 'nothing to lose', and he set about managing the team so they could play without fear. 'My job is to allow people to dream, make the impossible seem possible,' he said before the start of the 2018 tournament. Although they were told to remember to represent fans back home, the message to his players was that 'the guy next to you is the most important one going into this tournament'.

Southgate was, to the writer Richard Williams, perhaps the first England manager since Sir Alf Ramsey 'to decide on a system and then choose his players to fit the pattern': a distributor, Jordan Pickford, in goal; defenders who were good on the ball, like John Stones and Harry Maguire; wing-backs in Kyle Walker and Luke Shaw whose job was to stretch the play; and flexible attackers like Marcus Rashford and Raheem Sterling.

2018

Barney Ronay recalled an incident of abuse that happened to Sterling six months before the tournament, while he was playing for Manchester City: having thought that he was waiting for someone so he could sign an autograph for them, he was instead insulted with racial epithets. 'He shook himself off, went inside, played 90 minutes and scored twice in a 4-1 win,' Ronay said of a player who tried to dictate the narrative around black players, in particular when he compared coverage of two young Manchester City team-mates buying a house for their mothers.

White player Phil Foden was a 'starlet', while black player Tosin Adarabioyo was 'on £25,000 a week ... despite having never started a Premier League game'. To Sterling, such headlines 'fuel racism an[d] aggressive behaviour' towards black footballers. Foden admitted to having a difficult season in 2024/25, while Tosin was enjoying his first at Chelsea. He was yet to make a senior appearance for England, which meant he could still have declared for Nigeria.

In 2018, Southgate was also, Ronay wrote, 'ruthless in the best possible way, free from the constipated thinking, the sense of hierarchy, of repeating the same old failing patterns'. Out went Wayne Rooney and Joe Hart, and in came Pickford, Dele Alli and other 'biddable, willing, uncomplicated' young talent, some of whom Southgate had managed in the under-21 side. His team failed to reach the semi-final of the 2015 European Championship, where Harry Kane and Jesse Lingard gained useful international experience in the absence of Raheem Sterling and Luke Shaw, who were part of the senior setup that summer.

Writing for the ESPN website, *Fever Pitch* author Nick Hornby pointed out that the members of the 2018 World Cup squad were 'not celebrities ... those with no interest in football would be hard pushed to name a single member of the squad, let alone any of their wives or girlfriends'. He was equally keen to situate the tournament in the context of the negotiations over Britain leaving the European Union, for which the north of England 'voted overwhelmingly' even as three in four Londoners wanted to stay within the EU. Perhaps, Hornby continued, 'In the current climate the England team means different things to different people. What many of us crave is an England team we can like: one that plays fast, muscular, ambitious English football, beats the teams that are inferior to them and goes out bravely to the one that's better. It's not much to ask, but it would help an unhappy country to feel better about itself.'

A good run at the World Cup would not fix the structural problems that led to unfairness and precarity, nor would they magically solve the disagreements over the direction the country should take as it negotiated to leave the European Union. Yet, just as Bobby Robson suggested had occurred after the 1990 tournament, it would certainly lift the mood and allow fans to bask in the reflected glory of the team's success.

In 2017, four games into his time managing the senior side, Southgate told the BBC that young English players 'get big money for having achieved nothing', which lessened their 'inner drive'. He preached discipline, where it was more about creating the environment to succeed and less about controlling what players did. He was, however, unable to let his players relax on a free day while on international duty, something the FA put a stop to in November 2016.

'There was a perception of them across the world, a perception of English football, and I thought it was possible to change that,' he added in one press conference. Images of players swimming with inflatable unicorns and playing darts with journalists conveyed a sense of fun. This was a move also pioneered by the FA, which turned over £376m during the 2017/18 season, investing about a third of that into the national game. Nike had signed a decade-long kit sponsorship deal and Wembley, which came under the oversight of the FA, hosted 58 events including the annual American football matches and shows for Ed Sheeran's world tour.

Back in 2008, a few years before the England DNA was drawn up, Jamie Carragher was calling for 'a radical mental rethink' about the national team, which would include a focus on the tactical side of football; the contemporary England side of which he was part lacked 'the will to win at all costs' that benefits teams in knockout contests. There, it is 'as much about "knowing" how to win as it is about natural ability ... playing with your brain as much as your feet'.

Ten years on, Barney Ronay wrote, football in England 'only skims the cream' of its hundreds of talented players. It is 'in effect a privatised, outsourced industry' which acts against 'any wider sense of public benefit or municipal investment paying off': young kids progress to youth football, all under the aegis of their parent club who strive to win the Premier League and do well in European competitions, with little to no concern for the national team. It was up to the FA to instil a desire to represent the England side, which began at the younger age groups.

The role taken on by Lilleshall and the England Schoolboys programme in the 1980s had now been passed to the clubs and their youth academies. They had become assets for their balance sheet and commercial departments, marketable commodities who were the subject of a slew of bids at younger and younger ages. This replicated how football agents were trying to secure the signatures of them earlier and earlier, an unhealthy state of affairs which Michael Calvin examined in his book *No Hunger in Paradise*.

One of Calvin's interviewees was the England coach. Southgate thought that the best England players had 'intrinsic motivation' to do well. 'It's about dealing with the constant setbacks, the constant need to adapt and adjust,' he said, which included being in and out of the first team. To Calvin, 'Personal development is football's final frontier.'

The national team, in summary, would to Ronay 'remain trapped inside the limitations of its own domestic game, picking from the leftovers, asking for favours', even as winning the World Cup with England remains an aspiration. Speaking in 2024, captain and record goalscorer Harry Kane reminded players who had pulled out of a recent squad that 'England comes before club ... I want to start every game'. In 2017, Southgate similarly commended Wayne Rooney for being with the squad 'every single time without fail' despite his status as a 'multi-millionaire'.

David Goldblatt had written that, like much of British life, 'The new football economy is unfair but functional, wincingly unequal but never boring.' The open conclusion to *The Game of Our Lives* was to ask whether football was 'the canary in the mine of our impending global mediocrity and domestic fragmentation'. Happily, the 2018 World Cup put a pause on such thoughts, albeit after the departure of the UK from the European Union and the disastrous loss to Iceland at Euro 2016.

Alan Shearer tried to articulate the mood of England after that game, laying into the manager as 'tactically inept ... It looked to me like Roy [Hodgson] was making it up as he was going along.' A high-profile defeat always unleashes criticism of the worst order, and Shearer was keen to point fingers, once again, at the golden goose, 'We are blinded by the Premier League. We think it's the best in the world for talent. It's not. We are totally reliant on foreign players and managers for excitement. We are not as good as we think we are.'

'We haven't got leaders, they're all pampered, they're all [listening to] headphones and you can't get anything out of them,' complained Chris Waddle, who has also called modern-day players 'robotic ... athletes who can play two-touch football'. Alan Mullery, who played for England at the 1970 World Cup, echoed what Waddle thought, positing that the kids of the mid-2010s 'don't have the hunger now ... Everything's done for them. The academies are magnificent.'

This has also impacted players' leadership capabilities, with Mullery sad about the lack of English characters in the Premier League of the mid-2010s. In 2016, Gary Neville told Henry Winter, 'In the modern game there's an increasing lack of players who communicate on the pitch ... maybe society's changed.' Neville wrote in his memoir, moreover, that he was 'not convinced we ever quite had the depth in our squad to win a major tournament'.

The complaints continued. Jamie Carragher also pointed to a 'superiority complex' which was entirely without 'historical justification', especially given the home advantage the team enjoyed in 1966. Since then, as we have seen, England have lost 'every time we've played a quality side at the business end of a tournament', and neither have they overcome the odds and 'defied expectations'. Instead, England ought to enjoy being underdogs, 'ready to do everything and anything to win'. We remember the heroes' welcome the team received after overachieving at the 1990 World Cup.

John Barnes reiterated a fault he had spotted with English football as a whole, 'We rest on our laurels. We don't grow, don't evolve. While everyone else was looking at the technical aspects of football, we weren't. It was all "let's get stuck in", the good old British mentality.' On the topic of getting stuck in, prime minister Theresa May had to unite members of the cabinet who had set themselves either side of the debate to leave the EU, as if she was Sven-Göran Eriksson trying to assemble a midfield that couldn't play together.

Certain Conservatives, wrote political chronicler Steve Richards, 'had been fantasists for so long that they could no longer deal with the hard grind of reality'. One of them, Steve Baker, was more loyal to the Brexit cause than to his party, a drastic change from when 'loyalty to leader was almost a religious faith'. This was especially true at a time when the party had different leaders every few years, akin to a Championship club like Watford.

Boris Johnson, who had been installed as foreign secretary, was inside the tent waiting to swoop in and save the country from disaster. Simon Kuper had written a character study of Johnson in his book *Chums*, painting him as an opportunist who would do anything for success. His sister Rachel had revealed that his childhood ambition was to be 'world king' and, via jobs in journalism and politics, he was only a conveniently timed putsch away from 10 Downing Street. Compare this with the accidental manner in which Gareth Southgate fell into the role of England manager and, indeed, the manner in which May herself won party leadership uncontested in 2016.

May was criticised for not meeting the survivors of the Grenfell Tower disaster in June 2017, the defining event of her premiership that did not involve exiting the EU. The report into the inferno arrived in September 2024, listing a catalogue of avoidable errors from several different parties. A huge remediation project of similarly cladded buildings was already in motion, with the original developers taking responsibility for the task. Several former England internationals including Les Ferdinand, Alan Shearer and David James took part in a Game 4 Grenfell at Loftus Road in September 2017, the day after the national team beat Malta 4-0 at Wembley.

The government had also been in dispute with doctors. Back in 2015 there had been arguments over their working hours, particularly at weekends. Junior doctors were moved to strike when they did not accept a new contract offer, and over 100,000 operations and procedures were cancelled. This brought back memories of the strike action of 1975, but 40 years on, with a larger and more sedentary population, England was even more dependent on its health service.

It was still unwilling to fund it from their own pockets given that it was free at the point of use, while the government was equally cautious to work on ways to revolutionise it too quickly after the fiasco of the 2012 reforms. The Conservatives were equally trepidatious when it came to social care, after they announced and then withdrew a pledge to change how much people contributed to their residential care, in particular when they suffered from dementia.

Opposing such taxes were the Labour Party, led by Arsenal fan Jeremy Corbyn, who had been elected leader in 2015 and whose chief slogan was 'For the many, not the few'. Corbyn, whose son Ben is a scout and football coach, watches his team from a corporate box rather than within the crowd. 'We went to the football a few times and it created logistical problems,' Ben recalled to *The Guardian* in 2025, 'just loads of people wanting pictures and being adoring of him.'

The 2018 Budget was delivered in October by Philip Hammond, who raised the national minimum wage to £8.21 an hour. The Queen's Speech was cancelled in

2018 to allow for deliberations with the European Union, which also coloured the tone of the Budget. In 2017 the government agenda had included 'new national policies on immigration, international sanctions, nuclear safeguards, agriculture, and fisheries'. One clause sought to prioritise mental health within the NHS, and it announced a quick inquiry into the Grenfell Tower inferno, which would include advocacy for bereaved families.

Also in train was a commission for countering extremism, 'both across society and on the internet, so it is denied a safe space to spread'. Smartphones had by now become a menacing but useful feature of everyday life, the latest technology to become indispensable to people, who could be tethered to them when out and about. They could also send abusive, as well as kind, messages to players, which would increasingly be viewed by the people who managed their social media operations for them.

It has become routine in recent seasons for news stories to appear where clubs condemn abuse sent to players, and even their wives or girlfriends, after an error in a game. This sometimes seems like a displacement activity, to reframe the focus on a defeat into a defence of a player who has contributed to it.

Faceless social media companies, much like customer service chatbots, have become a scourge on contemporary life, but like racist abuse at football grounds it is a matter of educating people not to launch into abusing players in the first place. More worryingly, such criticism is also caused by a fan failing to win money in a bet because of that error, which has increased their emotional state at the moment they post the message.

England had bid to host the 2018 World Cup. Losing to Russia and gaining only two votes from the FIFA congress was 'a national disappointment', according to the government select committee review into the bidding process. The FA chairman David Triesman felt it was 'a millstone' to have to consider offering gifts or bribes, something that a *Sunday Times* report had investigated, and the BBC had aired allegations of, days before the award of the tournament. Triesman himself had to resign after being recorded accusing countries of wanting to bribe World Cup referees, pleading entrapment. It was not only England managers or prime ministers who could be caught being candid on a microphone.

A few months before the tournament was due to begin, diplomatic relations between England and Russia grew cold after the Salisbury poisoning, when the former military officer Sergei Skripal was suspected to have been given Novichok by Russian agents. Prince William accordingly did not travel to cheer England on, while Boris Johnson wrote an article for *The Sun* which denied the team would boycott the World Cup entirely, rekindling memories of discussions held to do the same in 1982 and 1990.

Johnson thought that this would have been 'unfair on the team, young athletes who have trained so hard for what is the summit of their careers', as well as fans who wanted to enjoy football 'without the intrusion of politics'. He added that, after all, Vladimir Putin did not own the trophy. The UK chose to expel Russian diplomats instead.

England's opening game saw them beat Tunisia in the last minute with the first of several goals they scored from a set piece, here a corner tapped in by Harry Kane. Against Panama, they scored five before half-time and won 6-1. Nick Hornby wrote for the ESPN website that the 'quick and ruthless' performance was unlike any other World Cup match England had played in the current century. A lack of debate about the compatibility of midfielders 'feels like a holiday' to him, as did the 'glorious respite' of not arguing about politics. 'The beauty of sport is that it simplifies everything,' he concluded, with life reduced to a good or bad result.

'We were getting used to this strange, entirely unaccustomed feeling of the steady hand,' Barney Ronay noted of Southgate, something which had been denied the England journalists in the disappointing 2014 tournament that was over within two matches. The team were now 'fun, likeable and charming', with the manager eliminating any cliques that marred previous squads even dating back to Southgate's time as a player. There did not seem to be a division between players of various clubs, as Rio Ferdinand and Rodney Marsh had both noted of previous England teams, which was all the better for team morale.

The presence of Jamie Vardy as Kane's understudy, one of those characters Alan Mullery had been waiting for, also brought some earthiness to the squad. 'I get abuse from opposition fans and give it back to them,' the Leicester City striker told *The Guardian*, 'but that's just me, and that's how it should be; it's only a bit of banter.' Vardy was the latest player to call representing his country 'probably the biggest thing in football' and to admit to throatily singing the national anthem, but he decided to retire from international football after the 2018 World Cup to prolong his career with Leicester.

The Euro 96 anthem 'Three Lions' was joined by a new version of 'Whole Again' by Atomic Kitten, which ended with the line 'football's coming home again!' 'You got the feeling people just really did need something to laugh at,' posited Ronay. The experience was all the better because it was shared and on non-paywalled TV. Unlike the Premier League or Champions League, there was no need to procure a Sky or BT subscription to watch the World Cup, which as usual was free to air on both the BBC and ITV.

Plenty of players were familiar even to casual English football fans: in the group game against Belgium, Ronay counted 23 players to have a Premier League club on their CV, including the match-winner Adnan Januzaj, who left Manchester United in 2017 without ever playing for England. Those arguments which were raised in 2013 were now redundant, especially with the rise of another United academy product, local talent Marcus Rashford.

This time around, England had made plans for penalties during the knockout rounds: they practised them at the end of training sessions, with players shouting to distract the takers, who would warn the goalkeeper where he would place the kick, forcing them to take better penalties. Finally, after defeats in 1990, 1998 and 2006, and with memories of the Euro 96 shoot-out against Germany, they would focus on something they had previously ignored, similar to the government enacting a smoking ban or paying state employees fairly.

Against Colombia, who took the game into extra time with the last kick of the initial 90 minutes, England won a World Cup shoot-out for the first time, in spite of Jordan Henderson's kick being saved. Jordan Pickford, however, reached up to prevent Carlos Bacca's from going in, with Eric Dier converting the winning penalty. It was also fortunate for England that their opposition's playmaker James Rodriguez, a star of the 2014 tournament, was injured for the game.

Speaking in 2025, Southgate had been overjoyed for Dier, 'In 1996, I had walked 30 yards to the penalty spot believing I would miss. In 2018, Eric had walked those same 30 yards believing he would score.' Winning the shoot-out meant that the team had broken down a barrier to victory, after he and his coaching team had brought in 'a belief and resilience' in the players. He hoped that all young men in England could use that moment to spur themselves on to success.

To Ronay, vice-captain Henderson was a 'cajoling presence ... a great team man and a player with just enough of that old pointing, shouting spirit', perhaps the kind Gary Neville enjoyed seeing in players. Thomas Tuchel would also recall Henderson to the side in 2025, despite the unpopularity of his brief sojourn in Saudi Arabia, which was seen to be at odds with his support for social causes while captain of Liverpool. It was no longer the case that off-field or social issues and footballing prowess were treated separately, although Henderson has since returned to English football with Brentford.

Dele Alli celebrated his goal against Sweden in the quarter-final with a dance inspired by the video game *Fortnite*. Jesse Lingard did the same against Panama, bringing youthful vitality to the team and tapping into a younger fanbase who might be familiar with the dance. The man who wished to be known as Dele came through at MK Dons as a teenage prodigy before signing for Tottenham, where he was burdened with the same extraordinary levels of expectation that Wayne Rooney and Michael Owen had.

A sharp downturn of form was eventually explained in 2023, when Dele spoke to Gary Neville about checking himself into rehab to deal with childhood trauma and his addiction to sleeping pills. It seemed Prince William's encouragement for footballers to open up about their personal struggles, coupled with Danny Rose's comments at the World Cup press conference, had borne fruit. 'Discussing mental health is not a sign of weakness,' the prince wrote of the 'brave and inspirational' player whose career has also included several injuries to his groin and hip.

Henderson, Dele and Lingard all started in the semi-final against Croatia, where England regressed to the mean. Kieran Trippier put them ahead early with a direct free kick but Croatia dominated and won it in extra time. Ronay wondered rhetorically why, when it came to football, England fans asked 'not just why aren't we better, but why do we think we should be?' At least this time around, Ronay wasn't asking supporters to apologise to the team for their many mistakes.

Paul Hayward pointed to 'a kind of lovesick idolisation' when England do well at tournaments, as the team had done in 2018 when fans watched matches in waistcoats in homage to Southgate's choice to wear one on the touchline. When it went wrong, however, 'addressing the failures in the system … was always secondary to the emotional response to "failure", the deep offence taken by the English when expectation collided with reality'. This schizophrenic approach to the team has never been healthy; again, looking back to 1990, it should be a matter of overachieving modest goals rather than expecting to win at all costs.

Writing for the website Football365, and echoing Nick Hornby's hopes before the tournament, Daniel Storey praised the 'meaningful distraction' the run to the semi-final offered. This was 'a team which we could believe in, a team moving in the right direction and a team in which we could have immense pride'. Significantly, as Hayward noted, Southgate also broke into the front pages of newspaper coverage, where the politics is usually found, and unlike other England managers the stories were not to do with his private life.

'His intelligence and decency were deployed by commentators as a rebuke to politicians and others in public life. Southgate was the real, modern England, fighting to be heard,' Hayward said, perhaps using journalistic licence in defining the 'real' nature of a country of millions of people and dozens of different accents. 'Here was a leader of substance who pursued the common good.' Again, the manager was an avatar for the nation, an easy shorthand who could exist in a world of images, memes and soundbites that sped past a scrolling news consumer.

Southgate might also boost the esteem English people felt about their home nation. Before the start of the tournament, the BBC's home editor Mark Easton had written an essay on English identity. 'England is treated like an embarrassing uncle at a wedding,' he began, with people just as keen to describe themselves as British as English. 'They are strands of the same national thread,' he wrote, but 'the English identity emerges as more exclusive while the British identity is seen as more inclusive'. Far from looking to its diverse national football team, ciphers for England were its history and landscape, 'a pre-industrial bucolic nation populated by well-mannered and virtuous citizens'.

In *The Times*, Matthew Syed hoped for another change after England's fine performance. For too long, managers were declared saviours before being knocked down when things went awry, what Syed called 'the cycle of deification and castration' which shifts the focus away from the sort of reforms needed at a structural level. He could just as easily be talking about the rush to anoint prime ministers as the next glorious leader, before the harsh reality of events and forces outside their control serve to knock them down.

Days after the 2018 World Cup concluded, the Department for Culture, Media and Sport parliamentary committee, which scrutinised matters of cultural and sporting importance, called Gary Neville to a meeting about the future of English football and the national stadium. He felt the FA was 'working with their hands tied behind their back' to improve the game, and that it ought not be forced into selling Wembley Stadium, 'a national asset', five years before all the debt had been paid off.

'You have just seen last week 26.6m people tune in to watch an England game,' Neville marvelled. 'What else does that in this country?' He was less enthused about the government selling off school playing fields: 'Twenty or 30 years ago I could choose 30 pitches locally to me. A lot of them are not there any more ... they are built on or they are sold.'

Over the past two decades, English football had 'lost faith in ourselves': under a third of Premier League players were English, and 'the balance has tipped too far' away from homegrown talent. It was no longer true that youngsters could reach the first team of the club who had developed them, so Neville proposed a quota, this time a 50-50 split between British and foreign players, which 'would represent what we are as a country in terms of acceptance and making sure we think about international relations, international employment'.

It was also worrying that no elite team was managed by an Englishman, when in past generations Bobby Robson and Terry Venables had both been entrusted with Barcelona. As for the FA board, 'It is a cobweb. Just pull it down.' In spite of everything Gareth Southgate and the England team had done in the weeks before the committee meeting, Neville was keen to remind MPs that a strong World Cup performance could not mask structural issues within English football as a whole.

All the same, as Nick Hornby wrote in one of his pieces for ESPN, it was time to be realistic about England's success in Russia. Perhaps the 'smart and serious' Southgate got lucky, with four wins, and losses to two very good teams in Belgium and Croatia. None of the six nations, moreover, had a population bigger than that of London, and Harry Kane's Golden Boot for the tournament's top scorer was achieved by 'three penalties, one deflection, a header and a tap-in from corners', all in the group stage. Hornby envied the Croatian playmakers who would 'control a game', although he would not have to wait long for Jude Bellingham to emerge as that talismanic figure for England.

Instead, Hornby's key English player at the 2018 tournament was cult hero Harry Maguire, who was – in his capital letters – 'One Of Us, the authentic representative of all the fans who wave flags of St George from Kettering and Coventry and Barnsley.' Once again, players were avatars for something quintessentially English, although even then figures such as Maguire were an anachronism. 'Our fondness for making virtues out of necessities indicates a desire for underdog status even when we're not underdogs,' Hornby wrote of a country whose domestic football teams dominated the annual money leagues. 'We're happier that way.'

Hornby ended his piece with what he believed to be any England manager's goal, 'To make the impossible become routine.' Southgate merely wanted it to be possible at all, but Hornby felt the calibre of the England team should deliver them to the final stages repeatedly. He would see the men and women reach four European finals between them within the next seven years as the FA's investment and the shrewd managerial appointment bore fruit, while British politics was marred by pandemics, parties and the dying embers of the Conservative government.

2022

'AS A NATION, we have too many troughs and not enough peaks.'

Stuart Pearce was referring to the England football team back in 2000, but he could just as easily have been commenting on the country as a whole.

In the epilogue to his book *Answered Prayers*, Duncan Hamilton described the last round of one-man shows Geoff Hurst was performing. He was, once again, 'expected to belt out all the hits' about events from long ago in 1966. The victors had done a similar tour, to public indifference, in the mid-1970s, and even in 2022 at Dudley Town Hall Hurst could barely pull 250 elderly people to a 1,000-seat venue.

The hat-trick scorer had sold his medal and shirt for a combined £240,000, with the latter finding a home in the National Football Museum beside the match ball, which Hamilton said was 'a little misshapen, like a balloon desperate for some air'. Gordon Banks had said that, if England did win the World Cup again, 'they'll stop dusting us down and bringing us out every four years'.

Hamilton concluded that the FA's treatment of those 11 men, whom Banks seemed to compare to an heirloom or the family silver, was a 'scandal'. Those players 'seem so much like the rest of us. They never saw themselves the way we saw them: 11 ordinary immortals.' When Hurst dies, and all 11 immortals are rendered mortal, England will feel, 'with profound regret and a little guilt', that they ought to have celebrated them more, even though their achievement will never die; as the final sentence of Hamilton's book read, they will be remembered as 'winners, shining in their youth'.

Six decades after those 20-somethings triumphed, events of 30 July 1966 have been replayed, dissected and mythologised. Paul Gascoigne for his tragedy and David Beckham for his celebrity have matched Hurst and his hat-trick, and there is a sense of ownership from England supporters for all three men. Is there a same sense for any of the 26 players who travelled to Qatar for the 2022 World Cup, whose allegiance was to their clubs rather than their country? After all, they are global ambassadors for their clubs, who help drive billion-pound TV deals which help fund their lifestyles and equip them for a life of riches which were denied to the team of 1966.

Does it matter more to an international footballer to play in the Champions League or Premier League than at a quadrennial tournament like the European Championship or World Cup?

The starkest reminder of this was when Ben White withdrew from the squad during the tournament. Writing in *The Times*, Henry Winter suggested that White would for ever be known as the man who refused to play for England, 'even if it is totally inexplicable'. As with Jamie Carragher in 2008, it may have been the case that the defender didn't want to travel if there was little chance of getting on to the pitch, but White refused to explain himself beyond citing 'personal reasons'.

The market dictates how much stars like White are paid, with clubs rich in money from sponsorship and commercial activity aside from those TV deals. Jack Grealish, Marcus Rashford, Phil Foden and Bukayo Saka had all come through the ranks of their hometown clubs as teenagers and had played hundreds of first-team games between them by the time the tournament came around. Borussia Dortmund's Jude Bellingham, aged 19, would finish his season as the Bundesliga's best player before following David Beckham, Steve McManaman and Michael Owen as the latest English *galáctico* at Real Madrid.

How many Bellinghams, though, had been lost to the English game in years past? In his book *Fifty Years of Hurt*, Winter wrote a lament for the decline of flair in English football, asking, 'How many skilful kids become fearful and alienated' when others had wanted to break their legs, enduring 'roughhouse tactics and balls launched into the mixer'? Belatedly and in a hugely welcome manner, a combination of the rules on player contact and a need to entertain people had encouraged flair players and made for a quicker game, aside from when it is stopped to review an incident via video.

This drive to increase skill levels came about thanks to the success of Pep Guardiola's Barcelona side, of which Gary Lineker, who scored 48 goals for England, approved and predicted would improve the national team when the young players matured. England stars Foden and Kyle Walker have both been part of the Manchester City team coached by Guardiola.

Far from the rigidity that Trevor Brooking and Glenn Hoddle once complained about, players had far more flexibility in their positions, and they were able to adapt to different shapes in defence, attack and transition. This is precisely what the FA sought to do with the England DNA project, initiated in 2013, to chime with the tactical and coaching developments that ran alongside increasingly technically gifted athletes playing on better pitches alongside and against international talents.

Nor were the players straitjacketed when it came to discussing social issues. They spoke in solidarity with the rights of black people, as they knelt down at the blast of a game's opening whistle. This debate took place in a media environment where clicks and outrage had become currency, and where it was far easier to debate symbols and gestures rather than deal with deep-seated problems with race or autocracies. England were one of a handful of teams who planned to wear a rainbow-coloured armband at the 2022 World Cup to protest the hosts' treatment of LGBT people, but they relented after threats of punitive action on the pitch.

The manager was equally keen to allow the players to express their views, treating them as people rather than automata. 'This had to be a team where we were united on how we saw it,' Gareth Southgate said at the end of 2021, the year of the delayed Euro 2020 tournament, 'and we could send a message to young kids watching that I think the lads maybe didn't realise how powerful that would be going into a tournament because they wanted to concentrate on the football.'

Southgate had told Paul Hayward, for his book on the England football team published just before the World Cup, that the topics he was asked about in one recent press conference included 'human rights Qatar, human rights Saudi Arabia, taking the knee, mental health'. He also acknowledged the economic recession, at the end of 2022, which coincided with the Qatar tournament, 'Life has been difficult for a lot of our people, so we want them to enjoy their football and have a journey with the team that brings some real happiness.'

As Nick Hornby had noted of the 2018 finals, the team's success would be both a piece of good news and a panacea.

Before the European Championship, Southgate had published the famous open letter to the country, which inspired a play by James Graham chronicling the events of the 2018 World Cup and took the England football team to the National Theatre stage. Writing in *The Times* in 2023, Graham compared the manager not to the prime minister, with whom he is usually paired, but to 'the Archbishop of Canterbury or the governor of the Bank of England'; football fans are thus equivalent to worshippers or savers who hang on the word of the man at the top of the tree. Southgate was a man who had been constant in his role while the country had indulged in a period of 'self-flagellation' after leaving the European Union.

To Graham, who has also written about the miners' strikes in Nottingham and parliamentary sessions in the 1970s, Southgate 'recognises himself and those around him as storytellers' burdened by the past, and his team 'seem to represent an idea of ourselves that we like, or miss, or have imagined but aspire to: decency, humility and a sense of good old fair play'.

Referring to those social issues his players were eager to tackle, and not just 'stick to football', it appears to the playwright that Southgate thought his players could be 'liberated in being their true selves' and 'on the same wavelength' as a typical England fan. Such a comparison was never made of Roy Hodgson or any earlier England manager.

The theme of Southgate's letter was the pride in representing England, of how players could start at Barnsley and Sheffield United and, as John Stones and Kyle Walker did, become 'one of the chosen few' to wear the shirt. 'When you go out there, in this shirt,' Southgate wrote in the letter which began with the words 'Dear England', 'you have the opportunity to produce moments that people will remember for ever. You are a part of an experience that lasts in the collective consciousness of our country.' He recalled watching the 1982 World Cup as vividly as royal weddings and the Queen's Silver Jubilee.

In 2021, with some self-deprecation that feels on brand for Southgate, he admitted to being less important than 'the kids and the dogs' at home. He did not wish, however, to be a nagging father to his players when it came to social media use. 'I trust them and know they are mature enough to make their own decisions,' he wrote, echoing his old national team manager Sven-Göran Eriksson's modus operandi of treating players like grown-ups.

He also commended fans who protested the introduction of the European Super League, without judging if it was a good or bad idea himself. England captain Harry Kane, whose employers Tottenham were one of the clubs wishing to break away, was 'proud of the fans for sticking up for what they believe in'. Prince William saw the league as a threat to 'the values of competition and fairness' of the English game, and the Conservatives were moved to fast-track the fan-led review into football, which was to be the responsibility of Tracey Crouch, the former sports minister who appeared in a previous chapter.

The review's focus was on the domestic game, whose top division's 20 clubs turned over £5.15bn in the 2018/19 season, with the next three divisions increasing their revenues to a total of just short of £1bn. England internationals received eyeballs on them from across the world as well as the thousands sat in the stadiums. A generation ago, it was harder to follow the exploits of Gary Lineker and Ray Wilkins, for club and country, because football had far less global reach, and satellite broadcasting had not developed accordingly.

It is incontestable that the TV deals that accompanied the new competitions of the 1990s, such as the Premier League and revamped European Cup, had made footballers more prominent as figures in the public eye, elevating them to the status of musicians or movie stars. David Beckham, who gave his name to a movie, was thus even better known than Diego Maradona. Billions of people could marvel weekly, rather than every four years, at Lionel Messi and Cristiano Ronaldo, in slow motion and via reverse camera angles. This could only benefit young English players, replicating their skills in academies, and go on to help the national team too.

Players were also more liable to be barracked, either in stadiums or via social media accounts. In his letter, Southgate offered advice to fans who might be tempted to racially abuse players. 'You're on the losing side,' he wrote, positing a society that had become 'much more tolerant and understanding' following the headlines that came in the aftermath of the murder of George Floyd, which sparked the Black Lives Matter movement into life. This made FA chairman Greg Clarke's use of the term 'coloured players' in a parliamentary committee session unfortunate and career-ending. Back in 2017, he had referred to accusations of institutional racism within the organisation as 'fluff', but there was no public outcry.

By the middle of the 2010s, David Goldblatt wrote, Afro-Caribbean players had 'found and staked their place in English football as they had done in the wider society', although there was still a scarcity of black managers which was disproportionate to the number of black players, something the FA was trying to change by adopting the Rooney Rule from the NFL. It would interview at least one ethnic minority candidate for every role within the England coaching staff.

Justin Cochrane combined coaching at Brentford with his role with the England team, while Ashley Cole and Chris Powell both gained roles with the national side on top of their own domestic coaching duties. It was an FA initiative launched in 2018, the Elite Coach Placement Programme, that gave Powell a chance to work with England.

Away from the training pitch, music played a role in reshaping how English football was viewed. John Barnes's rap in the middle of the 1990 World Cup song 'World in Motion' helped increase the visibility of black players outside of the pitches and sports pages. In 1996 'Three Lions' had, David Goldblatt wrote, a 'mawkish and sentimental masculinity' that appealed to non-football fans. Sunder Katwala, a writer who heads up the British Future think tank, summarised it as 'an English anthem about how to be at ease with being a middling power' while also harking back to the victory at the 1966 World Cup and Lineker's goals in 1986 and 1990.

By the time it was re-released in a version with sleigh bells to chime with the fact that the Qatar World Cup took place in November and December 2022, 'Three Lions' had become part of what Southgate called the nation's 'collective consciousness', much like the victory it hymned. Even if younger fans had not seen Bobby Charlton 'belting the ball' or could recall Nobby Stiles's victory celebrations, they can be informed about them as well as the other 'oh-so-nears' across the decades. 'I know that was then but it could be again' was the mournful, hopeful line that followed snatches of commentary from tournaments gone by.

The video to 'Vindaloo', a terrace singalong that soundtracked the 1998 World Cup, depicted 'a mongrel nation bound by its love of football, family and food', according to Goldblatt. He noted that, curiously, there had been no official England World Cup song in 2010; in 2006, talkSPORT put together a version of the *Dad's Army* theme song, roping in Geoff Hurst and Martin Peters.

In 2021, for the delayed Euro 2020 tournament, rappers Krept & Konan were deputed to write the official tournament song, 'Olé (We Are England)'. The tune found rhymes for squad members and had a chorus that predicted the team were 'bringing it home … get them a pint'. The pair told the BBC that 'everyone has a different definition of what English is', from council estates to pubs to fish and chips.

Songs like theirs sought to unite the English fanbase, something Southgate had seen fit to do in his time as manager. Whenever England played, Jamie Carragher wrote in 2008, 'You get this strange, largely subdued atmosphere that only comes alive when England score or attack. There's always a slightly sinister edge, too: you know the mood can shift from euphoric to vicious within the space of a few minutes.' Latterly, fans would take to flying paper aeroplanes on to the pitch, having grown accustomed to the functional football that helped England qualify for major tournaments.

Nonetheless, Southgate ended his 'Dear England' letter with a wish for parents and figures of authority to point to his team and commend them for representing England in the best possible manner. Reaching the final of the tournament, and coming a penalty shoot-out away from victory helped his cause.

On top of the quadrennial jamboree which provided entertainment in the final weeks of the year, Tim Minchin's musical adaptation of the Roald Dahl book *Matilda* enjoyed a screen version, while there was also a feature-length version of *Downton Abbey* and another adaptation of *Death on the Nile*, following the one of 1978. Romantic comedy *What's Love Got to Do with It* had a British Asian pair in the lead roles.

Across their years in government since 2010, the Conservatives had been keen to spread the wealth of the UK beyond London. First, George Osborne announced the creation of a Northern Powerhouse, then Boris Johnson made 'levelling up' the UK his key strategy, creating a department led by Michael Gove. The white paper, published in February 2022, promised billions of pounds to speed up broadband, build railway lines, establish freeports, improve high streets and move government departments outside London.

There was also a Community Ownership Fund, which would enable people to own local pubs and football grounds. This sort of measure would 'restore a sense of community, local pride and belonging'. The document boasted of providing funds for 'over 800 new grass pitches and 60 new artificial grass pitches'. Welling United were given over £400,000 to develop their ground 'for community use and future sustainability'. The Labour government closed the fund in January 2025, prioritising other areas of the economy.

Britain withdrew its troops from Afghanistan in 2021, taking their lead, as they had done in 2001, from a decision made by the American president. When Russia launched its assault on Ukraine in February 2022, the UK was still not protected from volatile energy prices, having not invested in storage capacity. As had happened in the 1970s, prices shot up, both at the petrol pump and at home. It also led to the eventual sale of Chelsea because after 20 years of Roman Abramovich's ownership, it was suddenly unsustainable for a Russian to own an English football club.

Outlining the government's agenda, the Queen gave her final speech in May 2022, the year of her Platinum

Jubilee. She began her address with a line about helping to 'ease the cost of living for families', something that had become starker than ever after the Covid-19 pandemic. Aside from a mention of Ukraine, there was no focus on matters abroad, unless you count 'action to prevent dangerous and illegal Channel crossings and tackle the criminal gangs who profit from facilitating them'.

The government sought to prevent public bodies engaging in boycotts that undermined community cohesion, and it would also seek to ban conversion therapy. Most pertinently for this discussion, an independent football regulator was also in the offing, following the fan-led review. This concluded that such a regulator would remove any conflict of interests and 'be accountable to fans, communities, clubs and to parliament', especially because many clubs 'are at a financial precipice'. As well as a shadow board, there was support for a Golden Share where fans could decide matters of 'identified heritage items' such as a club's name or its playing colours.

We have mentioned in an earlier chapter the popularity of footballers becoming immortalised in statues. There is an oddly outsized view towards bronze or stone embodiments of figures, almost as much as there is a clamour to award medals to them while they are alive. Cecil Rhodes's status in Bristol was toppled by activists in 2020 because of the money he reaped from the slave trade, while in London the statue of Winston Churchill was boarded up or guarded to prevent damage to it during public demonstrations. The government also sought to bring in legislation to curb such freedoms of protest, which included making it an offence to climb on to memorials and punishing offenders with fines and prison sentences.

The wretched mini-Budget of September 2022, for which prime minister Liz Truss did not ask assistance from the Office for Budget Responsibility, was mostly reversed, but one clause was not: the end of the cap on bonuses for the sort of banker who had endangered the economy in 2008. Steve Richards wrote in his book *Turning Points* that, in the week following the mini-Budget, '40 per cent of mortgage products had been withdrawn from the UK market'. Rishi Sunak, a Southampton fan, had been a banker with Goldman Sachs and still had a residence in California. It was he who took over from Truss as prime minister, significantly just before England travelled to Qatar to take part in the winter World Cup.

Flexible working patterns following the pandemic meant that fans were able to watch England's games more easily than they could in 2018. Public screenings had to compete with Christmas parties because the tournament had to be moved to the winter to avoid the extreme heat of the summer in Qatar. During the opening ceremony, the BBC aired a discussion between pundits which alluded to the corruption in how the country came to host the competition, the migrant labour used to build the stadiums and its stance on homosexuality.

Given the opposition to non-heteronormative people in Qatar, Southgate told *Pink News* that the England team needed 'to respect a country with a different culture, religion and traditions. But at the same time we have the responsibility and the possibility to shed light on aspects that can be improved.' With gay rights so well advanced in England – the FA spearheaded an annual visibility campaign which encouraged the wearing of rainbow-coloured laces – there was now a focus on trans issues, although much discussion seemed to be reduced to which person could use which bathrooms.

Happily, on the pitch, England won their opening game 6-2 against Iran, whose goalkeeper was withdrawn midway through the first half after a clash of heads, testament to the focus on player welfare. They followed this with a goalless draw against the USA, in front of plenty of empty seats. Those fans who did make the journey to the stadium booed the team at the final whistle.

The final group match was against Wales. England won 3-0, with two goals from Marcus Rashford, one of which came directly from a free kick. Before the player's interventions against Wales, Barney Ronay complained that England were 'rigid … like dutiful pedestrians', reporting once more for *The Guardian*. Rashford had form in being a catalyst for action: during the pandemic, the Manchester United striker had led campaigns for children's literacy and the supplying of school meals, and he also brought out several books. He inspired a wall painting in Manchester too.

Rashford's club form faded but it picked up at the right time before the World Cup. Speaking in a press conference at the tournament, he soberly said, 'You can't expect to go into games and just win because you think you have better players than the other teams.' He added that Southgate had raised the standard of training, which was 'intense', while the manager himself saw a 'different mentality' in this England side. Back in 2018, their ambition had merely been to win one game in the knockout stages; the clock that Greg Dyke had set up that ticked towards 2022 went unmentioned.

Rashford had been one of three players, along with Bukayo Saka and Jadon Sancho, to miss their penalty in the European Championship Final against Italy, a game marred by 6,000 England supporters forcing themselves into the stadium despite not having tickets. The families of Jordan Henderson and Harry Maguire were caught up in the storm. A review into the fiasco, published in December

2021, described it as 'a national shame'; the woman who led the review, Baroness Louise Casey, noted that FA staff had been worried what would happen if England had won the game.

Southgate, she wrote, 'stood up for the values we hold dear', with players who 'cut across so many divides', but they were let down by 'mindless thugs' who were 'the most intoxicated and aggressive crowd' Wembley had hosted. They threw fireworks, bottles and smoke bombs, and they broke down barriers, overpowering the stewards, before they breached both the gates marked for disabled fans and emergency fire doors. Casey wanted 'a national conversation about greater civility and responsibility that goes far beyond what one sport alone can do', and for the stadium to forbid entry to fans under the influence. In 2026, fans need to go through airport security-style gates to enter Wembley.

Out in Qatar, Southgate had used a 3-4-3 formation, which Antonio Conte had developed in a coaching career that had seen him come to England in 2016, first at Chelsea then later at Tottenham. He told Paul Hayward that, unlike in the 1980s when English coaches across the league adopted a uniform style, the rise of foreign coaches had brought 'a brilliant showcase of different coaching techniques, team formations, tactical approaches'.

Whereas Bobby Robson would be 'up the creek' if he tried to experiment, Southgate could trust that his players were intelligent enough to adapt to his ideas. He was also unafraid to drop star players if their conduct was unreasonable, as Raheem Sterling found in 2019 when he took out his frustrations on a team-mate in training.

The pathway to the senior team was improved by the lower age groups winning tournaments. The side that won the under-17 World Cup in 2017 with a 5-2 victory over

Spain included Phil Foden and Marc Guéhi; three months earlier, Dominic Solanke and Fikayo Tomori were among England's under-20 World Cup winners. The FA had ensured all age groups played in the same way, and that there was cohesion between coaches, who swapped ideas and recommended players to one another at the national centre in St George's Park.

England's last-16 game pitted them against Senegal, which ended in another 3-0 victory. The goals came from Jude Bellingham, Harry Kane and Jordan Henderson, with Jordan Pickford keeping a third clean sheet in a row. Sterling was absent having left Qatar to deal with a burglary at his home. Bellingham's performances, meanwhile, suggested he was the heir to Bryan Robson or Steven Gerrard, akin to what Barney Ronay called a 'midfield wildebeest' or, with an inevitable wartime reference, 'the Lancaster bomber'.

Ronay's fellow reporter Sean Ingle summarised the team's ethos as 'fun, accountability, responsibility', prompted again by Southgate 'radically sidestepping out of football's comfort zone' and taking ideas from coaches of other sports. The New Zealand rugby team were a template for the 'good citizens' the coaching staff wanted the England squad to be, which causes one to wonder if there would have been a place for former captains John Terry or Wayne Rooney in the team of 2022.

Performance coach Owen Eastwood, drafted in from the All Blacks, preached the Maori concept of *whakapapa*, where individuals had tribal roles and, in a sporting context, could leave a legacy. Hence, since 2019, England shirts have had an embroidered legacy number corresponding to the player's debut relative to the history of the team; Kieran Trippier was 1222, Harry Maguire 1223. 'Clubs have done that very well and we haven't always managed that,' Southgate said in 2021, adding that players in certain positions in the England team, be they goalkeeper or striker, had a responsibility to leave that role in 'a better place for the next person who comes and recognise what the people before you did'.

Before the quarter-final against France, Southgate revealed that he had had to hire more security outside his house. There was none of the criticism which had been levelled at the three black players in 2021 when Harry Kane missed the chance to equalise with a penalty in the France game, having already scored one earlier in the match. 'We win and lose as a team' was his manager's post-match comment after the 2-1 defeat, recalling Alf Ramsey's reluctance to criticise Norman Hunter after contributing to Poland's goal back in 1973. Nor was there any gnashing of teeth from England supporters, as there had been in 1998 over Beckham, 2006 over Rooney or 2016 over the entire side.

Suitably alarmed at this, Henry Winter began his match report for the *Sunday Times* with 'Where is the fury?' He directed this at the manager and the players, 'one of the best groups ever assembled', rather than the fans, and he called for Southgate to take a seat on the FA board rather than in the dugout. 'The majority of his players are coached at club level by better coaches than Southgate,' he added.

Winter's fellow *Times* writer Jonathan Northcroft looked to the future and the foundations Southgate had constructed. He had refreshed a 'tired' England team by debuting multiple teenagers, just as the FA had wanted, who had won tournaments at youth level. But having earlier lost to Croatia in 2018 and Italy in 2021, England had failed in a knockout game for a third time in four years – although against France they did not go on to lose from a winning position.

This 'serial failure', Winter wrote, cried out for 'ruthlessness' and 'a winner's attitude'. Did the manager, like Ramsey in 1973 against Poland, bring on a substitute too late, after keeping his starting XI unchanged until the 80th minute? And why did the FA's plaintive message of 'it was not to be' not acknowledge the 'cold survey of resources to results'?

In any case, over summer the England women's team had won the Women's European Championship, beating Germany after extra time in a final at Wembley. The game was broadcast on the BBC and covered by newspapers. Sonia Sodha of *The Observer* was there and found there was 'no hint of an edge to the electric atmosphere'. The 'positive and inclusive patriotism' of the England team could amend the 'populist culture wars' of the government, the latter including the debate over the taking of the knee, on which more shortly.

In 2022, England was still two years away from a new broom in government, although the Labour Party was now under new management thanks to the leadership of human rights lawyer Keir Starmer. In a conversation with the *High Performance* podcast in 2023, he compared his position as opposition leader to the England football manager 'where everybody can do your job better than you'.

After the Brexit Party had stood aside before the 2019 general election, the Conservatives won a majority of 80 seats, securing 365 of them and extending Boris Johnson's term as prime minister. Johnson attended the Euro 2020 semi-final in an England shirt, then sent a message on the day of the final, declaring 'football's coming home!' He was also caught on video celebrating Harry Kane's goal against Germany in the tournament.

By the time England went to Qatar, he would no longer be prime minister. Southgate was a man of probity and decorum compared to Johnson, who was given a fixed penalty notice after a party took place in the Downing Street offices when the country was supposed to be under the lockdown rules which he himself imposed. It was the Chris Pincher affair which led to his downfall, as it emerged that Johnson had appointed him as a government whip despite knowing about an incident that had happened in a private members' club. As he had done when questioned about the party, he changed his story when it became clear that his initial line was untenable.

Had the World Cup been held in the summertime, Johnson's July resignation would have occurred right in the middle of the tournament. Criticising the politician in an interview with Sky News after the Euro 2020 final, Gary Neville called him and Southgate 'poles apart. You can be a leader and be a gentleman. You can be ruthless and have empathy and compassion.' In another interview with *The Guardian*, he recalled the daily pandemic briefings given by Johnson and health secretary Matt Hancock.

'They were lying to us,' Neville said. 'People were losing their lives or unable to go to loved ones' funerals. Meanwhile, those ministers were scheming and giving contracts to their mates. A few months in, I realised: "They're proper wrong 'uns, this lot."' Nor was Johnson someone Neville wanted in his Manchester United side, 'All my life, I've been in teams where you look after one another. This lot don't think that way. They're in it for themselves and on the take.'

He added, 'It's damaging our country, our integrity, our international standing. We're a laughing stock. Gone were the days when it was the England team and its supporters who were letting the side down, with the government intervening to legislate against hooliganism or helping nudge the FA into doing the right thing. Even though players like Kyle Walker and James Maddison would be splashed over newspapers for what they were doing in their private lives, it was Hancock who was forced to resign after being caught on camera kissing a woman who was not his wife.

Neville also mentioned how Hancock, who was setting up loans for friends to help supply PPE for hospital workers, had publicly suggested that players take a pay cut. Premier League footballers had, however, already met to organise a fund and defer their wages during the pandemic. Later in 2020, with fans still not allowed back in stadiums, the league's governing body agreed to help lower-league clubs with grants or loans. Neville wondered why Hancock had singled out footballers, inferring that perhaps figures from finance or enterprise could have forsaken their bonuses or taken a drop in their own salary.

Like Gary Lineker and John Barnes before him, Neville has widened his punditry to take in social as well as football issues. The rise of long-form audio media like podcasts and YouTube videos has allowed public figures to comment on anything at all: they might not have done their research, and based their arguments on feeling rather than fact, or put forward jingoistic sentiments. This has ruined the punditry career of Joey Barton, capped once for England, who picked arguments with other public figures who successfully sued him for libel, but it has elevated Neville and Lineker to the type of figures who sometimes lead the news agenda with their pronouncements because of the size of the audience they command.

'I think when most people are tuning in to watch Gary Neville they want to hear about the football and watch the football,' said prime minister Rishi Sunak. 'They don't want to discuss politics.' Neville, who justified his own role as a pundit at the tournament by choosing to 'highlight the issues and challenge them', had mentioned how at the time the Conservative government was 'demonising' nurses, railway workers and emergency service personnel.

As for Lineker, his comment in March 2023 about home secretary Suella Braverman using language about migration that was similar to that used in Nazi Germany led to a days-long media story. Far from the debate being about government policy, it centred on whether *Match of the Day* would or would not be taken off air that weekend. Eventually the broadcast went ahead with no analysis and only abbreviated match highlights.

Such a news story provides one example of how media organisations, in particular on the online side, prioritise clicks and outrage, much as how politicians try to create wedge issues to divide the electorate, or indeed how football pundits adopt controversial positions to drive engagement with the broadcaster paying them for such opinions.

As manager of the national team, Gareth Southgate sought to unite, not divide, which only made the press and politicians less amiable in comparison. The collapse of public trust in members of the latter two professions has lasted several decades, even as both such people use the England football team as a vector for stories and opportunistic opinions, or else stand up in parliament and discuss them.

In the House of Lords, which cannot make laws but can suggest amendments to legislation, Michael Dobbs referred to the people who abused the black England players in 2021 as 'not football supporters. They are sick. They are scum. They are cowards because they hide behind the anonymity of social media.' Baroness Uddin noted that the team served 'to unify a divided nation, which stood with the profoundly thoughtful leadership' of the manager, while another lady, Baroness Jones, brought up the 'dog-whistle comments' that foment racist sentiments.

This surrounded the issue of players kneeling to show there was no room for racism in football. Home secretary Priti Patel called it 'gesture politics', and she did not condemn those who jeered the players. Johnson only commented on it after the abuse in the wake of the final, wishing the abusers would 'crawl back under the rock from which you emerged'. Could the abuse after the final have been lessened with stronger government response to the initial knee-taking, or would there have been racist sentiments expressed regardless of it?

Speaking at Prime Minister's Questions, Johnson spoke of being 'proud' of the team, whom Keir Starmer called 'young, diverse and humble … the very best of modern Britain'. His first question to Johnson was about the initial comments on taking the knee, which the PM refused to directly address, instead mentioning how Ms Patel had also suffered from 'racism and prejudice' and how 'no one should boo the England team'. Starmer retorted that the government line on knee-taking was evidence of 'trying to stoke a culture war. They have realised that they are on the wrong side and now they hope that nobody has noticed.'

Starmer concluded, 'I will tell you the worst kind of gesture politics: putting an England shirt on over a shirt and tie while not condemning those booing is the worst kind of gesture.' And just what is it, Starmer added rhetorically without expecting an answer, 'that this England team symbolises that this Conservative Party is so afraid of?' Tyrone Mings, one of England's black players at Euro 2020, wrote that the government 'don't get to stoke the fire, and then pretend to be disgusted' when racism unleashes itself.

In October 2019 there had been a debate in parliament about racist abuse towards England players in a match against Bulgaria, which led to the game being stopped twice. England could have walked off the pitch near the end of the first half but chose not to do so. 'Enough is enough,' said the minister Nigel Adams, who reserved positive words for Mings, who was making his England debut and was the player who drew attention to the chanting. 'I feel more sorry for those people who feel they have to have those opinions,' he said.

Labour MP Anna Turley echoed Southgate's view that England needed to get its 'own house in order'. She was keen to highlight the paucity of leadership roles held by ethnic minority staff, although she failed to mention the elite coaching programme of which Chris Powell and Ashley Cole were part. 'How can we expect the young people of the future to see a career in football unless the FA looks more like the society it represents?'

As has been outlined across this investigation, the England team and the FA are avatars for the country itself. Thanks to the sport's visibility and expansive coverage, football also brings global political issues into sharp focus, as it did when Saudi Arabia's PIF group bought control of Newcastle United in 2021. Three of England's 2022 World Cup Squad played for the Magpies: Nick Pope, Kieran Trippier and Callum Wilson.

As mentioned, Mike Ashley had been the owner of the club since 2007, having bought it from the property developer Sir John Hall. He loaned the club money, and sold it to a fund which, despite its promises to the contrary, represented a foreign government spearheaded by the Crown Prince Mohammed bin Salman. With the assistance of the British government, who were allies of the Emirate nation and sold them weapons, the Saudi investors were allowed to purchase the club.

Writing in *The Guardian*, David Goldblatt saw contemporary English football as 'political theatre'. He felt the Newcastle deal emphasised the country's 'morally diminished place in the world'. Ashley had run Newcastle 'like a business', one which was 'doomed to mediocrity' when competing with the super-clubs based in London, Manchester and Liverpool. Goldblatt yoked the club's situation with the 'tepid' promises Labour made to bring regeneration to the city, as well as the wealth that came to the financial centres of the country, which were able to serve precisely the kind of Gulf-based rich people who had just bought Newcastle.

'We have allowed the private to trump the public,' Goldblatt concluded, aware that Newcastle had become another English asset to fall into foreign hands. Gareth Southgate, speaking in 2023 after Jordan Henderson had signed for a Saudi Arabian club, asked in response to the player's critics whether people should cease working 'for companies that the Saudis own in London' or refrain from buying Saudi oil. Once again, the England manager was being asked to address geopolitical issues in a way many of his predecessors were not; Sven-Göran Eriksson spoke more about his midfield than about the invasion of Iraq, although the Swede did comment that he was 'never going to be for war'.

In 2021, at a Royal Television Society event, Southgate had spoken of the modern type of management style. 'We've moved from a time in our lives when the boss was the boss,' he said. 'In whatever industry it was, he banged the desk, he shouted, and you jumped. You were fearful of losing your job. It wasn't a culture of "We're all trying to work together to achieve a common goal".'

Key for him was to manage players individually, rather than enforce a uniform style upon them, 'We have a range of lads who don't want any profile off the field, who keep themselves to themselves, to guys that are comfortable and able to speak from a position of strength and are confident in the messaging they give.'

Writing in *The Guardian* during the Euros in July 2021, Shaista Aziz commended England for 'playing for all of us' even though people like her, from a Muslim background, 'know we are a tiptoe away from racism and bigotry'. Sunder Katwala of the British Future think tank, which aims to foster a 'confident and welcoming Britain, inclusive and fair to all', wrote that sporting events that bring millions of people together grow ever more important in a more fragmented society.

'It is harder to find positive recognition of England outside of the sporting sphere,' he noted unhappily. 'Our football team has told the story of who we, the English, are today, while other national voices and institutions have failed to speak for England.'

Katwala's words came from a report titled *Beyond a 90-Minute Nation*. More than any other symbol of Englishness, co-writer Steve Ballinger noted, the England football team can 'embody and promote inclusive English identity, belonging equally to people from all ethnic backgrounds'. When it comes to the St George's Cross, it is the Rashford effect, when England are playing in a tournament, that helps people feel more welcome when they view a symbol which is often misappropriated by bad actors.

In terms of social cohesion, Southgate himself added, things had changed since England reached the Euro 2020 final. 'With the national team, there is more at stake than just the football and we recognise that,' he said. 'The most heartening thing, for me, has been the people who have come up to me celebrating their feeling of connection to the team, who are Muslim, Hindu, Sikh, Afro-Caribbean. The change in that over the last 18 months has been remarkable.

I didn't realise how disconnected we were, particularly from those communities. That's what this group of players has done. They've been relatable.'

Five decades after English footballers would hop on a bus alongside fans who were on the way to watch them go about their work, there was parity of esteem again.

2026

'WHERE IS our perception of ourselves as a nation?' Gareth Southgate asked Paul Hayward in one of the most memorable lines of the latter's biography of the England team. 'It's come from one bloody good day, really.'

That day is now 60 summers ago. The likelihood is that, just as Harold Wilson had been back then, it will be a football-loving Labour prime minister who will travel to North America and Mexico to watch England play in the 2026 World Cup, which returns the tournament to a liberal democracy after Russia and Qatar.

Having appointed a foreign coach in 2001 and 2007, England went for a non-Englishman again in 2024. Perhaps they were inspired by the success of Dutch manager Sarina Wiegman, whose Lionesses took the Euro 2022 trophy at another home tournament.

Thomas Tuchel had won the Champions League with Chelsea and the domestic leagues with Paris Saint-Germain and Bayern Munich.

In March 2025, Sky Sports presented a documentary on the decline of English managers. 'The pool of English coaches at the elite level of the game is pretty shallow,' opened reporter Rob Dorsett, who headed to St George's Park. He talked to Ian Foster, who coached England under-19s to a European Championship win and was in charge of Plymouth Argyle for three months during the 2023/24 season. 'There's a view that English coaches don't have a certain style,' Foster said, who argues that their strength is in adapting to various tactics.

There is also a section of the programme which wonders if foreign ownership of top clubs contributes to a lack of English managers. 'This country has become the new Hollywood,' argued Howard Wilkinson, the man who helped draft the blueprint for English football in the 1990s. 'It's exactly the same as in employment everywhere: if there's a place where being good at your job earns you more money, then you will naturally seek to be in that place.'

An England manager has more control when it comes to picking his squad than a Premier League one, where the players are sourced by a director of football. However, the national team's players are limited in one significant respect, in a way that does not apply to the nationality of the manager. In his match report on England's defeat to France at the 2022 World Cup, Henry Winter had written that appointing a foreign coach like Tuchel would be 'cheating', given the investment into the FA's coaching hub at St George's Park. His colleague Alyson Rudd used the same word, adding that it would be 'rather pathetic' to call on a 'less matey, more demanding' German, although unlike Sven-Göran Eriksson or Fabio Capello at least Tuchel had coached in England.

On his appointment in October 2024, Tuchel applauded the 'one of a kind' character of English players, as well as their 'determination, grit and hunger'. He clearly knows the history of football in the country and what supporters look for in their team, even though English football has adopted the modern advances in technical and tactical ability. In conversation with the media at his first press conference, Tuchel called his new role 'the biggest job in world football' and apologised for having a German passport.

His aim, as per the contract he was given, was to 'put the second star on our shirt' by winning the World Cup. He would also veer away from political discussion, pleading that he be allowed 'to focus on the football'. There was still English representation on the coaching staff in the presence of Anthony Barry, who had worked with Tuchel at Chelsea and Bayern Munich. The head coach, he said, departed from 'the English idea' of formations and structure by focusing on behaviour and positional play.

In a global marketplace, Englishmen had finally ventured outside the British Isles in numbers to play their football. By the time he picked his squad for post-season international fixtures in May 2025, Tuchel was able to look to other leagues, rather than limiting himself to the Premier League. Jude Bellingham and Conor Gallagher were both playing for clubs in Madrid, Harry Kane for Bayern Munich, Jordan Henderson for Ajax and Kyle Walker for AC Milan. Ivan Toney, meanwhile, was out in Saudi Arabia.

Paul Hayward, who covered England between 1996 and 2020, including at six World Cups, summarised the cycle of tournament reporting: '1. We can win it. 2. The spirit has never been better. 3. It's time to deliver. 4. We'll do it for the fans back home. 5. Sorry.' Tuchel sought to turn the fifth point from sorry to starry.

As with Eriksson after the 2005 defeat to Northern Ireland, however, it only took one loss to throw things into disarray. In Tuchel's case, it came in a friendly against Senegal in June 2025, where, after four clean sheets in World Cup qualifiers, an experimental team conceded three times, which once again led to a significant chunk of the crowd booing the team. Morgan Gibbs-White apologised after the game, saying, 'We let the country down. We let the badge down.' The manager told people to 'stay calm ... The World Cup is not next week.'

They were not helped by a close 1-0 victory over Andorra, exhibiting the way England fans still thought they should be winning easily over lesser opposition who put 11 men behind the ball and were more interested in not losing so heavily. As with fans of Premier League clubs, it was as if they were customers demanding results at every level of competition, with newspapers once again amplifying the criticism and not considering the context of the game. It is interesting to note that the home fixture against Andorra was held at Villa Park, with Wembley earmarked for a Coldplay gig which was postponed because of planned strike action on the London Underground (tube works never take place when England play a match at the national stadium).

At the 2024 European Championship, comments by Gary Lineker about England's poor performance against Denmark in a group match were put to captain Harry Kane. He retorted that Lineker and Alan Shearer, in their role as pundits, had 'a responsibility' to offer constructive criticism to instil confidence in the team. For Lineker's part, he thought journalists were 'too scared' and not 'brave enough' to ask the question themselves, which is odd given that in his day they were unafraid to go in two-footed in their criticism and make managers' lives miserable.

England did go on to reach the final of the tournament, losing to Spain. Writing a message before the game, prime minister Keir Starmer, who was a week into his new job, commended the team for their 'graft and hard work ... You have united the country.' The editor of the *New Statesman*, Jason Cowley, compared Starmer to Southgate, 'They are both cautious, pragmatic men from the home counties. Their speech patterns and diction have a certain low-toned flatness. Their lack of radicalism and charisma have been repeatedly noted by their detractors. They both prefer long-term plans and are not easily knocked off course by events or mob rage.'

Like Harold Wilson before him, Starmer is a Labour man who loves his football. In 2023 he told the ArsenalFanTV channel about his Sunday kickabouts, 'The moment you go on the pitch, it doesn't matter what you do for a living, it's just a completely different code. People from all sorts of backgrounds come together to win.' He thought the same about the crowd who watched Arsenal, where fans 'all do different things. You've got all these people, these thousands of people here in this stadium … They come together for one purpose, one common goal: cheer on Arsenal.'

As his biographer Tom Baldwin wrote, 'Football has always normalised what isn't quite normal for Starmer. When he was young, his overbearing father would not allow him to watch TV, so he would avoid school playground conversations about what had been on the night before by kicking a ball around instead.'

The habit of newspapers to frame new developments as 'a blow' to a named member of the cabinet is akin to how injuries are described as similar setbacks for football managers; the frowns or smiles worn by chancellors denote the state of the economy, matching how these managers become avatars for entire clubs. Cutaways during TV coverage of matches show them celebrating or stewing in the dugout, hymned or berated with predictable 'sacked in the morning' chants. This drives a narrative that can be picked up by pundits, who can offer bite-sized views on TikTok or long-form debate on podcasts, which have taken the post-match pub conversation and turned it into club-specific brands. Lineker's Goalhanger production company and his agenda-setting *The Rest Is Football* is the market leader.

These days, the interest in English football has made discussion around it, and the monetisation of it, a career opportunity, both for ex-professionals like Gary Neville and fan pundits like the team at ArsenalFanTV. In *The Game of Our Lives*, David Goldblatt listed the increasingly immense revenues of top-division clubs, which had risen from £170m in 1992/93 to £1.3bn in 2005 to £2.3bn in 2013. Truly, Premier League football was 'the right product at the right time in the right place'. Added to this was the lifting of the ban on online gambling sites whose logos, from the 2026/27 season, will not be placed on the front of club shirts, although they will be present on their sleeves.

The relationship between football and gambling, which grew out of the Gambling Act of 2005, has been hugely lucrative for clubs, replacing sponsorship from cigarette advertising which had been banned in 2003. In the 2024/25 season, *The Telegraph* reported, the 20 Premier League clubs earned £500m from their sponsorship deals, while Sky Bet has enjoyed an association with the Football League since 2013. Stoke City are owned by the Coates family, who also own betting company Bet365, although they must abide by rules limiting their losses, which discourages them from spending their profits on the club in the manner that Jack Walker could do with Blackburn Rovers in the 1990s.

Rather than compiling accumulators for multiple sets of results, gamblers could bet on individual matches and, eventually, place in-play bets on events in those matches, encouraged by pitchside adverts which proliferated during football coverage. In fact, whereas gambling was prohibited on TV advertising across Europe, the UK allowed it, with the message 'When the fun stops, stop' appearing onscreen to discourage addiction. Fans of Chelsea and Norwich City both successfully appealed to their clubs to cancel contracts with online casinos or gambling operators.

Just as politicians could not use insider knowledge to wager the date of a general election, something two Conservative candidates and the party's chief data officer were alleged to have done in 2024, for which they would go on trial, so footballers were forbidden from placing bets on matches, whether the games involved their clubs or not. Among several professionals who were caught doing so, Ivan Toney was found to have gambled on over 200 games, including 13 during the 2017/18 season. In 2023 he was banned from playing for Brentford, although this did not serve to jeopardise his place in the Euro 2024 squad.

Aware that Toney was suffering from an addiction, Gareth Southgate said that it was imperative that the wider football industry acted to rehabilitate him; by not shutting the door on his England career, it would give the striker 'additional motivation ... I like his personality, his belief and the way he goes about his job'. Once again, the manager was treating the player holistically, aware what playing for England meant to the striker. Daniel Sturridge and Kieran Trippier were two other England players who were suspended for betting on matches. The rise of fixed-odds betting terminals and gambling on smartphones made it more likely that people would fall into the kind of addiction from which Toney suffered.

Peter Shilton has written extensively about his own addiction, with two betting companies sending him Christmas hampers thanking him for gambling so much of his money on horse racing. He once lost £20,000 in a single day. 'Not only was there an adrenaline rush of excitement when I won,' he wrote in the *Daily Mail*, 'but also when I lost, because there was the thrill of thinking

I would then find a winner to recoup the losses.' Having tackled his habit, Shilton now helps others tackle theirs.

A review into the Gambling Act was published by the government in 2023, which approved of the ruling that restricted the broadcast of adverts that included the presence of notable footballers, given that it could entice children to gamble. Then there was Football Index, a so-called betting platform that was actually akin to a pyramid scheme which let gamblers place three-year bets that tracked how players performed over a period of years; it ran high-profile TV adverts and sponsored Nottingham Forest, before it went bust in 2021.

The platform was the topic of a debate in April 2024, with MP Liz Twist saying that victims, who lost a total of £134m, 'were misled and instead believed themselves to be investors taking risks, hedging funds and building a portfolio, something that would be normal for those who engage in the stock market'. A combination of a failure of regulation, the enticement of vast sums of money and a passion for football, at a time when access to gambling was available on a phone in one's pocket, contributed to a wretched situation, albeit one which did not involve any of the game's key stakeholders.

A decade on from the publication of David Goldblatt's book *The Game of Our Lives*, the sums of money in football have become even more gargantuan. TV deals are larger than ever before, with a £6.7bn four-year deal agreed in 2023, up from a three-year £5bn one. For a few seasons Amazon Prime had screened several matchweeks per season, encouraging people to sign up to its service which predominantly allowed people to speed up the delivery of products they had ordered from its vast store. Meanwhile, the FA celebrated a much smaller four-year TV deal to screen the FA Cup, with 'more games available than ever before' thanks to fewer of them kicking off at 3pm on Saturday.

In its 2023/24 accounts, the FA boasted a profit of £64m from a turnover of £551m, a £70m improvement on the previous year. About £170m was invested back into English football, including the delivery of grass pitches across the country. The annual report was introduced by Debbie Hewitt, the FA chair, who noted how Britain and Ireland would be the hosts of Euro 2028, which would 'showcase the positive role that football can play in bringing communities together'. Hewitt added that the FA had removed the need for FA Cup replays in some rounds to ease the burden on 'fixture congestion and player welfare', all the better to help the international team too.

The England men's team had been ranked in the top five of the FIFA rankings since October 2018, greatly helped by the training provided at St George's Park. There was also the introduction of a new system for signing players from abroad that would incentivise clubs to 'deliver playing opportunities' for English players. These foreign signings would have to make a so-called Elite Significant Contribution to their new club, who would in turn enjoy four rather than two such players the more they played homegrown squad members.

FA chief executive Mark Bullingham mentioned the 100 kitchens that have been installed or refurbished for grassroots clubs, a key reminder that the FA does not just look after the teams and the trophies. Emirates and Nike were on board as key partners, and the organisation also had a charity fundraising drive for the Alzheimer's Society. Alongside Taylor Swift's concert residency and the Champions League Final in 2024, Wembley hosted a wrestling event for the second successive year, although by this time American football fixtures had moved to Tottenham's new stadium.

Goldblatt concluded his book with a thought about the England team. He argued that it had represented 'an unruly exercise in nation-building' and was 'an experimental imagined community of the protean English nation'. Perhaps the idea of the football team as a symbol of a nation, with all its imperfections, makes it a national discussion point akin to a branch of the armed forces or the church. James Graham's comparison between the Archbishop of Canterbury and the England manager might be accurate after all.

The team also brings together players of different heritages but who all play under the same banner. The 2022 World Cup squad contained Bukayo Saka, whose parents are both Nigerian, and Jamaica-born Raheem Sterling, while Jack Grealish and Declan Rice picked England over the Republic of Ireland, where their grandparents were from. For every player they have gained in this way, however, England have also lost out on the opportunity to call up several other players.

In 2017, Wilfried Zaha declared for Côte d'Ivoire, his country of birth, after coming through the age groups for England and playing two games for the senior team. Stuttgart-born Jamal Musiala chose to sign professional terms with Bayern Munich after being developed as a younger teenager by Chelsea; he has become a mainstay of the German national side. Cameron Carter-Vickers is one of many Europeans to have declared for the USA.

Conversely, after coming through to play for Watford's first team, Amin Nabizada joined up with England's under-18s a year after training with the Afghan national side; he can still represent both nations and, if given the chance to do so, will declare his allegiance to the benefit of his career.

Speaking to *The Times* in 2019, former head of elite development Dan Ashworth said 55 of 75 players under the age of 15 who were on the FA's radar were eligible to play for more than one country. 'We cannot be arrogant enough to assume that if you're living in England you automatically want to play for England over any other country,' he added, in spite of the attractive presence of St George's Park as a hub and the recent success of the age group teams in international tournaments.

The national side, wrote Goldblatt, was 'one of the very few civic institutions where Englishness was publicly on display' and around which one could build 'a contemporary sense of national identity'. The women's team, known as the Lionesses, have contributed to this, not least by reaching three consecutive tournament finals between 2022 and 2025, winning two European Championships and losing to Spain in the 2023 World Cup Final.

It did not seem to be a coincidence that, when Chloe Kelly gave a post-match interview after England beat Spain on penalties to win Euro 2025, she spoke of being 'proud to be English'. The side had branded themselves as 'proper English' throughout the championships, with striker Alessia Russo defining it as being 'very dominant on the ball' and fighting as a team 'until we can't run any more'. In a reminder of Terry Butcher's bloodied shirt in 1989, goalkeeper Hannah Hampton had to stem the bleeding from her nose during the quarter-final shootout, coincidentally against the same nation, Sweden.

In 1993 the FA took control of women's football in England, both the domestic game and the national team. In the 1980s it had been run by a group of volunteers under the banner the Women's FA, which was abolished after financial difficulties. A decade later, the movie *Bend It Like Beckham* made women's football more visible, and England's games at the 2005 Women's European Championship, in stadiums exclusively in the north-west of the country, were broadcast live on the BBC.

A report from what was then the Culture, Media and Sport select committee in July 2006 outlined the state of play in the women's game. It called on the lifting of the restrictions on mixed football, where boys and girls could not play together after the age of 11, which hindered girls from continuing to participate at all in the sport after primary school. They also suggested women's football 'carve a niche for itself and establish its own territory where it can shine and attract support'. This was at a time when Manchester United paused their women's team, in 2005, while Arsenal galloped away with several league titles, remaining undefeated four years in a row.

The FA introduced the Women's Super League in 2011, which was semi-professional until 2018, and a women's side represented Great Britain at the 2012 Olympics, beating Brazil 1-0 at Wembley with a starting XI of ten Englishwomen and a single Scot. Many of those English players had been part of the side that lost 6-2 to Germany in the Euro 2009 final under manager Hope Powell. Also in 2012, the FA spearheaded a programme for girls' football, which included a commercial strategy, and from 2015 the Women's FA Cup Final became an annual event at the national stadium. The England women's team, meanwhile, played their first game at Wembley in 2013 and have drawn larger crowds there in the ensuing decade.

The PR has not been entirely positive, however. In 2017, striker Eniola Aluko spoke out in public against the racial treatment and bullying of former England manager Mark Sampson, who was in charge during the run to the semi-finals of the 2015 World Cup. More happily, high-profile sponsorship deals, including with Marks &

Spencer, made individual Lionesses visible away from the pitch, while the appointment of former England men's international Phil Neville, who led the side to the semi-finals of the 2019 World Cup, also increased the team's profile. The defeat against the USA included a sending-off, a missed penalty and a goal ruled out for offside, which made for exciting TV, if also for inevitable disappointment.

In the press conference before the final of the 2022 Women's European Championship, the climax of a tournament hosted in England, captain Leah Williamson said, 'For every success we make, for every change of judgement or perception or the opening of the eyes of somebody who will now view women as somebody with the potential to be the equal of her male counterpart, that can create change in society.'

Williamson had grown up looking up to Kelly Smith, Rachel Yankey and Faye White, who in turn passed the baton to the 2022 squad. It is interesting to note that Mary Earps and Jill Scott inspired news coverage after using swear words on the pitch, although far more often it was their football that did most of the talking.

After England won the final thanks to an extra-time goal by Chloe Kelly – 'Lionesses bring it home' was the splash headline of *The Times* – *Guardian* journalist Suzy Wrack noted the 'reciprocal relationship' of women's football in England, which was 'decades, if not a century' behind the men's game. Her colleague Jonathan Liew warned against a repeat of what happened to men's football in 1992, where eyeballs led to revenue and, in turn, to some destructive aspects of the game including 'immorality, inequality and exploitation'. There was also the paradox of female players at Arsenal and Manchester City benefitting from the sponsorship deals with, respectively, Rwanda and Abu Dhabi.

In *The Times*, Henry Winter warned that the achievements of the Lionesses should not be compared to the men's team 'as a stick to beat' them with for their lack of success. Nor did he wish for Ellen White's goalscoring prowess to be bracketed with that of Wayne Rooney. Once again, Winter's concern was for an English coach to replicate Wiegman's achievements, and for the knowledge to be shared equally between the men's and women's teams at international meet-ups.

Such exchanges happened at St George's Park, where the talent pathway from youth to senior football was being facilitated as part of the FA's Blueprint for Success that would build on the England DNA that ran through the pathways for both men and women. The document included an ambition to give young schoolgirls the same access to football as boys.

Unconsciously paraphrasing the select committee report of 2006, Liew admired how the Lionesses had 'managed to carve out its own vision of what football can be … Many of the England team are openly in same-sex relationships and nobody really cares.' Former player Karen Carney, who would compete on *Strictly Come Dancing* in 2025, posited that the country could build on the team's legacy, starting with allowing more girls to play football in PE lessons. Ian Wright echoed this after the victory in the final, demanding that interested parties like the FA and Premier League make it more accessible for girls to watch games both in person and on TV.

Carney led a review on behalf of the government into women's football, publishing her findings in July 2023 in a 128-page report. By this point the FA had given control of the Super League to a private company, which would raise the standard of the game both by increasing investment from sponsors and broadcasters, and by growing the fanbase; this, it was hoped, would feed into the national team just as the Premier League was meant to do in 1992.

As at the time of writing this book, however, there are issues within the domestic game, including a pipeline problem with homegrown talent, where there are not 'enough players who can readily progress into first team football'. To compensate for this, in an inverse of what Greg Dyke proposed in 2014, the English game should welcome more talent from abroad and thus bring with them more of the desired attention and sponsorship.

There was, however, an issue over English players 'left to sit on the benches of top-tier teams to fulfil their homegrown player requirements', which were a minimum of eight per team. Such a quota had its pros and cons, although there was also the opportunity for women to be registered to two clubs in a season, something which benefitted Michelle Agyemang, one of the breakout stars of the 2025 Women's European Championship.

In common with the modern concern for the mind as well as the body, Carney had spoken about the depression she suffered during her playing career. She recommended mandatory performance psychologists, as well as increased maternity provision and post-football career support. In common with government pronouncements about being 'world-beating', the review wanted the English game to be 'best in class in terms of player care and support' and, equally, called for 'a best in class matchday experience and broadcast product'. Perhaps the English game would 'set the standards for women's professional sport globally'.

Interestingly, when it comes to broadcasting, Carney saw 'an obvious gap' for women's football at 3pm on a Saturday, when no men's football is allowed to be shown live so as not to impinge upon live attendance figures; Sunday at noon was agreed, with Sky broadcasting the majority of games. This replaced the previously common time of 2pm on that day, which often clashed with Premier League coverage. Several games across the season, especially local derby games, take place at the men's home ground at affordable, family-friendly prices.

The more attractive the game looks, at domestic and international levels, the greater the retention of fans, players and coaches; the precedent was the way in which the Premier League changed how football was looked upon in the 1990s. Instead of Paul Gascoigne's tears set to the music of Puccini in a gallant semi-final defeat, it would be two tournament wins that would propel investment into the women's game in England. It may well be that in 2027 the Lionesses triumph at the World Cup in Brazil, but an improvement on the men's team's dreadful exit at the group stages in 2014 would be a useful start.

For all the good work the Lionesses have done to unite the country when they play in those major tournaments, according to Jamie Carragher in his 2008 autobiography, England is 'divided, not only in terms of prosperity but by different regional outlooks. For some of us, civic pride overpowers nationality.' The importance of metro mayors in recent years, who have been given powers over their local areas from Teesside to the West Midlands, builds on this.

Andy Burnham, mayor of Greater Manchester, places importance on redeveloping Old Trafford to match the Etihad Campus which Manchester City's owners built around the existing Commonwealth Games stadium. 'The more ambitious the club is, the better it is for us,' Burnham said, 'because then the benefits will come out to our residents for decades to come.'

The new Old Trafford would need government funding to improve transport links, something that was already strong when the Olympic Stadium was built in

Stratford. Football, as Burnham put it, can 'rebalance the rewards of growth' to the north of England and lead to the construction of new homes and infrastructure, something that chimed with how successive governments wanted to spread the country's affluence outside its southern cities.

This was especially crucial given the difficulties surrounding the development of the HS2 rail link, which incurred increased costs for compensating, or avoiding inconvenience to, people who lived on the proposed route, leading to an abandonment of the leg that took trains from Birmingham to Manchester and Leeds.

It is much harder to improve transport links and infrastructure than to turn around the fortunes of an England football team, although the challenges of winning international competitions pose a difficulty for managers, who receive much wider criticism when it goes wrong. Governments can, as we have learned, step in to tilt the national game in the right direction, and in March 2024 the Conservatives introduced the Football Governance bill, which would lead to the inception of an independent football regulator.

The England team may be at the top of the pyramid, but the country's national game, stewarded by the FA, relies on strong, nourished roots. One of the pillars of the legislation was to protect the cultural heritage of clubs that develop players who represent the national team. Speaking in 2023 after the publication of the white paper that resulted from the fan-led review, minister Stuart Andrew became the latest politician to justify government intervention into the national game. 'The industry has been given more than ample opportunity to reform itself and has repeatedly failed to do so,' he said. 'Independent regulation for football will make the game more sustainable, and mean fewer fans and communities have their clubs put at risk.'

2026

The England manager, however, was sceptical. 'It's another VAR waiting to happen,' Gareth Southgate said; just as how video assistant referees offered another opinion on the decisions of an on-pitch ref, so a regulator would become another layer of bureaucracy in judging the fitness of owners of a football club. After all, the FA had been slow to adopt recommendations from the select committee report in 2011, and before that it had taken two decades to bring in banning orders to prevent overseas travel and stamp out hooliganism at the turn of the millennium.

Running a club properly these days means adhering to the Profit & Sustainability Rules that cap losses over a three-year period at £105m, although accounting tricks could initially help spread transfer fees over several years via amortisation. This would, in part, stop clubs from spending vast amounts of money buying foreign talent and nudge them into bringing through their own players, which would be useful for the national side. Following the example set by Bukayo Saka, Marcus Rashford and Phil Foden, Myles Lewis-Skelly at Arsenal, Kobbie Mainoo at Manchester United and Curtis Jones at Liverpool have all emerged as regulars for their clubs, which have put them in contention to play at the World Cup in 2026.

Lewis-Skelly's rise mimics that of Marcus Rashford a decade before him, including the presence of a strong maternal figure in Marcia Lewis. Lewis is the woman behind No1Fan.club, which supports parents with advice as their children rise through the youth ranks of their club and into the professional game. As she told *The Guardian* in June 2025, it was important for her to keep her England international son, who scored on his debut, grounded. 'You've still got your chores to do. You still need to empty the dishwasher, tidy your room,' she said.

It is likely that, in the lead-up to the tournament, a select group of commentators and pundits will be on the lookout for wedge issues to create debate that drives a narrative away from formations and player selection. During Euro 2024 it concerned the colour of the England flag stitched discreetly on to the back of the shirt. The leaders of both major political parties were critical of the decision by Nike to add blues and purples to the design, even though it looked back to the training kit worn by the 1966 squad. Prime minister Rishi Sunak thought nobody should 'mess with' a flag which was 'a source of pride, identity [and] who we are'.

Another politician who raised the issue of the flag on the shirt was, predictably, Reform UK leader Nigel Farage, who became the member for Clacton in July 2024. He had hosted a regular show on GB News since its launch three years beforehand, which brought shock-jock polemic-style broadcasting to the screen. Over his long career in politics, Farage has been very attuned to anything over which he could make political capital. It could be refugees crossing the English Channel in small boats, the closure of his bank account with Coutts or the toppling of statues of men who profited from the slave trade. Farage is for ever ready with a comment for a TV debate show on his own channel or one with far greater viewership.

In 2023, Farage had appeared as a contestant on *I'm a Celebrity …* to direct eyeballs towards him and his new party, Reform UK, which encouraged people to 'join the revolt' against the staid political system. He recruited Rupert Lowe to stand as MP for Great Yarmouth, a seat he won before being ejected from the party the following year.

Lowe was a familiar figure to football fans. He had initially helped with the process to find Southampton a new ground and then became chairman. Lowe also sat on the FA board, and in 2004 he had proposed, in a personal intervention, that the association pass responsibility for several aspects of how it runs English football to the leagues; the following year, Lowe incurred the ire of Southampton fans after they were relegated from the Premier League, and in 2009 he was back at the club when they called in the administrators.

In a *Guardian* interview in 2003, in which journalist Jim White described him as 'an outsider trying to bring a bit of order and sense to the unreal world of football', Lowe said that a football club was 'like any other business. Its purpose is to make a profit.' Yet, thanks to clubs overreaching with their expenditure, football mimicked society in running 'an economy based on liquidity not reality ... The structure of football has been weakened.' For this, Lowe blamed the fans, who 'have encouraged their board to go and spend money they haven't got'.

Speaking in parliament in a debate about the introduction of a football regulator, Lowe advised against bringing in checks and balances, especially on one of Britain's few 'success stories ... The Premier League projects unrivalled soft power.' He felt that regulation 'would deter foreign investment and add bureaucracy'.

Predictably, Farage railed against Thomas Tuchel's appointment as England manager. He justified his disappointment by saying there had been 'a resurgence in a sense of what it means to be English in an unashamed way'. Reform UK were keen to capture this spirit, leeching support away from the Conservative Party in the type of towns which had voted for them in 2019 after Farage's outfit of the time, the short-lived Brexit Party, entered a pact not to contest any seats.

Reform UK's appeal to English patriotism placed them in dangerous company: Stephen Yaxley-Lennon, a former football hooligan who calls himself Tommy Robinson, founded the English Defence League, which was hostile towards the Islamic religion and its followers. In 2020 he was banned from attending all England games after being caught on film punching a fellow fan.

Such prejudice existed in the same country where openly queer women Billie Eilish and Chappell Roan could top the UK charts, as they respectively did with 'Guess' and 'The Subway' in 2024 and 2025, and where a Muslim player, Tottenham's Djed Spence, could make his England debut in September 2025. By this time, six per cent of the UK shared his faith, so once again the football team looked like its wider population.

And what is Englishness anyway but a slippery and elusive concept which can be bent into shape by those wishing to define it for themselves? Writing in *The Times* in 2024, Scottish-born Hugo Rifkind, son of former Conservative home secretary Malcolm Rifkind, thought that Scotland, Wales and Northern Ireland 'have something to define themselves against'. Conversely, England is a country 'without real national dress, with no parliament, with a new accent every five miles and with a head of state shared with the neighbours and also with Papua New Guinea'.

His colleague David Aaronovitch commented during the Lionesses' run to victory that England as a country was 'unable to progress', doomed to keep up the old rivalry with Germany and standing only for 'sports teams and Shakespeare'. Conservative MP Robert Jenrick summarised Englishness as roast dinner, literature and landscapes.

The further away we are from the Victorian era, David Goldblatt noted of the time of amateurism and fair play, as well as the codification of football's rules, 'the more football has kept those notions imaginatively alive'. In a secular world where Christianity is far less popular than it was even a generation ago, football provides a conduit 'for collective energies, identities and shared meanings'. Over and above any domestic club, the England football team perhaps provides the strongest form of these.

By entering the qualification stages for the World Cup every four years, England hope to pit their own identity against those of other nations, albeit through the medium of a rules-based game that involves putting a football in a net. To do so, they invest in developing homegrown coaches or else reap the dividends of foreign-born coaches plying their trade in England.

If every player is fit to start, the team that plays at the 2026 World Cup will have plenty of world-class talent who, in the past few years, have tested themselves against the best players in Europe on a monthly basis. The global brand of the Premier League might have led to far fewer Englishmen playing in the top division, but these footballers are far more aware of their international opponents than in the days where it was harder to scout and analyse the likes of Pelé and Diego Maradona.

Mercurial managers can still make a difference, much as how Alf Ramsey and Bobby Robson could galvanise their teams. Thomas Tuchel has been hired in the absence of any better English candidate, and it will be proven to be the correct appointment if he goes beyond Gareth Southgate in leading the side to a World Cup Final victory. Unlike Southgate, however, he has not been given the role to set the long-term culture or engage with domestic politics. He has not uprooted his family from Germany, given that his contract expires in the summer of 2026, and he confessed that he would only sing 'God Save the King' once he has been able to 'earn the right' to do so.

England's key playmaker Jude Bellingham plays in Madrid, so he is far removed from the country's politics as he challenges himself in La Liga. In spite of his astonishing goal in the last minute of the Euro 2024 game against Slovakia, he felt he was made a scapegoat for the team's defeat to Spain in the final. This came at the end of a tournament where he learned that English journalists had visited members of his family without telling him first. 'That's something I kept to myself,' he said, adding, 'I don't think that's fair. I think that crosses the line of respect.' Bobby Robson and Graham Taylor would sympathise with the young player.

Throughout this book, I have tried to compare England as a nation with its football team. There were moments when I thought that certain comparisons were too facile or tenuous, but I believe I have summarised how football has been a political focus for each governmental administration. Bids to host the 2006 and 2018 World Cups were ambitious projects which ultimately failed, and the role of the Football Association has occupied several sports ministers as the FA moved away from its amateur ethos to a more professional group of executives in charge of a vast budget in a commercially driven environment. It is to their credit that the FA's annual turnover is now over £500m.

The England team's dozen games a year provide a united focus for the country which is otherwise split into tribes, be it Manchester City or FC United of Manchester, Green Party or Reform UK. Paul Gascoigne, David Beckham and Wayne Rooney still create news in their 40s and 50s because people remember the exploits of their 20s and 30s. Their narratives are more involving than that of a politician, who has often come up anonymously through research departments where they have learned how to become electable. Their job has been summarised as honest opportunism, exploiting division and convincing the electorate to lend them their vote so that they can put in place the kind of policies that improve their lives and, more significantly, benefit the party's donors and financial supporters.

These politicians cannot, however, affect their mood in the way Jude Bellingham's acrobatic goalscoring or Jordan Pickford's shot-stopping can do. Nobody has written a modern 'Three Lions'-type anthem about the Labour Party. Few listeners to a political speech punch the air, and comparatively fewer people are engaged in local elections than in a World Cup qualifying game. The membership of political parties has cratered in the years since England won the tournament, with a more individualistic nation focusing less on improvements in society than their own personal advancement.

On top of this, branding and advertising has played its part in politics, with slogans like Take Back Control often replacing detailed policy to better leave an impression on voters. The 1970 election, which turned party leaders into pseudo-celebrities, was a harbinger of the current age of mononyms like Boris, Nigel and Keir. Footballers and politicians are found in the front sections of newspapers and in neighbouring videos in a typical social media feed. Reform UK even sold a football shirt at their 2025 party conference.

The England team continues to be feted and celebrated as one of few tangible national symbols. Even if an English person only tunes in to watch important matches, and even then only curiously and without any knowledge of the latest talismanic figure in the dugout or on the pitch, the option is there for them to show the pride in their nation, and wave a St George's flag, in a way it is often difficult to do politically.

As Bobby Robson noted in 1990, success at a World Cup can change how a nation feels about itself. In his time as manager, the narrative around England supporters was dominated by hooliganism and violence. The threatening behaviour outside Wembley Stadium before the Euro 2020 final, and the social media abuse of players who committed the crime of missing a penalty for their country was a reminder of those bad days and of how football can throw light on how elements of society behave. Political figures can use the popularity of the game to offer change, all the more so because TV pictures make fans' actions more apparent than the shady machinations of business figures or bankers.

The energy shortages of the 1970s, clashes with mineworkers in the 1980s and foreign warfare of the 2000s affected people's lives more than Kevin Keegan or Jeff Astle missing key chances or Wayne Rooney losing his cool. Yet those footballing moments brought together millions of English people in a common and politically neutral cause. Today's international player rarely declares his allegiances to a political party; he is more likely to appear in a video with Prince William talking about mental health, or to run his own foundation to support worthy causes.

Politicians, however, need no invitation to support the England team. It seemed so out of character for the Conservative Party to depart from the squad's wish to take a knee during Euro 2020, and then to oppose Nike's tampering with the colour of the St George's Cross on the back of the England shirt at Euro 2024. This is part of a modern trend of finding symbols over which to argue rather than addressing the root causes of race or patriotism. Gareth Southgate was commended for following his players in addressing social issues, and he was turned into a leading man on the London stage for his efforts.

The team that won the 1966 World Cup, and the manager who inspired Duncan Hamilton's book *Answered Prayers* are part of the national story much as Harold Wilson, Margaret Thatcher and Tony Blair are. Their victory on what Southgate called 'one bloody good day' left a legacy that cannot be repealed in the manner of English law passed by a government.

It is less likely that someone will attempt to topple the statue of Bobby Moore outside Wembley Stadium than interfere with those of politicians like Thatcher. It is hard to conceive that Blair will inspire one, although Paul Gascoigne and David Beckham might. Regardless of any physical representation of them, the folk tales from the 1990 or 2002 World Cups in which the pair respectively starred will be told over and over again; this book and dozens of others are guilty of perpetuating this.

Acknowledgements

THE IDEA for this book came to me on a train into London, which goes past Wembley Stadium. If I looked at the England team's performance during every World Cup qualifying period or tournament, would I be able to map it on to how the country was being governed? Could Harold Wilson and his chancellor Denis Healey imitate or depart from Alf Ramsey's taciturn approach to managing a football team? Would Tony Blair match Sven-Göran Eriksson for charisma, or Glenn Hoddle for revolutionising his tactical approach to his job? How would I manage when comparing Gareth Southgate to the prime ministers he outlasted?

The book became less of an exercise of this type than an attempt to lay out the evidence, using dozens of journalistic sources and player memoirs, and prompt some conclusions in you, the reader. It was interesting to read back over Hansard, where politicians' words are written down as a political record, and see common through-lines between eras, especially over attitudes towards the FA. In much the same way, it was fascinating to compare England managers and players over the last half-century, discovering how the latter group balanced their club obligations with striving for international success.

I am indebted to books by Henry Winter and Paul Hayward, respectively *Fifty Years of Hurt* and *England Football: The Biography*, as well as David Goldblatt's *The*

ACKNOWLEDGEMENTS

Game of Our Lives. Thanks go once again to Jane Camillin at Pitch for green-lighting the book in a World Cup year, thanks to Gareth Davis and Andrea Dunn for spotting a handful of errors in the manuscript, and to Duncan Olner for designing an eye-catching cover. Thank you to my partner Vanessa for her continued support in my literary ventures. She obtained her British citizenship just before I embarked on this book, and she shared my joy when England's excellent Lionesses retained the Women's European Championship in 2025.

My half-siblings Jacob, Joseph and Lily-Harper will likely be watching the 2026 World Cup from New York City. Born to a French mum and an English dad, they will possess three allegiances to teams in the tournament, in that very modern manner where globalisation has created porous ideas of national identity. Perhaps they will be attracted by the white shirts with three lions on it, as well as the stories alluded to in the song 'Three Lions', as much as they will by the English attacking talent on display.

Our nephew Hugo, son of my brother Richard and his wife Alice, has no such issues: he is English through and through, although he will not remember any of his first World Cup given that he will only be two years old, just as I had been in 1990. Luckily, through documentaries, books and the song 'World in Motion', I am up to speed on England's performance in Italy, with those two extra-time victories and a penalty shoot-out defeat. I have since watched, as you too might have done, repeated failures to emulate the 1966 side, although this book has taught me to respect and admire those defeats, and to celebrate the players who represented their country across the decades.

In a volatile political landscape where England is riven with factions and vested interests, and where 18 months into their time in charge a Labour government is finding it far harder to lead the country in 2026 than the equivalent new team did in 1999, a book like this can act as nostalgia for how things were and as an impetus to act on how things are. The current England side are greatly different to their predecessors but they share the same goal: winning the most important international tournament in order to bring joy to those who share in victory and to make them forget about the sort of troubles in society that politics wishes to alleviate.

Whatever happens over the summer, and in the 2027 Women's World Cup in Brazil, there will be new memories made and new stories told, adding to the ones in this book which have served to enrich the tale the nation tells of itself.

Bibliography

Adams, T., *Sober* (London: Simon & Schuster, 2017)

Beckham, D., *My Side* (London: CollinsWillow, 2003)

Bowles, S., *The Autobiography* (London: Orion, 2004)

Brooking, T., *Trevor Brooking* (Manchester: Granada, 1982)

Butcher, T., *Both Sides of the Border* (London: Weidenfeld & Nicolson, 1987)

Calvin, M., *No Hunger in Paradise: The Players, The Journey, The Dream* (London: Arrow, 2017)

Campbell, A., *The Alastair Campbell Diaries: Volume One, Prelude to Power 1994–1997* (London: Random House, 2010)

Carragher, J., *Carra* (London: Corgi, 2008)

Charlton, B., *My England Years* (London: Headline, 2008)

Charlton, J., *The Autobiography* (London: Corgi, 1996)

Croker, T., *The First Voice You Will Hear Is...* (London: Collins Willow, 1987)

Dale, I. (ed.), *The Prime Ministers: 55 Leaders, 55 Authors, 300 Years of History* (London: Hodder & Stoughton, 2020)

Dein, D., *Calling the Shots: How to Win in Football and Life* (London: Constable, 2022)

Downie, A., *The Greatest Show On Earth: The Inside Story of the Legendary 1970 World Cup* (London: Arena Sport, 2021)

Dyer, K., *Old Too Soon, Smart Too Late* (London: Headline, 2018)

Edworthy, N., *The Second Most Important Job in the Country* (London: Virgin, 1999)

Eriksson, S-G., *Sven: My Story* (London: Headline, 2013)

Evans, C., *Don Revie: The Biography* (London: Bloomsbury, 2021)

Evans, T., *Two Tribes: Liverpool, Everton and a City on the Brink* (London: Bantam Press, 2018)

Ferdinand, R., *#2Sides* (London: Blink, 2014)

Ferguson, A., *Managing My Life: My Autobiography* (London: Hodder and Stoughton, 1999)

Francis, T., *One in a Million* (Chichester: Pitch, 2019)

Fynn, A., & Guest, L., *The Secret Life of Football* (London: Queen Anne Press, 1989)

Gerrard, S., *My Story* (London: Michael Joseph, 2015)

Glanville, B., *The Story of the World Cup* (London: Faber & Faber, 1997)

Glanville, B., *England Managers: The Toughest Job in Football* (London: Headline, 2007)

Goldblatt, D., *The Game of Our Lives* (London: Penguin, 2014)

Goldblatt, D., *The Ball Is Round: A Global History of Football* (London: Penguin, 2006)

Hamilton, D., *Answered Prayers: England and the 1966 World Cup* (London: Riverrun, 2023)

Hardman, I., *Fighting for Life: The Twelve Battles that Made Our NHS, and the Struggle for Its Future* (London: Penguin, 2023)

Hayward, P., *England Football: The Biography, The Story of the Three Lions 1872–2022* (London: Simon & Schuster, 2022)

BIBLIOGRAPHY

Heskey, E., *Even Heskey Scored* (Chichester: Pitch, 2019)

Hoddle, G., with Davies, D., *My 1998 World Cup Story* (London: André Deutsch, 1998)

Hoddle, G., *Playmaker* (London: Harper Collins, 2021)

Hopcraft, A., *The Football Man: People and Passions in Soccer* (London: Collins, 1968)

Lansdown, H., & Spillius, A. (eds.), *Saturday's Boys: The Football Experience* (London: Willow Books, 1990)

Lineker, G., & Baker, D., *Behind Closed Doors* (London: Arrow Books, 2019)

Marsh, R., *I Was Born a Loose Cannon* (London: Optimum, 2010)

Matthews, S., *The Way It Was: My Autobiography* (London: Headline, 2000)

Merson, P., *Hooked* (London: Headline, 2021)

Neville, G., *Red* (London: Corgi, 2011)

Owen, M., *Reboot: My Life, My Time* (London: Reach Sport, 2019)

Paxman, J., *Black Gold: The History of How Coal Made Britain* (London: William Collins, 2021)

Pearce, S., *Psycho* (London: Headline, 2000)

Richards, S., *Turning Points: Crisis and Change in Modern Britain, from 1945 to Truss* (London: Macmillan, 2023)

Robson, B., *Farewell but not Goodbye* (London: Hodder & Stoughton, 2005)

Ronay, B., *How Football (Nearly) Came Home: Adventures in Putin's World Cup* (London: HarperCollins, 2018)

Samuelson, E., *All Together Now: How Wimbledon Fans Brought Their Club Back Home* (Chichester: Pitch, 2021)

Seaman, D., *Safe Hands: My Autobiography* (London: Orion, 2000)

Shilton, P., *The Autobiography* (London: Orion, 2004)

Souness, G., *Football: My Life, My Passion* (London: Headline, 2017)

Storey, D., *Gazza In Italy* (London: HarperCollins, 2018)

Taylor, G., *In His Own Words* (Hemel Hempstead: Peloton Publishing, 2017)

Taylor, R., & Ward, A., *Kicking & Screaming: An Oral History of Football in England* (London: Robson Books, 1995)

Tossell, D., *All Crazee Now: English Football and Footballers in the 1970s* (Chichester: Pitch, 2021)

Winter, H., *Fifty Years of Hurt: The Story of England Football and Why We Never Stop Believing* (London: Bantam Press, 2016)